SEEDS

SEEDS

Supporting Women's Work in the Third World

Edited by Ann Leonard

Introduction by Adrienne Germain
Afterwords by Marguerite Berger, Vina Mazumdar,
Kathleen Staudt, and Aminata Traore

THE FEMINIST PRESS
at The City University of New York
New York

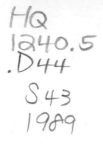

Printed in the United States of America on acid-free paper by McNaughton & Gunn.

92 91 90 89 5 4 3 2 1

Library of Congress Cataloging-in-Publication Data

Seeds: supporting women's work in the Third World/edited by Ann Leonard; introduction by Adrienne Germain; afterwords by Marguerite Berger . . . [et al.].
    p. cm.
  Originally published in a pamphlet series Seeds.
  ISBN 0-935312-92-7 (alk. paper): $29.95.—ISBN 0-935312-93-5 (pbk.: alk. paper): $12.95
    1. Women in development—Developing countries—Case studies.
I. Leonard, Ann, 1945–   .   II. Seeds (New York, N.Y.)
HQ1240.5.D44S43 1989
305.42'09172'4—dc20   89-23329
                                                   CIP

This book is an outgrowth of the Seeds pamphlet series on women's income-generating activities. Project direction and administrative support for Seeds are provided by the Population Council. A grant specifically for the publication of this book was made by the United Nations Development Fund for Women (UNIFEM). Support for the Seeds project over the past ten years has been provided by the Carnegie Corporation, the Ford Foundation, the General Service Foundation, the Government of the Netherlands, the Inter-American Foundation, Oxfam America, the Population Council, the Rockefeller Foundation, UNICEF, and the Women and Development Office of the United States Agency for International Development.

Cover photograph: Garland maker, member of the Working Women's Forum, Madras; by Marty Chen
Text design: Paula Martinac

The Seeds Steering Committee dedicates this book to the memory of William O'Neill Sweeney. Bill Sweeney was a friend and mentor, a creative source, and an ongoing inspiration to our work. It was due to Bill's openness to new ideas and focus on providing people with the information they need in the most suitable format that the Seeds approach came into being. His wit, his warmth, and his generosity of spirit attended the birth of the Seeds pamphlet series and continued through his participation as a member of the Seeds Steering Committee until his passing in July, 1987.

Contents

Preface

Today, as in the past, the vast majority of women in the world work. In the developed world, despite the numerous gains women have made in the workplace, most female workers still receive a fraction of the compensation paid to their male counterparts. In the less developed countries, most women earn outside the modern wage sector of the economy where their income, whether generated in cash or goods, is an important and often vital contribution to the support of their families. Yet most development programs* continue to overlook women's involvement in the economy. When they do focus on women's work, it generally is to provide training for some type of home-based handicrafts activity, which rarely is economically viable and often is seen more as a welfare measure than a means for women to gain self-sufficiency. The United Nations Decade for Women (1975–1985) brought attention to these problems and to the real need for information about income-generating programs for women that provide them with a cash income, involve them in decision making as well as earning, and are based on sound economic criteria.

In the late 1970s, a pamphlet series of case studies, called Seeds, was begun to meet this need. This book presents nine of the eleven studies

---

*The term "development" as used throughout this book refers to the process by which poorer nations of the world increase productivity and their provision of basic services, frequently utilizing financial aid, commodities, and transfer of technology provided by already developed countries and/or international assistance organizations.

that have been published to date, together with additional material that places the studies within the broader context of women and development in all regions of the Third World. In the late 1980s, while there has been significant growth in the number and success of income-generating programs for women, much more still needs to be done, and the demand remains, from an ever wider audience, for information about creating and sustaining such programs.

The Seeds series came into being when women staff members involved in addressing women and development issues within three international development agencies became aware of the need for information that could serve as both resource and inspiration for those working at the grassroots level in development and, at the same time, underscore for those involved in designing and funding development projects around the world the importance of targeting resources to assist women to generate income. These three women were Adrienne Germain and Kristin Anderson, program officers at The Ford Foundation and The Carnegie Corporation (two major private foundations), respectively, and Judith Bruce, associate at the Population Council (an international, non-profit organization having a long-standing concern with women and development issues). They approached Bill Sweeney and Ann Leonard at the Ford Foundation, who were publishing a successful photojournalistic pamphlet series documenting innovative approaches to communication within population and family planning programs. They had in mind a similar pamphlet series focusing on women's income-generating activities. Sweeney and Leonard greeted the idea with enthusiasm.

The next step was formation of a Steering Committee to oversee the goals and operation of the publishing project. The committee is a small group of individuals actively involved in the area of women's income-generation activities, who are able to contribute their time on behalf of their organizations and to work in close enough proximity to New York City to be able to get together frequently enough to keep the work on the pamphlets moving forward.

Ann Leonard was named editor of the series, and also a member of the Steering Committee. The committee determined that each pamphlet would document one project and that the authors would be women who either had journalistic skills and were knowledgeable about or had access to a specific project, or someone actually involved with the project who possessed the writing skill necessary to bring the project's experience to life for an outside audience. The narratives were originally published (and new ones continue to be produced) as separate pamphlets in order to facilitate distribution and make them easy to read by development practitioners and policy makers at the local level and within international development agencies. However, not long after the series commenced, another audience for the material emerged: resource centers on women's economic roles, development organizations committed to educating their supporters in industrialized countries about the process of economic and social change, and university-based training programs for development practitioners. It was primarily with this latter audience in mind that the idea for a Seeds book was brought to fruition.

Each of the nine chapters of this book contains an original Seeds pamphlet, updated where necessary and slightly adapted for publication here. These chapters document projects that are based on women's own initiatives and solidarity; that encourage broad changes in participants' socioeconomic status and personal sense of worth; and that are economically viable. Project leaderships share a broad vision of women's potential and challenge such existing structures as gender roles, middle-merchants,* moneylenders, or institutions that have heretofore excluded or exploited women.

The Seeds case studies portray women's traditional roles in saving, production, and income generation in their "spare time." They also demonstrate ways in which women can build on these skills and activities to enhance their productivity and their income. Several of the case studies describe courageous strategies to move into "male" occupations—construction work in Jamaica or public transport in Kenya. The chapter on handicrafts provides an in-depth treatment of the pitfalls of projects based on traditional stereotypes about women's "proper" work.

Each study represents the strongest, most unique women-generated and women-led enterprises that can be identified. In the beginning, it was difficult to locate such projects because there were few that could meet the Seeds criteria. Today more are thriving than can possibly be documented. Many of the projects documented here are small in scale (fewer than fifty participants) because most women's economic enterprises are relatively small, such as the Mraru bus project in Kenya, the Markala soap and cloth dyeing cooperative in Mali, the Kingston Women's Construction Collective. But others focus on much broader efforts that reach large numbers of women, such as the Working Women's Forum in India and the Bangladesh Rural Advancement Committee. Together they are indicative of the range of activities and strategies that are possible.

In addition to the case studies, this book provides contextual material for the student, teacher, and practitioner in the field of women and development. The Introduction by Adrienne Germain, now Vice-President

---

Middlemerchant is used in this book in place of the term *middleman.*—Ed.

of the International Women's Health Coalition, describes the evolution of women and development activities throughout the last two decades. The first three afterwords present commentaries on the meaningful role these documentations play from the viewpoint of three prominent activists from Third World regions: Vina Mazumdar (Asia), Aminata Traore (Africa), and Marguerite Berger (Latin America and the Caribbean). A final afterword, by Kathleen Staudt, professor of Sociology at the University of Texas, El Paso, features some practical suggestions for use of this book in a classroom setting, based on the experience of the author and her colleagues Marianne Schmink and Gay Young in using the case studies in their courses.

All the members of the Seeds Steering Committee, past and present, have been richly rewarded by participation in the development of the Seeds pamphlet series, and now the publication of this book. We hope that the publication of *Seeds* will allow some of the experience gained by women working together to help themselves to reach an ever-expanding audience, thus generating a better understanding of the crucial economic contribution women make in support of themselves, their families, and their countries.

Ann Leonard
for the Seeds Steering Committee

Acknowledgments

In addition to those organizations providing financial support for the Seeds Publication Project that are acknowledged on the copyright page, the efforts and encouragement of a number of individuals and institutions have been instrumental in making the Seeds pamphlet series a success and in the resulting publication of this book. Since 1981, project direction and administrative support for Seeds have been provided by the Population Council. Editorial policy for the project is set by the Seeds Steering Committee.

Over the years a number of thoughtful and committed people have contributed their time and energy to Seeds as members of this committee. They are: Kristin Anderson, Marty Chen, Margaret Clark, Adrienne Germain, Anne Kubisch, Cecilia Lotse, Karen McGuinness, Katharine McKee, Jill Sheffield, William Sweeney, Anne Walker, and Mildred Warner.

Day-to-day administrative and editorial responsibilities are carried out by Ann Leonard, as editor and administrator, and Judith Bruce, Senior Associate of the Population Council, as project advisor, both of whom are also members of the Steering Committee. The committee is particularly grateful for the encouragement and support extended to the project by the Population Council's President, George Zeidenstein, and Vice President and Director of the Programs Division, George Brown.

Introduction

Adrienne Germain

As countries of Asia, Africa, and Latin America emerged from colonial rule beginning in the 1940s, they faced daunting challenges: to build their economies, establish political structures, and provide social services such as education and health care. These newly independent countries came to be labeled "developing," "less developed countries" (LDCs), "Third World," and the "South."

Western countries, known as "developed," "industrial," "donors," or the "North," recognized that the economic development of the Third World is essential not only for the survival of their people, but also to meet the North's need for raw materials and markets. In 1948, the North began to allocate funds to assist Third World governments in their national development efforts, and today continues such assistance directly through bilateral relationships with individual Third World governments, and indirectly through the multilateral agencies of the United Nations system (for example, UNICEF and the World Bank) and private voluntary agencies.

There have been vigorous debates, within and across Third World countries and between the South and the North, over the definition and objectives of "development," the proper roles of richer countries, and the values that drive development assistance. These debates have focused on differences between the economic and political power of the North and the South, and on class and other differences within Third World countries that often inhibit development. Until recently, these debates rarely examined the ways in which gender differences affect and are

1

affected by development. Yet, in both North and South, girls and women have had substantially less access than boys and men to resources (such as credit, technology, and education). They have had less control over resources and very limited access to decision-making positions.

The Genesis of Women in Development Programs

Before 1970, few women worked in international assistance agencies. Those who did were junior in rank and generally confined to the head office, except for field trips. Men in these agencies interacted largely or solely with elite men in the Third World, where government and development institutions were dominated by men. Virtually everywhere, studies of women's position and roles and analyses which contrasted male and female experiences were considered irrelevant, if considered at all. Women were known only as the bearers and rearers of children, their voices rarely heard publicly or in the corridors of power.

Whispers of change began in the early seventies. In the West, the women's movement was beginning make inroads within international development organizations both in terms of staffing and programming. At the same time, the landmark study, "The Report of the Commission on the Status of Women in India," authorized by the Government of India in 1972 and published by the Indian Council of Social Science Research, brought attention to the desperate plight of women in poverty. Papers commissioned for a United Nations World Population Conference, held in Bucharest, Romania, in 1974, assessed various aspects of women's status relative to their fertility rates. In a widely discussed and controversial speech at that conference, John D. Rockefeller III, a leader in the population field, asserted:

> The final element of reappraisal I would like to discuss is the role of women in society.
> Women contribute in numerous ways to the national life of every country. In most developing countries women are crucial to the economic standing of the family because they are responsible for food crops, they supplement family income through home-based arts and crafts, they are often the head of the household.
> But unfortunately women are often discriminated against in education and employment or excluded from such opportunities altogether. . . .
> For all these reasons, new and urgent attention to the role of women must be a vital characteristic of any modern development program. What happens to women in the course of development efforts needs to receive careful consideration from both internal planners and external supporters. This will be essential to assure achievement of national economic

goals, but that it is also compatible with universal standards of human dignity and justice. . . . (Rockefeller 1974).

At about the same time, the United Nations declared 1975 to be International Women's Year, since recognition was now growing that, despite the U.N. Charter, the Universal Declaration of Human Rights, and other such instruments, women were gaining much less than men from development. Many women, in fact, seemed to be losing resources, status, and power as men became more educated, moved into the modern cash economy, and learned to use new technologies (Tinker and Jaquette 1987).

In 1975, the U.N. sponsored the World Conference for International Women's Year in Mexico City, which provided an exhilarating forum for an exchange of ideas and experiences among women from all over the world. Out of the conference came a new sense of solidarity and a common purpose: the advancement of women for their own benefit and for the benefit of their families and societies. The conference helped women recognize that many common challenges and problems confront women across classes and cultures throughout the world, though the interventions required for change vary substantially across countries. The conference produced an agenda for an international decade for women centered on equality, development, and peace. Equality (women's rights), development (alleviation of poverty), and peace were to be achieved at both national and international levels through the addition of women to staffs of major institutions; through development of projects specifically for women; through policies and programs to give women equal access to opportunities for education, employment, political and social participation; and through the establishment of various special mechanisms such as national ministries of women's affairs, the U.N. Commission on the Status of Women, and special offices in donor agencies.

For many Western women working in development agencies and on research, the conference crystallized what they had heard from Third World women for several years: poor women, like poor men, give priority to production and income generation as a matter of survival for themselves and their children. Papers for the conference and the infant literature on women and development clearly documented, however, that where women's production and income needs were recognized, emphasis tended to be placed on traditional female sectors, especially handicrafts, and the idea of assistance for women was most often based on concepts of welfare or relief, rather than on economically viable employment strategies (Germain 1976–77).

During the first half of the United Nations Decade for Women (1975–1980), women working in development agencies both in the West and in the Third World struggled largely alone to achieve the Decade's goals. Considerable prejudice existed within agencies, as well as in society, forcing women to make substantial personal and professional sacrifices to advance the cause.

At about the same time, during the late seventies, several other trends and themes emerged in Third World development circles that would support women in their productive roles. For example, Robert Mac-Namara, then President of the World Bank, in a seminal speech in Nairobi, called for the Bank's entry into development approaches that previously had been considered "unbankable," and which definitely included women's entrepreneurial efforts.

Concurrently, the United Nations International Labour Organization (ILO) discovered the "informal sector," that part of the economy in which people are self-employed rather than employed in salaried jobs. Enterprises in the informal sector fall largely outside government or union control or protection. The locations of these enterprises may often be legally questionable (street vendors), illegal (the black market), and vulnerable to all manner of abuse by the public or authorities. Nonetheless, the informal sector plays a critical role in both household and national economies: millions of poor people generate their only income from enterprises in this sector and at least half of them are women.

It was also during the late seventies that women re-discovered the "new household economics," a branch of economics that recognizes and analyzes the household as the basic social unit of production and economic decisions. Development economists, who had rarely looked at households, began to re-examine household strategies in terms of the allocation of income and labor. A series of seminars by the New York-based Agricultural Development Council, which sought to stimulate gender analysis in household studies, revealed the extent of girls' and women's economic contributions to household survival and helped lay the foundation for programs to support women's productive as well as reproductive roles (Weisblat 1975; Binswanger et al. 1980).

Development think tanks, such as the Overseas Development Council, identified gaps in meeting basic human needs such as housing, education, and health care. They described strategies for new approaches to development that would give priority to meeting these needs, and to building up "human capital" for development as opposed to earlier strategies that had focused extensively on infrastructure, export-oriented agriculture, and industry. This approach was designed to balance economic, growth-oriented models of development pursued by the World

Bank and other major funding organizations. At the same time, calls for a "new international economic order" reverberated in the corridors of the United Nations, causing it and other development agencies to focus on the economic imbalance between developed and developing countries and to examine underlying structural causes of poverty and underdevelopment in the Third World.

All these efforts, however, focused almost solely on class differences. The burden of proving that gender is significant and that women are vital to national development and the alleviation of poverty fell on a small group of individuals from development agencies and in Third World countries who were specifically concerned about both women's rights and women's poverty. Most had few, if any, financial resources to command and worked in the traditional female or welfare sectors of health, nutrition, family planning, and education. Those in economic sectors—agriculture, industry, employment, banking—and elsewhere often were reluctant to risk their professional standing by promoting attention to women. Some women, like so many men, rejected the concern about women's rights and productivity as a culturally imperialistic notion of Western women, as a "luxury" that poor countries could not afford, or as a major distraction from women's critical reproductive function.

Empirical research, dialogues, and debates in national and international development forums slowly led to some breakthroughs. The U.N.'s International Labour Organization, studying the informal sector, revealed the extent to which women both produce and market in this sector. Similarly, household level analysis revealed not only women's major contribution to total household income and production, but also the fact that they, more than men, tend to use all their income to meet their families' basic needs for education, health care, and food. A major review of rural development strategies in Africa by the World Bank came face-to-face with the fact that, although most subsistence farming in sub-Saharan Africa is done by women, development projects had excluded them entirely (Lele 1979). Detailed descriptive portraits of very poor women in India as well as newer survey data, revealed that anywhere from 15 to 65 percent of poor households in Third World countries and in the United States are headed by women (Gulati 1981). These women have been divorced, deserted, or widowed; they live in polygamous households to which men fail to contribute; their partners are disabled or earn too little to support the family; or, in some cases, these women choose to live on their own with their children. Labor force surveys, after some of their definitions were adjusted, revealed that women were much more economically active than anyone previously had assumed. Studies also documented women's lack of access to improved technology, credit, basic education, skills training, land, and other resources that would enable them to increase their productivity.

While these facts began to make clear the pragmatic need to support women in their effort to contribute to family income and national development, the question remained "how?" How to help women produce and generate income in economically viable ways? How to do this and, at the same time, support and complement their other major responsibilities—child rearing and household management? How to do all this and respect women's basic human rights?

Many women felt it imperative to consider whether integration into the prevailing systems, strategies, and institutions of development, integration in fact into the prevailing economic structures, was the most viable and moral approach or whether, in fact, the structures and strategies themselves should be changed. In 1979, participants in a Bangkok meeting of Third World and Western women concerned with development, organized by the U.N. Asian and Pacific Center for Women in Development (APCWD), reached this consensus: those present cared not only about equality and development but also about "women's dignity, autonomy and (broader) socio-economic change—in short, not merely . . . improving women's lives within existing structures of inequality and oppression, but . . . changing women's lives, not merely with equality but with liberation. . . ." (Antrobus 1987, 50)

Prior to 1985, when the Decade for Women officially ended with a World Conference to Review and Appraise the U.N. Decade for Women in Nairobi, a network of primarily Third World women activists and policy makers established Development Alternatives with Women for a New Era (DAWN). They sought to redefine the nature of "economic development," the "equality, development, and peace" goals of the U.N. Decade and their own vision of a

> . . . world where inequality based on class, gender and race is absent from every country, and from the relationships among countries. Where basic needs become basic rights and where poverty and all forms of violence are eliminated. Each person will have the opportunity to develop her or his own full potential and creativity, and women's values of nurturance and solidarity will characterize human relationships . . . (Sen and Grown 1987, 80)

Women in Development Today

The Seeds pamphlet series, from which this book was developed, is one of many remarkably diverse projects and institutions that have emerged during the last twelve years, along with the United Nations Decade for

Women. Others include international women's networks such as DAWN, described above, or AAWORD, the African Association of Women for Research on Development; large-scale credit projects for the rural poor, such as the Grameen Bank in Bangladesh, 80 percent of whose 413,000 borrowers are landless women; the Self-Employed Women's Association of Ahmedabad and several other large "unions" of self-employed women in India, each of whose memberships may exceed ten thousand; Women's World Banking, an international financial intermediary to advance and promote entrepreneurship among women by guaranteeing loans for thirty thousand women valued at $4.6 million to date; the United Nations Development Fund for Women (UNIFEM) and other U.N. agency programs that underwrite credit and income generating schemes for women throughout the Third World; and women in development offices in major bilateral aid agencies, such as U.S.A.I.D. and others.

As suggested above, and embodied in the Seeds cases, a great deal has been learned about the productive roles of women, especially poor rural women hidden from public view (Abdullah and Zeidenstein 1979). Women's studies programs and courses have emerged, not only in the United States, Canada, Europe, and all parts of the West, but across Asia, in Latin America, and in parts of the Middle East. A burgeoning literature—books as well as articles—is finding its way not only into special courses, but into mainstream courses and departments concerned with agriculture, education, population, rural development, economics, and other fields.

Development rhetoric is also changing: no longer is it "culturally imperialistic" to be concerned about women's opportunities and rights at policy levels. U.S.A.I.D.'s Fund for Africa, established in 1988, mandates that the full range of women's productive contributions be recognized. Major development leaders, such as Mr. F. H. Abed, Director of the Bangladesh Rural Advancement Committee, and Dr. Md. Yunus, Director of the Grameen Bank, have recognized that "women are the managers of poverty." Though the totals are still small, more women now than in 1975 hold positions of influence in development agencies and in governments. The momentum is great and the lessons learned substantial.

Challenges for the Future

But we are still in for a very long haul. As Vina Mazumdar suggests in her afterword, political consciousness and power remain elusive. Exclusion of women continues at senior levels in most institutions. Ruth Sivard's landmark 1985 survey clearly documents that, by most measures, women's position in the Third World has remained the same or even deteriorated since 1975:

> Despite the key role that women have in Third World economics, they have been largely by-passed in development strategies. Throughout the world, women are still disproportionally represented among the poor, the illiterate, the unemployed and underemployed. They remain a very small minority at the centers of political power.

Even after having achieved greater visibility, women continue to lose, in aggregate terms, more than they gain in development. Most women's projects remain small and on the margins of mainstream development efforts, and deeper, more fundamental problems are emerging. As the world economy stumbles, and the Third World debt crisis looms ever larger, evidence is emerging that once again girls and women are suffering disproportionately: the "feminization of poverty" is now a global phenomenon. The root causes of poverty and inequality are not, however, solely economic. DAWN's analyses, among others, suggest that political and socio-cultural crises in the eighties, interacting synergistically with economic problems, pose far more complex development challenges than heretofore recognized. These require fundamental alterations in world economic structures. DAWN and other development specialists propose that capitalist or growth-oriented models of development are part of the problem, not the solution, and that alternative approaches to development are needed. For example, Peggy Antrobus asserts that "support for income generating projects (within growth-oriented development models) in preference to programmes which attempt to address structural issues, or empower women," may actually impede or delay fundamental contextual adjustments (1987, 60).

Whether we accept existing structures and development models, or strive to alter them, at least three challenges face us in the decade ahead:

Upscaling, increasing the number of women who have access to income generating projects that exist or are created;

Deepening, supporting participants in multiple ways so that they are truly empowered; and

Mainstreaming, insuring that both the projects and the women are central to overall development efforts, whether those efforts are within existing structures or are challenges to them.

Upscaling is possible, but usually only when planned from the outset. It may occur through systematically expanding outreach efforts and by building infrastructures that can serve more participants. Examples in this volume include the Working Women's Forum in India and the Bangladesh Rural Advancement Committee. Upscaling can also be done through careful nurturance of "branches" under the same central management or technical assistance program, as in the SIRDO waste management technology in Mexico or the FUNDE loan program for market women in Nicaragua. Other ways would be through "spin-offs" in which some of the original leaders or participants develop their own enterprises, or through "copy" organizations created by observers of the originals, as has happened with several nongovernmental rural development organizations in Bangladesh.

Many lessons have been learned about each of these upscaling strategies. Perhaps the most important is that direct replication rarely works, because the original conditions, leadership, and vision are not replicable. But success stories, especially those that document mistakes and shifts in tactics as well as accomplishments, can serve as examples, not models, and as sources of inspiration. A second important lesson is that income-generating projects grafted on to organizations that have their own agendas, such as family planning, and that do not have access to the necessary expertise, usually do not work. The design and execution of viable employment and income-generating projects require special skills.

Whether remaining the same size or expanding under any of the patterns listed above, *deepening* the projects requires action on three levels. The first is identification of viable means of increasing the income that women can generate in the activities they undertake through projects such as those documented here. This has proven exceedingly difficult and no clear answers are yet available. Sometimes, technical assistance with design and marketing of products the women produce and tactics such as wholesale purchase of raw materials can enhance efficiency, productivity, and sales. Projects originally based on individually controlled enterprises can experiment with group enterprises that have higher returns, but require more capital and skills. These are expensive and many have foundered due to political or interpersonal problems, inability to manage large capital or sophisticated technology, and other related problems.

The second aspect of deepening has to do with the types of support or input the projects offer. Participants often demand that income-generating projects deepen or broaden their scope to include literacy and other technical training, health advice/referral and/or health insurance, organizing skills, legal information, and more. The strongest projects, including several Seeds cases (India's Working Women's Forum, the Jamaica Women's Construction Collective, the Bangladesh Rural Advancement Committee), respond to these demands and thereby enable women not simply to earn income but to control its use and take command of other aspects of their lives. Some projects—like those of Bangladesh and India—originated with the objective of empowering women more broadly. Others, with more limited resources, skills, leadership, or money, can gradually move in this direction provided the commitment is there.

A third and fundamental dimension of deepening is the fundamental approach to women: does the project see them as targets for assistance, or as autonomous human beings with the right to manage their own lives? For many women, such autonomy is new and even frightening. If projects are truly to empower women, economic investment is not sufficient. Programs also must invest in helping women to develop a sense of self worth and to learn how to make decisions and exercise control, both as individuals and through group action.

Deepening projects to encompass educational, organizational, and consciousness-raising components has been important and effective in many settings. But, as Aminata Traore and others suggest, a wider and more fundamental vision is necessary for *mainstreaming*. Rather narrowly conceived programs to help women gain access to occupations dominated by men (Jamaica Women's Construction Collective) face exceedingly difficult obstacles. They ultimately may be able to assist only a small number of women, unless they are used as leverage to change policies on recruitment, admission to training courses, and the like. While symbolically important, such projects may use resources that, if differently allocated, might benefit many more women. The case study of the women involved in forest conservation in Nepal clearly demonstrates that only a carefully planned strategy can influence government agencies to include women in major development sectors and that to insure successful implementation women's traditional roles must be recognized. Similarly, the SIRDO waste management technology in Mexico took note of women's key roles in community health and sanitation and benefitted by working with and through women to achieve their program objectives.

Full inclusion of women, not simply in development but in their societies on an equal footing for the benefit of all, requires fundamental changes. Ultimately, sustained efforts to upscale, deepen, and mainstream women's projects will empower women to contribute to changes in the prevailing structures. The challenges, if anything, are becoming greater. UNICEF has documented that governments, facing severe shortages and structural adjustment pressure from the International Monetary Fund, are cutting back on basic social services while at the same time expecting women to provide these services on their own.

Antrobus eloquently underlines the fact that such an approach is both exploitive and counterproductive in the long run (1988).

With the conclusion of the United Nations Decade for Women in 1985, one major impetus for fundamental change ended. If we are to meet the challenges of poverty and achieve social justice and peace, we must continue to work to ensure that women are recognized as fully competent human beings, with equal rights to control resources, make decisions, and take full advantage of opportunity. We must fight the exploitation and subordination of women. The Seeds case studies exemplify these values and also demonstrate that women are fundamentally altruistic: they work not only for their own benefit but for the benefit of their families and their societies.

> What we have managed to do . . . is to forge grassroots women's movements and worldwide networks . . . to begin to transform (the subordination of women) and in the process to break down other oppressive structures as well. . . . We have learned . . . that the political will for serious action by those in power is contingent on women's organizing to demand and promote change. . . . (Sen and Grown 1987, p. 22)

References

Abdullah, T. and S. Zeidenstein. 1979. ''Women's Reality: Critical Issues for Programs and Design.'' *Studies in Family Planning: Learning About Rural Women,* vol. 10, no. 11/12, November/December. New York: Population Council.

Antrobus, P. 1987. ''A Journey in the Shaping, A Journey without Maps: A Caribbean Experience of Women and Development Programmes during the U.N. Decade for Women (1975–1985).'' Unpublished manuscript, cited with permission of the author.

Antrobus, P. 1988. ''The Gender Implications of the Global Economic Crisis.'' Lecture at the Woodrow Wilson Center, Princeton University, May. Cited with permission of the author.

Binswanger, H.P. et al., eds. 1980. *Rural Household Studies in Asia.* Singapore: Singapore University Press.

Bruce J. and D. Dwyer, eds. 1988. ''Introduction.'' In *A Home Divided: Women and Income in the Third World.* Stanford, CA: Stanford University Press.

Cornia, A. et al., eds. 1987. *Adjustment with a Human Face: Protecting the Vulnerable and Promoting Growth.* Oxford: Clarendon Press.

Germain, A. 1976–77. ''Poor Rural Women: A Policy Perspective.'' *Journal of International Affairs,* vol. 30, no. 12, Fall/Winter.

Gulati, L. 1981. *Profiles in Female Poverty: A Study of Five Poor Working Women in Kerala.* New Delhi: Hindustan Publishing Corporation.

Indian Council of Social Science Research. 1975. *Status of Women in India: A Synopsis of the Report of the National Committee on the Status of Women.* New Delhi: ICSSR.

Lele, U. 1979. *Design of Rural Development: Lessons from Africa.* Baltimore, MD: Johns Hopkins University Press.

Leslie, J. 1987. "Time Costs and Time Savings to Women of the Child Survival Revolution." Paper prepared for a Rockefeller Foundation/International Development Research Centre workshop, "Issues Concerning Gender, Technology and Development in the Third World," New York, February 26–27. Washington, D.C.: International Center for Research on Women.

MacNamara, R.S. 1973. Address to the Board of Governors of the International Bank for Reconstruction and Development, Nairobi, September 24. Washington, D.C.: IBRD.

Rockefeller, J.D., 3rd, 1974. "Population Growth: The Role of the Developed World." International Union for the Scientific Study of Population, Lecture Series on Population, World Population Conference, Bucharest.

Sen, G. and C. Grown. 1987. *Development, Crises, and Alternative Visions: Third World Women's Perspectives.* New York: Monthly Review Press.

Sivard, R.L. 1985. *Women . . . A World Survey.* Washington, D.C.: World Priorities.

Tinker, I. and J. Jaquette. 1987. "U.N. Decade for Women: Its Impact and Legacy." *World Development,* vol. 15, no. 3, 419–27.

Weisblat, A. 1975. "Role of Rural Women in Development." New York: Research and Training Network, Agricultural Development Council, October.

Introduction

1

AFRICA

1
Village Women Organize: The Mraru, Kenya Bus Service

Jill Kneerim

The Mraru Women's Group, like many community women's organizations around the world, is an example of a deeply-rooted tradition of association and self-help among women. In 1971 the group began to gather its resources to solve a common problem—transportation. They raised money, bought a bus, and began a public transport service that made money. Then they were faced with other difficult tasks such as reinvesting profits, serving members' broader needs, and maintaining a strong economic base. The Mraru Women's Group has shown unusual creativity and persistence in identifying common needs and organizing to meet them. They have also demonstrated that a small, private organization with few resources can effectively call on the skills and resources of other agencies, both public and private, to help them achieve their goals, while remaining independent and self-reliant. It is hoped that their experience may be an inspiration to other such groups and that other women will be able to profit from the lessons learned by the women of Mraru.

The women in Mraru got angry one year. The nearest market center for this cluster of eight small villages in the Taita Hills of Kenya was the town of Voi, about 12 kilometers away. You can't carry heavy goods to market or a sick child to the clinic on foot over that distance. There

---

Except for the update section, this chapter was originally published as the pamphlet *Village Women Organize: The Mraru Bus Service* in 1980 by the Seeds Publication Project.

The Mraru bus *(Jill Kneerim)*

aren't many buses to Voi, and almost all are fully loaded by the time they reach Mraru. If there is any space, it goes to the men, not women. Men first: that is the tradition in the countryside of Kenya, and for women the tradition is to resign themselves to it. But in 1971, the Mraru women decided to do something else. They decided to buy their own bus.

This sounds like an unusual decision, and it was. How could a handful of rural women with no regular incomes, in a country where few women own property, collect enough money for the down payment on a vehicle and then persuade a bank to lend them the balance? It sounded like a daydream. But six years later, with the bus paid for and running a regular route to Voi every day, the Mraru Women's Group had declared a dividend to its early shareholders and was building a retail shop with its profits.

The Taita women in Mraru are not wealthy or well educated or in any other way noticeably different from village women in other parts of Kenya, or even other parts of the world. Virtually all of them raise large families and produce the family's food in *shambas,* small plots owned by their husbands. They earn some cash by selling maize or cassava root or goats they have bred (when they can get these goods to market) or from trade, buying small quantities of goods at wholesale to sell at retail.

In a good year, a typical woman in Mraru may make 1,000 Kenya shillings, about US $130, which she usually spends on the family: school fees for the children, the food she doesn't grow herself, corrugated roofing for the house.

The Mraru Women's Group

In 1970, forty-seven women in the several villages of Mraru joined together to form a club affiliated with the national women's organization Maendeleo ya Wanawake ("Women's Progress" in Swahili). They chose as chairperson Eva Mwaluma, a member of the Taita/Taveta County Council at the district headquarters in Wundanyi.

The Mraru group met regularly to learn about crafts and homemaking and to talk over their problems. Eventually, one of the problems they talked about was transportation into Voi. A year of drought was making trading particularly important, yet all of them were having trouble getting to the market in Voi. There had even been some desperate cases of women or babies lost in childbirth because there was no way to get to Voi's maternity clinic. The women decided that the best solution to this problem was to buy their own bus.

In rural Kenya, most transportation is provided by private entrepreneurs. Even the country buses—dented, patched, and repainted old products of Mercedes-Benz and British Leyland that toil along the country roads from town to town—are private property, not a publicly run service. Virtually every route they take, as well as many they never get to, is also traversed by smaller conveyances called *matatus*. These jitneys sporting flamboyant slogans in Swahili are a familiar sight all over the country, hurtling along loaded to twice their stated capacity with the conductor hanging off the back step shouting out the destination.

In August, 1971 the Mraru women started saving for their bus. They agreed that, over time, each member should contribute at least 200 shillings (about $27), which would be the value of one share. Like many other groups of women in Kenya who form savings societies, they met every month, and each member contributed what she could afford. Those without money brought eggs, hens, fruits—anything of value. These contributions were given a cash value and entered in the record book along with cash payments for the month. At one typical meeting, they collected 793 shillings. Next day, the funds were deposited in the Mraru Maendeleo ya Wanawake savings account at the post office in Voi.

Small things accumulate. By 1973, they had saved 27,000 shillings ($3,600). That was sufficient capital for Eva Mwaluma to go to Mombasa, some 170 kilometers away, to place an order for a bus with the

Cooper Motor Corporation. This was the beginning of a long process. Construction of the bus body would take time and could not begin until an order was placed. The Cooper branch manager figured out the costs. The bus, an 11,760-pound British Leyland diesel with an aluminum body and seating for twenty-one passengers, would cost 111,780 shillings, including finance costs. Cooper would require a down payment of 47,800 to release the bus. The group would have to raise 21,000 shillings more just for the down payment. In addition, they would have to get a very substantial loan to cover the remainder of the purchase price, and their only collateral was their determination to succeed. The bus itself would not be considered collateral because rough, overcrowded roads and reckless drivers make vehicles too vulnerable.

Nonetheless, the group's spirits were high. It seemed possible that their dream could become reality. Some of the more skeptical members now began to deliver more money, and the women held fund-raisings to collect donations from outsiders. (Public fund-raisings—called *harambees* after the national motto meaning "join together"—are a widespread, popular tradition in Kenya begun by the first president, Jomo Kenyatta.) More women joined, and the possibility of obtaining a loan began to improve. A government social services worker in Mombasa lobbied with the Cooper Motor Corporation and persuaded its managers that this group was worth taking a chance on. The company was able to obtain a commitment from National Industrial Credit (East Africa) Limited in Nairobi to lend the Mraru women more than half the purchase price on the strength of the Cooper manager's sworn assurance that if any payment was late, he personally would go to Mraru to collect it.

By early 1975 the bus was in the warehouse in Mombasa and ready to go. According to size, weight, and capacity, it was a *matatu,* but it appeared considerably more imposing than most *matatus.* It looked like a scaled-down, brand new country bus, with a separate door for the driver, a center aisle with double seats facing forward on either side, an emergency escape door in the rear, a side entrance for the passengers, and a generous luggage rack on top to hold loads of bagged charcoal, crates of chickens, and bundles of firewood. There it was—the real bus. Cooper's sales manager had a sign painted for the display space above the bus windshield and, on his own time and at his own expense, drove the bus from Mombasa to Mraru to show the women what was almost theirs.

The last push became urgent because now that the bus was there to be seen, other customers in Mombasa wanted to buy it. But, the Mraru Women's Group treasury was 6,800 shillings short of the required down payment. In their first three years they had raised 27,000

Joan Mjomba, right, talking with the vice chairperson of the Mraru group, Polina Danson *(Jill Kneerim)*

shillings; in the fourth year they raised 14,000 more. But they needed a total of 47,800.

Last-Minute Rescue

It is never easy to discover what makes for success, but whatever the magic was, the Mraru Women's Group had it. In the previous ten years, women's groups of various kinds had been forming all over Kenya, but most of them were smaller and had a more traditional focus such as handicrafts, savings, farming, or raising livestock. In 1975, women's groups received more attention than usual because of International Women's Year. More than 70 percent of adults in rural areas of Kenya are women, often left behind to keep the home and raise the children while their husbands migrate to the cities for wage-paying jobs. In trying to plan ahead for rural development, Kenya had begun to take account of what women were doing and were capable of doing. The Mraru Women's Group was surely a fine example and one becoming well known in the Coastal Province.

At that time, the chairman of Maendeleo ya Wanawake for the district of Taita/Taveta was Joan Mjomba, who had grown up in one of the villages of Mraru. Although she no longer lived in Mraru, she joined the group to show her enthusiasm and support. In early 1975, at the

Government-sponsored provincial seminar for the International Women's Year, she described the Mraru women in glowing terms and urged the provincial office of social services in Mombasa to make a special example of it in its reports for the Women's Year.

The sense of excitement about what the Mraru group had achieved so far was not surprising. After all, the group had started with no assets, no special talents, and no wealthy members, yet it had saved an incredible 41,000 shillings in just three years. Now it was on its way to persuading a bus company and a bank to break tradition by lending money to a group of women.

A crucial factor in finally securing the bus was one of the government's provincial social workers in Mombasa, Terry Kantai. She personally guaranteed a loan for the final 7,000 shillings needed for the down payment. Then she, the Maendeleo organization and the Mraru Women's Group organized a *harambee* fund-raising to show the bank and Cooper Motor Corporation that they could rely on this group to pay off its debts. At the end of the ceremonies the group had collected 3,013 more shillings from 484 donors—enough for the first two payments on Terry Kantai's loan. With the complete down payment now available and the skeptics convinced, the bus could at last be released from the warehouse. Jubilant, the group hired a driver, and on May 3, 1975, Eva Mwaluma, and the treasurer, Mary Frederick, went to Mombasa, claimed the bus, and drove it back to Mraru. Next day, the shining white bus began plying the route between Mraru and Voi.

The Mraru women now had a full-scale business on their hands. They had insurance and registration fees to pay, they had to buy petrol and pay for maintenance, and they had to meet a monthly debt-retirement payment of 4,088.90 shillings over a period of eighteen months. In addition, they had three full-time employees: the driver; the conductor, who collects fares and issues receipts; and an inspector. At first the Mraru women hired a woman as conductor, but the customers sometimes proved too rowdy for her to handle so a young man was employed for the job. The inspector, however, is always a member of the group who rides on every trip to be sure fares are collected and accounted for. This is a demanding job and she gets paid for it. At the end of each day the receipts are taken to the group's treasurer in Mraru who verifies the total and enters it in the books. The next morning the inspector deposits the money in the bank at Voi.

Each passenger pays 3 shillings for the one-way, 12 kilometer trip from Mraru to Voi. The bus leaves the main intersection in Mraru (the junction of two dirt roads) at 8:00 A.M. every morning and continues back and forth to and from Voi, with four or five stops in between, as long as there are passengers who want to make the trip. In a refreshing switch on the original situation, members of the group get first preference when there are too many passengers for one load.

A day's gross for the bus service can vary from 120 to 800 shillings; on market days and holidays it can reach several thousand. The bus also is available to hire for special trips. A typical one was made for the Taita/Taveta Education Board, transporting school choirs from one town to another at a charge of 400 shillings per round trip. If a job requires an overnight stop, the driver, conductor, and inspector are paid a small allowance for overnight expenses.

Diversification

The bus proved an excellent investment. Demand for its services was so lively that the driver worked seven days a week and was given vacation pay instead of time off. In a year and a half, the debts were paid and the Mraru Women's Group began a new savings account. By 1977, they had 12,000 shillings in the bank and were accumulating more all the time. The group then declared half the money as a dividend and targeted the remaining funds for a new enterprise, a *duka* or retail shop in Mraru. The dividend, distributed in proportion to each woman's shares, was a stunning success. Women who had never owned anything in their lives, and many who had pursued this project despite their husbands' disgruntled complaints, now were receiving a return on their investment. News like that spreads quickly. The group had 68 members at the time of the dividend; within two years the number had grown to 195. Many of the new members were women with more ready cash than the first group; quite a few of them could afford 200 shillings outright.

The *Duka*

Almost as soon as they were able, the women decided to invest in another enterprise. The bus, though a good earner, seemed too vulnerable. They again chose a business serving the local market; however this time it was not movable, but a solid asset. The women applied to the Taita/ Taveta County Council for one of the plots in Mraru that the Council had specifically set aside for such use. Again drawing on outside expertise for estimates of costs and needs, the Mraru women decided to start small, with only a shop. At a future date they would hope to expand the building to include quarters for employees of the bus service and the shop, an office, a meeting room that could double as a classroom, a kitchen, an indoor toilet, and five bedrooms that would serve as a small hotel.

The shop: "We'll never be counted bankrupt with that there." *(Jill Kneerim)*

The shop and three small rooms made of cement block with corrugated roofing would cost 55,000 shillings; stocking the shop would cost another 22,000. The funds came from new members who had been joining under the impetus of the dividend and the group's savings of 6,000 shillings in profits from the bus—an amount which was growing every week. With plans approved by the Council, construction of the *duka* began in February 1977 and was completed six months later. The Government Social Services Department made a loan of 10,000 shillings to the group to help stock the *duka,* even though their advisors were concerned that the shop might be being built a few years too soon in the general scheme of things.

Elina Mwaizinga, a member of the group, became the full-time salaried shopkeeper. Rising early from her bedroom behind the shop, she opens the doors at 6:00 A.M. and does not close them until 7:00 in the evening. This is her daily schedule except for Sundays when she closes the shop for a few hours at midday to go to church, and on the days she goes to Voi to buy supplies from the wholesaler. The *duka* stocks simple household items: aluminum cooking pots, skin-toning cream, malaria tablets, canned cooking fat, nipples for baby bottles, pyrethrum insect spray. Its biggest sellers are sugar and tea. Wholesale costs, of course, are one of the major expenses of the shop. So is Elina's salary: 300 shillings a month. While the shop's location is not ideal for a retail business, since the population that can reach it easily is small, it does have 195 unswerving customers who will not buy their goods anywhere else. Members pay the same prices as other buyers, which are more or less equivalent to the standard retail prices in other shops. Although all of them patronize the *duka* faithfully, their business isn't taken for granted. At the annual year-end meeting and party, members are invited to show shop receipts for purchases of more than 50 shillings, which entitles them to an item off the shelves. "That's to please the customers for coming," says Elina.

Although the shop is not nearly as profitable as the bus, it represents a solid asset. "The thing we are proud of is that investment," says one of the members. "We will never be counted bankrupt with that there." The cement-block building could always be rented in hard times. It could even be sold, but the group is determined never to have to do that.

Further Development

As a registered women's group, the Mraru group is eligible for continuing assistance from the government, including advice on further investment to protect against any problems in its other businesses. On the advice of government social workers, the group has begun raising goats and studying for self-improvement. These more traditional pursuits of women are both substantially underwritten by government funds.

The Taita Hills area is extremely dry at times, which makes goat raising a better investment than farming. Besides, almost every woman in Mraru is skilled in raising goats. The Women's Bureau in Nairobi, with funds from UNICEF, provided the Mraru Women's Group with one hundred goats, plus two prize male goats to help them develop their stock. The male offspring are sold for meat at about one year of age, the females are kept for breeding.

Group members added thirty more goats to the herd, and the village of Mraru also contributed by granting the women's group free use of grazing land on one of the hillsides about half a mile from their shop. A goat herd, whose salary is 240 shillings a month, is the enterprise's largest operating expense.

The major capital expense was a building to house goats and goat herd: 350 shillings for poles on which to plaster clay walls, 700 shillings for corrugated roofing sheets, and 150 shillings for the builder. The builder and poles were paid for by members' donations, but the money for the roof came from the profits of the *duka*. As it turned out, the shop was not quite profitable enough to cover the whole cost, so the side toward the hill is roofed with empty tin cans cut open and hammered flat, contributed from members' households.

Unfortunately, goats are a more vulnerable investment than canned

Left to right: The group's chairperson, treasurer, instructor in home economics, and vice chairperson singing the song, "Maendeleo ya Wanawake" *(Jill Kneerim)*

cooking fat, and the first year of this undertaking was a year of drought. Some of the animals died, including one of the prize he-goats. In order to protect their stock, the Mraru women sold a number of the remaining animals so they would have the cash to expand the herd when the rains returned and grazing was good. As of May 1979, the herd stood at forty-eight goats and the rains were blessing the hillsides.

The group began one other new enterprise at about the same time, this one aimed more at personal improvements than profits for the treasury. Here again, it received substantial government assistance. The Social Services Department donated two sewing machines and the salary for a teacher to live in Mraru and give classes in sewing and family health. The Department also gave the group 3,000 shillings for sewing materials. A monthly fee of 10 shillings per participant pays for small supplies like needles, thread, and buttons. The teacher, Dora Malemba, works full time and lives in a room behind the *duka*. She holds classes for one group of women in the morning and another in the afternoon. Her twenty-eight students, who almost never miss class except in the planting season, spend a good part of the sessions working on the two sewing machines. Although this project was intended for personal improvement, many of the dresses, jackets, tablecloths, and children's clothes the women produce are sold next door in the shop. In the first eight months of classes, the group made almost 1,000 shillings on the sale of these items.

In addition to sewing, Dora teaches the women about health and family planning. She works every day from a lesson plan she has devised in advance. Classes are informal with women wandering back and forth from the *duka* and babies tied to their mothers' backs or playing on the floor.

Organization

The group still meets once a month, at which time money is collected and the number of shares increased. Women who do not attend meetings are fined. (This is a general tradition in Kenya, to keep up attendance at all kinds of meetings.) One share in the group is still worth 200 shillings, and the women have set eight shares as the maximum any individual may buy. "We don't want to have some women who are better than others," the chairperson has said. In fact, the aim is to bring every woman's holdings up to eight shares so all will be equal, but that probably will have to wait until the group again has enough income to declare a dividend.

For business purposes, full-scale meetings are clearly too cumbersome, so the group has elected a committee of nine members to consider policy, look into problems, and make recommendations to the full membership. The majority rules, and election is done by secret ballot. The committee, which meets once every three months, unless a pressing matter requires an extra meeting, is also responsible for choosing the group's officers—chair, vice chair, secretary, vice secretary, and treasurer. These women in turn have their own special duties. The work of the treasurer and secretary are demanding enough to warrant their being paid a monthly fee of 100 shillings each. The secretary records the amount of money deposited monthly by each member and keeps a cumulative tally so it is clear where members stand in their ownership of shares. The treasurer has the daily job of counting the bus receipts and entering the total in the books.

None of the officers has had special training for her job. The treasurer, for example, has a secondary-school education but no background in accounting. Once the books were set up by a professional accountant, she has had no trouble maintaining an accurate record of the group's financial transactions. The professional accountant, from the County Council office, is hired by the group to go over its books once a year. This underscores one of the secrets of the Mraru group's success. From the start, it has sought and received professional assistance. Government social service workers have counseled the Mraru women on how to organize, on investments, and on the details of running a business. The group has had the invaluable counsel of Terry Kantai, first as an employee of the government's Social Services Department in the Coast Province and now as director of the Women's Bureau in the national government. They also have received advice from members of all levels of the Kenyan Ministry of Housing and Social Services, the Community Development Assistant of the Department of Social Services, the District Social Services office, and the County Council.

The Maendeleo ya Wanawake national organization is also available for counsel and instruction. Maendeleo can lobby with various government divisions on behalf of any one of its member groups and command far more attention than a single group, even one as substantial as the Mraru group. The extraordinary energy and enthusiasm of Joan Mjomba, first as district and then as provincial chair of Maendeleo, was likewise an advantage other groups might well envy. None of these advisors, national or local, intrude on the Mraru women, who clearly would be able to resist interference if they needed to. But obviously the women do not operate in a vacuum. If they want further counsel on any matter they can usually get it.

Crisis

Despite its growing diversity the group has had only one substantial moneymaker, the bus. But years of steady use on rough roads have worn it out. By the time the bus was four and a half years old, repair bills began to equal earnings and the group decided it was time to turn the machine in for a new one. At this point, the Mraru women met their first major setback.

In the years since their first purchase from Cooper, inflation had been rampant worldwide. Added to that, Kenya had a foreign exchange crisis that forced the government to place high tariffs on goods from abroad. The bus the women now wanted to order was slightly larger than their old one, seating twenty-six rather than twenty-one. Cooper was willing to give them good trade-in value for their old bus—60,000 shillings— and beyond that, they had 31,600 in savings. This would almost have bought their old bus outright in 1975, but in 1979 the Cooper managers shook their heads. Now a new bus, with insurance, registration fees, and interest on a loan included, would cost about 310,000 shillings. Although the group had a flawless record for repayment of loans, money was much tighter now and the best loan Cooper could arrange was for

Elina and the shop. As the members see it, "The [shop] is the child of the bus." (Jill Kneerim)

a maximum of two years. That would mean monthly loan retirement payments of nine or ten thousand shillings. The Cooper manager and Eva Mwaluma agreed that the income from the operation of a single bus could not sustain such payments.

Some of the group's decisions now had to be evaluated in a new light. They had chosen to invest in the *duka* rather than save for a new bus. While the Cooper Motor Company was sympathetic, they had to have a minimum cash down payment much larger than the group's savings. The *duka* should have been sufficient collateral for a long-term loan, but the land and buildings in Mraru have not yet been surveyed and centrally registered with the Ministry of Lands and Settlement in Nairobi. This means that there is no deed to the building and, without a deed, no bank will grant a mortgage.

As of this writing, the group's dilemma remains. The old bus, too tired to continue as is, has been retired and sits in the Cooper yards in Mombasa. Although Cooper has ordered the new bus, it will not release the vehicle without first receiving at least half of the total price in cash— approximately 60,000 shillings more than the group can currently muster. The Mraru Women's Group clearly needs to raise more capital, but its only substantial source of income is the bus service, and that is not running. The women of Mraru are experiencing some of the old problems they had almost forgotten: once again it is difficult to get to Voi.

Although they can now make simple purchases nearby at their own shop, individually they have less money to spend because they cannot get to Voi to trade.

However sobering, the setback seems temporary. The group has assets: its old bus, its building, the shop's inventory, the goats, the goat herd's building, over 30,000 shillings in cash, and goodwill in many places. It seems likely they will find some way of obtaining the loan they need. The strong spirit that has carried them through so much hasn't wavered. They discuss their plans for more goats, the hotel, and with the encouragement of the Cooper sales manager, the hope that after they get the new bus on the road they might reclaim and restore the old bus so they would have the wherewithal to give each vehicle proper servicing while still keeping up a regular schedule. Some of their advisers, anxious that the group not overextend itself in one area, have raised questions about expanding the bus service. It will be the women of Mraru, however, who ultimately make that decision. And whichever choice they make, their story augurs well for women and development in Kenya.

Update

A June 1987 letter from Eva Mwaluma reported the following developments since 1980.

The group did purchase a second bus, which it operated for seven months. Then, due to the high monthly payments, labor costs, and mechanical problems which developed "too soon," the bus service again had to be discontinued. Despite a large donation received from a supporter of the group, they were unable to get another bus on the road. They would now like to purchase a *matatu* or jitney which would be less expensive to operate and could compete more easily with other *matatus* in the area.

The group has gone ahead with construction of a hotel behind their store. Ten rooms have been built and some are already rented, providing the group with a monthly income. The shop and the goat raising project continue to operate successfully.

_____ Lessons _____

The story of the Mraru Women's Group is a story of courage, ingenuity, and persistence. Members have learned a great deal about the rewards and the problems of economic enterprises, information that can be useful to women in other countries:

1. **It is important to select a product or service for which there is a strong local demand.** Both the women and their communities needed better transportation services. The demand for a small retail shop was evidently less strong so the immediate returns have been smaller. The *duka* does, however, have the advantage of being a firm asset, potentially usable as collateral.
2. **The choice of product or service should be subjected to the most vigorous possible economic analysis to determine its economic viability.** The bank knew the bus could not last long on rural roads and set credit terms accordingly. This seemed troublesome, but in the end served the women well by holding them to realistic economic criteria. The loans provided for the *duka* and the goats were given on much more lenient terms and perhaps this should not have been.
3. **Available support services from individuals and agencies should be used to the fullest possible extent without creating dependency.** Small groups often need assistance, especially in the early stages. All countries have resources such as government agencies, national women's organizations, community leaders, and international organizations that can provide advice and assistance. Drawing on their experience can often help solve difficult problems or bring new ideas and energy into a project. But the group also must exercise its own judgment as to what advice to accept or reject. Autonomy is important, too.
4. **The design of the project should be kept as simple as possible, especially in the early stages.** It is generally best to start small, with one or two products or services and a clearly defined market. Decisions on diversification and expansion should be made with the same care as the original choice. Similarly, the project should require only a small staff, easily supervised by the group, at least at the outset.
5. **Any group undertaking an income-generating project must organize carefully and provide a paid staff to carry out basic operations.** In Kenya, women's organizations have a strong tradition of doing this, and can rely on both the government and the national women's organization for guidance in selecting officers, developing guidelines for savings and investment activities, recruiting and supervising project staff, etc. It is crucial that the procedures and principles agreed upon be followed consistently so that all members benefit and contribute fairly. Officers who have specific responsibilities should be chosen on merit and replaced if they do not perform properly.
6. **Most countries and cultures have long-standing traditions on**

which women's organizations and projects can build. In Kenya, the long tradition of *harambee,* working together, is surely an important source of strength for the Mraru women, not only in building their economic strength but in developing a broader competence to sustain their families and their communities.

Further Information

The Mraru Women's Group can be reached at: Box 163, Voi, Kenya. It is an affiliate of the Maendeleo ya Wanawake Organization, whose national headquarters are at P.O. Box 44412, Nairobi, Kenya.

For general information about women's groups in Kenya write to: Women's Bureau, Ministry of Housing and Social Services, P.O. Box 30276, Nairobi, Kenya; or, National Council of Women of Kenya, P.O. Box 43741, Nairobi, Kenya.

The Song of Maendeleo ya Wanawake

Maendeleo ya wanawake	Women's progress
Ni lengo letu la daima	Is forever our aim.
Maendeleo ya wanawake	Women's progress
Ha yana budi kutunzwa	Must be our pursuit.
Waume wetu sikilizeni	Our husbands, listen
Kwa utulivu na makini	Tentatively and carefully.
Maendeleo ya wanawake	Women's progress
Ha yana budi kutunzwa	Must be our pursuit.
Afya nzuri na hali nzuri	Good health and well-being
Ya watu wote wa nyumbani	For everyone in the family
Ya tegemea ya tegemea	It depends—it depends!
Maendeleo ya wanawake.	On women's progress.

2

The Markala, Mali Cooperative: A New Approach to Traditional Economic Roles

Susan Caughman and Mariam N'diaye Thiam

The Markala Cooperative resulted from the resolution of a group of poor women in rural Mali to seek paid employment. When the twenty original members joined together in 1975, their goals were to earn a regular salary and to learn marketable skills. By 1981, these goals had been achieved. The women have established a successful cooperative business based on the production and sale of dyed cloth and laundry soap. In learning the necessary skills, they sought out job training unavailable to most women in rural Mali. Although they were helped by capital grants from several voluntary agencies, the members financed their own lengthy training through earnings. The experience of the Markala women has already inspired other cooperative businesses in rural Mali. It has also demonstrated that creating off-farm employment opportunities for women is a vital element of rural development projects.

The town of Markala, population eight thousand, is located on the Niger River, about 300 kilometers from the Malian capital, Bamako. Mud houses arranged around central courtyards make up the town's two residential neighborhoods. Once a rural, agricultural settlement like most throughout the country, Markala underwent a significant change when a dam and network of canals and dikes were constructed around the town

---

This chapter, except for the update section, was originally published as the pamphlet *The Markala Cooperative: A New Approach to Traditional Economic Roles* by the Seeds Publication Project in 1982.

31

Members of the cooperative *(Susan Caughman)*

to provide irrigation for large-scale agricultural endeavors that would produce cash crops such as rice, cotton, and sugarcane. The construction and maintenance of the irrigation system brought thousands of laborers, semi-skilled workers, tenant farmers, and supervisory personnel to the area from all over Mali and from neighboring countries as well. Most of the men of Markala now work as wage laborers and not as farmers. Similarly, the traditional work of women has undergone a significant change.

Malian society places a high value on women's financial independence and Malian women always have played an important role in support of the family. There is a clear division of responsibilities for men and women. For example, men are expected to provide housing, wood, and a staple grain such as rice or millet. Women provide their families with clothes and the ingredients that make up "the sauce," the stew of meat or fish, vegetables, and spices that is combined with rice or millet to make up the traditional Malian meal. On the farm, women wove cloth from cotton grown in their husbands' fields and grew vegetables for the sauce in their own garden plots. Today, in towns like Markala, not only the men, but the women too must earn money in order to buy both clothing and food. However, unlike the men, they have not benefited from the training programs and employment opportunities opened up by the irrigation project.

To make matters worse, 1968 to 1973 was a period of severe drought in the Sahel region of West Africa. Although it did not bring starvation to Markala, it did cause great hardship. Staple foods became difficult to obtain and rose dramatically in price. The cost of millet, for example, escalated 800 percent between 1973 and 1975.

In order to earn money, Markala women engage in a variety of income-generating activities such as small-scale trading and food processing. These ventures, never very profitable, became totally inadequate in the inflationary economy that followed the drought. So in 1975, at the suggestion of a local official of the Ministry of Agriculture then residing in Markala, a group of local women came together to discuss their problems and what might be done. They were determined to do something to improve their economic situation and eliminate the insecurity of their lives. They decided to join together in a form of economic organization—a cooperative.

Setting Up the Cooperative

For the Markala women, the decision to join together in a cooperative was a daring step. Though collective work groups are common in Mali, joint ownership of resources is very unusual, especially with non-relatives. However, the pressure to earn needed funds had become intense and the old ways no longer were proving to be adequate. So, putting personal misgivings aside, the group decided to move ahead with plans for a cooperative.

A major incentive to undertake a cooperative business was the desire to learn new trades. Many economic activities in West Africa are the province of certain ethnic groups or families, the necessary training passed down from one generation to another. The women viewed the cooperative as an opportunity to receive new skills training just as the men had received training through the irrigation project.

In a series of meetings that took place over three months in 1975, the women discussed their problems and what they might do to earn money. Before beginning any business activity, they agreed on some ground rules:

- The group would be open to any woman in the town who wanted to participate.
- The membership fee would be low, so no one would be excluded because she had little money. (The initial fee of 1,000 Malian francs

(MF), about $2.50, was lowered to 100MF (25¢) when it was discovered that many women otherwise could not afford to join.)

• The main purpose of the cooperative would be income generation. From the onset, members rejected activities such as literacy training and health education as irrelevant in light of their financial needs.
• All important decisions would be made by the group members. The women would not call on local political or government officials for leadership, as similar groups in Mali often did. Though they would be careful to discuss their project with local authorities, the members would retain responsibility for decision making.

The women first considered the problems they hoped to solve and then decided what business activities might best meet their needs. As traders and food processors, their incomes were erratic; each day brought a new anxiety about feeding their families. Thus they needed not only a larger cash income but a steady one. Any seasonal activity, such as gardening or fishing, would not be suitable. They needed an activity with flexible hours, because child care and household chores took time each day. Members also wanted to increase their ability to find employment as individuals, not just as a group. They needed to learn skills that would permit them to earn a living wherever they might be.

In the end, cloth dyeing and soap making seemed to best meet their requirements. These skills, they felt, would be valuable for each member whether or not the group enterprise succeeded. Several other considerations were important in their choice. The necessary raw materials were available locally and both cloth and soap were always in demand. Even more important, cloth dyeing and soap making are traditionally female occupations in Mali. The women's unusual venture was already the subject of controversy in town, so they felt it was essential to choose activities considered by their community to be appropriate for women.

Approximately two hundred women expressed an interest in joining the cooperative and most attended one or more of the planning meetings. However, community skepticism and the prospect of a long training period dissuaded most of them from continuing with the cooperative. By the end of 1975, twenty determined women began working in borrowed rooms in the back of a local school and the Markala Cooperative was in business.

Trial and Error

To begin the cloth dyeing the cooperative, with the assistance of a Ministry of Agriculture official, received a $600 grant from a United Nations project in Bamako that provided the initial capital necessary to purchase

Women preparing to dye cloth *(Susan Caughman)*

cloth, dyes, and string, and to hire a well known cloth dyer to come to Markala from the capital to train the members. The cloth-dyeing process proved to be complex and the women found it useful to divide themselves into two groups. One group concentrated on mastering the techniques of dyeing with clay, a traditional art of the Bombara, one of Mali's ethnic groups. A sure eye and a steady hand are required to paint accurate designs on hand-woven cloth using a small stick. Many months of practice were necessary before the women were producing saleable cloth. The other group chose to learn tie-dyeing. Patterns are tied, wrapped, and sewn on to white cloth, which is then dyed in a vegetable or chemical bath. When the threads are removed, a white pattern remains on the colored cloth. This technique proved even more difficult to master than clay dyeing.

The first two years of cloth production were marked by heavy losses, which members chalked up to training costs. Still they remained determined to perfect their skills and in 1977 and 1979, members participated in advanced training programs held by the American Friends Service Committee (AFSC) in the Gambia and Mali. By 1979 the women felt their products were equal to those of Mali's better known cloth dyers.

It took an equally long time for the members to master the soap-making techniques. The women first hired local soap makers to teach them a process using fish oil. But they encountered difficulties: fish oil was not always available and, in any case, its strong odor made the soap saleable only when no other was available. Then the group experimented with shea butter, an oil made from the nut of a local tree, but they were unable to produce a soap that lathered well.

Then in 1979 the Ministry of Agriculture, with the collaboration of the American Friends Service Committee, began offering technical, financial, and marketing assistance to women's producer groups in Mali under a program called FEDEV (for Women and Development in French). FEDEV hired a Ghanaian soap maker, Peter Donkor, to advise the group. He suggested combining two different oils to produce an odorless soap that lathered well. Donkor also introduced a new soap-making process in which the oils, caustic soda, and water are boiled over a wood fire. Up to that time the group had made soap using the "cold process" method of stirring the ingredients together.

Boiling not only produced more soap with the same amount of oil, but it also eliminated the odor. The new boiling process was somewhat more difficult than the stirring technique because it required accurate measurement of raw materials and quick judgement about how much water to add. But thanks to their years of experimentation with oils and caustic soda, the women learned Donkor's new techniques rapidly. Within a week they were able to produce a high-quality laundry soap. Donkor returned in a few months to help the group install two soap-boiling tanks, which gave them the capacity to produce several thousand bars of soap a week.

Steps Forward

By 1978, cooperative membership had grown to fifty. Most of the members come from the lower income strata of Markala. The majority are married women older than thirty; 64 percent of the marriages are polygamous with household duties shared between one to three co-wives. Only eight of the members have attended primary school and none completed their studies; two members speak some French, the national language. Yet by 1979, despite low incomes and continued criticism of townspeople who, seeing no financial gain, accused the women of wasting their time, cooperative members had not only become technically proficient in two major skill areas but were well on their way to establishing their group as a viable business.

One important step was to register the group as a producer cooperative under Malian law. This procedure, which is necessary for recognition as a legal entity by the government, was long and complicated. It is unlikely that this group of illiterate women would have been able to complete the required bureaucratic procedures without the assistance of FEDEV staff.

Another problem was solved when the group gained a permanent workshop, after several years of temporary locations and storage problems leading to a terrifying incident in which a child tried to swallow caustic soda. With a grant from NOVIB, a Dutch voluntary agency, a cement building was completed in 1979; it consisted of a large room with shaded porches on either side so that workers could move outside during the hot months.

Along with the other visible evidence of the members' newly acquired skills—dyed cloth and good-quality soap—the building brought about a change in the townspeople's attitude toward the group's venture. Skepticism changed to admiration, and over time the cooperative found itself with many requests for membership. Local officials, astounded that a group of illiterate women owned a major building, began to consider the cooperative as a genuine business venture rather than writing it off as a social club as they had in the past.

Organization

In addition to problems in acquiring technical skills, the members faced difficult decisions about how to manage their business. Since the women had no tradition of sharing resources, managing the cooperative's assets was a key area of potential difficulty. Committees were set up and the members elected officials and bookkeepers. The daily work schedule was set up to permit a certain amount of flexibility, according to members' duties at home. Women in polygamous marriages, for example, whose cooking duties were less frequent, were required to be present more often than members who had to cook each day.

Because one of the women's goals had been to assure themselves a minimum stable income, they decided to pay each member a regular monthly salary from cloth-dyeing profits. This monthly salary began at 2,000 Malian francs ($5) in 1976 and had increased to 4,000 MF ($10) by 1980. Though small, it represents an important source of security for members.

Meeting the payroll each month remained the highest priority even when the cooperative had little income. Members often borrowed against expected profits or paid themselves with funds that might more profitably have been reinvested in raw materials. But despite the strain, members feel strongly today that without that regular salary they would have found it difficult to persist during the years of apprenticeship.

Woman pounding cloth as part of the dyeing process *(Susan Caughman)*

Facing another controversial issue, it was decided that each member would be paid the same monthly salary regardless of how much each woman produced. In part this decision reflected the difficulty of measuring individual production levels. On soap-making days, for example, everyone helps in measuring oils, weighing caustic soda, boiling the mixture, filling the molds, and later cutting the batch into small pieces. Similarly, a piece of cloth might have been tied by one woman, dyed by two others working together, and rinsed by a fourth; the threads might have been removed by a fifth. For this reason, the members decided to view profits as belonging to the entire group and to divide them equally.

On philosophical grounds, too, a majority of members felt that equal salaries were necessary to promote group unity and discourage jealousy and quarrels. Many of the women feel today that the group's survival is due to the equal payment system. But some cooperative members resented the inequity of a system that rewarded all members equally—even those who were less talented or hardworking.

In an attempt to respond to this criticism, the members devised a quota system. A small sum is subtracted from the monthly salary of any woman who does not meet minimum production and attendance quotas. In practice, however, this system has not resolved the tension between those who prefer to sacrifice some profit in order to keep the group alive and those who view the equal payment system as exploitation.

Difficult decisions like these were often made only after months of discussion. But through solving problems together, the group became loyal and cohesive. In the beginning, the women had joined in the hope of individual gain; but a commitment to the cooperative venture began to be important as well. When the cooperative had fifty members, the group decided that the high cost of training new members required them to close the cooperative until their finances were more stable.

Marketing

For the first few years, the cooperative's revenues came almost entirely from the sale of dyed cloth. As members became more skilled, their production gradually increased until it outstripped local demand. Although the cooperative's cloth is much admired by local women, few can afford to buy more than one piece a year. Thus the cooperative faced a marketing problem.

In 1976, a modest store, La Paysanne, opened in Bamako. Operated by FEDEV, it is designed to market the products of rural cooperatives. As it grew, it marketed an increasingly large percentage of the Markala Cooperative's cloth. By 1980, almost all the cloth produced by the cooperative was sold on consignment in Bamako.

The store provides the cooperative with a reliable marketing outlet, access to a wide clientele, and a regular gross revenue averaging about 400,000 Malian francs (approximately $1000) a month. Participation in the store also has other benefits: it has forced cooperative members to improve the quality of their work and provides them with a source of raw materials at wholesale prices.

However, marketing cloth through the Bamako store also presents a number of difficulties:

- First, transportation between Bamako and Markala is costly, making frequent trips by members to pick up raw materials and deliver finished cloth difficult.
- Second, information from the store about the colors and styles that appeal to clients is slow to filter back to the dyers. The cooperative therefore cannot adapt production rapidly to changes in demand.
- Third, since all cloth is sold on consignment, there is often a three-to-six month delay between the purchase of raw materials and the receipt of payment for dyed cloth. Lack of capital frequently forces the co-

operative to borrow against future sales in order to buy more raw materials and continue production.

- Fourth, the cooperative depends almost entirely for its income on a retail outlet 300 kilometers away where management decisions are made with little input from cooperative members. Even though the Bamako store is a non-profit organization that exists only to market cloth produced in rural cooperatives, the Markala women have hesitated to involve themselves in its management. They regard it as an urban affair.
- Fifth, a high percentage of the store's clients are temporary foreign residents, an unreliable market on which to build a business.

For these reasons, as well as because of the low profit margin on dyed cloth, cooperative members have begun attempting to find ways to diversify their sources of income. A millet-grinding mill seemed a good possibility, since Malian women often pay to have their millet ground outside the home. However, the cooperative's soap-making business seems to hold the most promise of increased revenues, since its quality is appreciated in Mali and factory-made soap is often in short supply. But so far, problems with unavailability of raw materials, packaging, and marketing have limited the group's income from this product.

Members sell soap directly to individual buyers at the cooperative. They are seeking merchants to sell the soap in other Malian towns, but transporting it in large quantities will require packaging the soap to prevent it from drying out, a problem the cooperative is addressing. In the future, members hope the greater success of their soap-making venture will permit them to rely less on a single product, dyed cloth, for their income.

Finances

Record keeping has been another source of problems. The cooperative women preferred to call on the services of their own members rather than involve outsiders in their finances. As a result, the two literate cooperative members were chosen as bookkeepers. The bookkeepers devised their own record-keeping system and kept careful track of all expenditures as well as attendance, production, and soap inventories. As the cooperative's business has grown, adding new activities and involving more complex transactions, these systems have become less and less adequate. The members need reliable and timely information about the profitability of the cooperative's ventures in order to make decisions about purchasing raw materials or changing production schedules. Although the group has sought bookkeeping assistance from the local

On soap-making days, everyone helps in measuring oils, weighing caustic soda, and boiling the mixture. *(Susan Caughman)*

cooperatives agency, in the end they devised a unique and unorthodox system of their own. The group has assigned the responsibility for keeping track of the income from different ventures (one batch of soap or one month's sale of cloth for instance) to different illiterate members. In their view, this method balances the two literate members' control over written records and spreads responsibility for finances widely. While their system complicates attempts to gain an overview of the cooperative's finances, it is one that members value highly. The cooperative's members need innovative assistance to design a flexible accounting system that incorporates their own methods with traditional bookkeeping techniques, and helps them prepare profit and loss statements.

Lack of working capital has been an ongoing source of difficulty. Members must stretch the cooperative's resources each month simply to meet the payroll and buy raw materials for the next month's production. Thus, they are unable to stock raw materials when prices are low—an especially important consideration for soap making because shea butter, the staple oil, is harvested and processed in August and September each year and triples in price later in the year. Members would like to increase cloth production but they cannot afford to invest in cloth and dyes and then wait six months to receive the income from sales. Recently, however, the group received a working capital grant from Oxfam-America to permit investment in raw materials and thus allow an increase in production.

The cooperative's decision to remain as independent as possible has meant that profits build slowly. The grants received by the cooperative (totalling some $75,000 over seven years) cover only specific projects— the cooperative's building, for example—or short term training programs. The day-to-day costs of salaries, water bills, transportation and a host of other operating expenses that keep the cooperative functioning are supported from profits generated by cloth sales. The members themselves subsidized their own lengthy job-training process—an expensive effort that kept salaries low for many years.

The fact that their income from five years of work has been low has only strengthened the women's resolve to increase their earning power. As cooperative production expands, the members hope salaries can be increased.

Though the members are not yet satisfied with the financial return on their venture, their commitment to the cooperative is unswerving. They are expansive about the benefits gained. The Markala women see their occupations before they joined the cooperative as inconsequential: "I was doing nothing, so I joined the cooperative." It is a source of great pride to these women that they are now skillful cloth dyers and soap makers with a place of employment and a monthly salary. Their daily anxiety of the past has been replaced by a new security. Many of the mem-

(Susan Caughman)

bers, confident of their own ability to earn money in the future, are teaching their skills to their daughters so that they too will be employable.

Because the cooperative salary meets only a small proportion of the women's monthly expenses, many earn additional income at night using the skills learned through the cooperative. "Before I had no trade," said one of the women, "Now I am able to meet my expenses. I can tie cloth or make soap at home at night."

The women value the support of their sister cooperative members highly. "If I need something, if I have difficulties, I am helped by a cooperative member." They feel that working in a group has been highly beneficial. "Some people have better ideas than others so when you work together you learn."

The financial advantages of the group extend beyond the monthly salary. Cooperative members have formed a rotating savings club to which each contributes from her salary. Each month in turn, two members receive 25,000 Malian francs (approximately $50). For most members, who are unable to save at all because of the cost of feeding their families, this club represents their only chance to assemble a significant sum of money. Most use the money to pay back loans or buy clothes for their children. But several have invested their savings—one in a cart that she hires out, and another in a soft drink business. The cooperative also has a special fund to help members in emergencies, such as family illness.

These achievements have not gone unnoticed. In addition to gaining their neighbors' approval, the Markala women have attracted official attention. The FEDEV program, inspired largely by the example of the women in Markala, now assists some twenty groups in Mali. Many of them have sent members to Markala for training and women from other countries have visited Markala to learn about the cooperative's experiences. (See Appendix.)

Update

Despite difficult times in Mali due to the local economic situation, the Markala Cooperative continues to be active. Fewer travelers to Mali has reduced demands for some types of cloth produced by the cooperative. However, a recent order from a Japanese company is providing them with at least one export market. FEDEV now operates as an independent entity—the last foreign advisor left in March 1987. A general assembly has been created which includes representatives from each of the member cooperatives.

The soap-making component of the project continues, with the group making both hard and soft soap. There is a stable market for the cheaper soft soap because, with economic conditions so difficult, many families must buy this variety even though it does not last long and is less economical in the long run.

Like many women's groups in Mali, the Markala Cooperative has started a vegetable garden to serve the local market.

_____ Lessons _____

The persistence and initiative of the Markala Cooperative has demonstrated that poor nonliterate women can collaborate successfully on economic ventures. Perhaps most importantly, through their action and the organization of their cooperative business they have made an important statement about the role of women in rural Mali. Rural women who are responsible for feeding their families require job training and employment opportunities that will provide them with a steady income. Although increased agricultural production is an important goal of rural development projects, the cash needs of women, on and off the farm, must also be considered if family living standards are to be raised.

Those who wish to increase incomes among rural women can learn a number of useful lessons from the experience of the Markala cooperative:

1. **The initial activity undertaken by a cooperative should promise a clear and immediate benefit to the participants.** Experts would probably not have advised cloth-dyeing as a start-up activity for women in rural Mali. Profit margins are small, training is long and marketing, difficult. But the members believed cloth-dyeing would be useful to them whether or not the cooperative survived, and they were willing to commit themselves to mastering the necessary skills. Thus cloth dyeing was ideal for the early years when the cooperative was fragile and group spirit was minimal. Now that the cooperative is stronger and more cohesive, members can move on to less conventional, more profitable activities.

2. **Women should choose the structure of their own organizations, even if their decisions appear illogical to outsiders.** The Markala women organized their cooperative in ways that defy commonly accepted business practices. Regular salaries were paid regardless of income; all members received equal salaries despite widely varying production records; untrained members were elected to keep the cooperative's books. Yet these unorthodox rules represent rational responses to members' own evaluation of their overall social and economic situation. Donors and government agencies should make sure members understand the costs of such decisions and should seek compromises that maintain the women's own priorities while increasing profits.

3. **Appropriate technical assistance is vital.** Without outside advice the Markala group would not have achieved its goal of job training. One of the most important services that can be provided is to identify useful advisors and skills while allowing the cooperative to decide the direction of the project. In this case, officials of the Ministry of Agriculture provided technical advice but also put the women in contact with donors that could help them.

4. **A delicate balance must be maintained between self-reliance and adequate levels of outside financial and technical assistance.** The members were anxious to maintain their independence; they therefore avoided relying on any single donor or government service. Their independence has been expensive, since the members have borne heavy costs for training and project development—costs that might have been covered if the project had been sponsored by an agency or a voluntary organization. The resultant lack of capital has limited the cooperative's growth and kept members' salaries low. On the other hand, highly subsidized projects often fail once subsidies are withdrawn. The Markala group's stability seems assured since they have learned to function autonomously in the face of a wide range of

problems and a sometimes adverse financial situation. Donors and beneficiaries must work together to structure financial assistance that encourages self-sufficiency without forcing poor women alone to bear the financial risks of experimental projects.

5. **Bookkeeping and management are as important as production skills if a small business is to succeed.** In their enthusiasm for training that would benefit all members, the women concentrated on soap-making and cloth-dyeing skills. They neglected technical training for those members chosen to keep the books yet were unwilling to hire a trained outsider to serve as manager or bookkeeper. As a result, the lack of timely and good accounting information has limited the cooperative's profitability. When planning projects, the importance of such skills should be emphasized.

6. **A flexible, long-term perspective is essential.** It took several years for the members to develop their job skills, and even longer for the women to build confidence in one another. By starting simply and adding projects only as the members felt ready, the group stabilized and strengthened their project. Rigid project designs and unrealistic time frames should not be imposed; six years after the group was formed, the members of the Markala cooperative view their work as having just begun.

Appendix: Femmes et Developpement

The Markala Cooperative's success has been primarily a product of the hard work and determination of the members. However it also has been helped to a great extent by the existence of rural outreach programs. As noted earlier, a local Ministry of Agriculture official brought the group to the attention of donor and government agencies. Then in 1976, the American Friends Service Committee (AFSC), in cooperation with the Ministry of Rural Development, established a women and development program, Femmes et Developpement (FEDEV), in Mali. This organization has been able to provide training for the women and an outlet for the sale of their cloth. Until this time, effective, governmentally supported, rural extension (outreach) services to assist the efforts of women's groups had been rare. The following description of FEDEV shows how such structures, established within government ministries, can play a vital role in helping rural women to develop skills and establish viable businesses.

The FEDEV project is quasi-governmental in character, reporting directly to both the Ministry of Rural Development and the AFSC. It also reports to the government office responsible for supervising the work of private voluntary organizations in Mali. The Director of the Division of Rural Promotion and Training assists FEDEV by assigning staff (rural extension workers), informing local officials of FEDEV activities, and integrating FEDEV programs with other government and private efforts.

Now active in five of Mali's seven regions, FEDEV works primarily through district level rural extension workers known as *monitrices*. These women are connected with rural multi-service centers where they work with village women on health and social needs. At this writing there are ten *monitrices* assigned to work with FEDEV. FEDEV provides advice, training (such as training in tie-dyeing, soap making, bookkeeping, and general cooperative management), and resources that allow women to expand their role in the community into the area of income-generating activities. They receive a bonus for their work with FEDEV which is in addition to their regular activities. FEDEV also has provided a number of small motor bikes to facilitate the *monitrices'* travel in rural areas.

The FEDEV program operates as follows. When a *monitrice* has identified a group of women desiring to start an income-generating project, she assists them in finding suitable space for their enterprise and makes arrangements for them to receive training in needed skills, such as soap making, tie-dyeing, gardening, rug making and others. FEDEV provides the training and assists the women in organizing themselves as a business (electing officers, selecting a bookkeeper, deciding on cost of shares, dividends, salaries, and so forth) in what is called a "precooperative" structure. Becoming a cooperative in Mali is a complicated legal process that generally is not undertaken until a group has demonstrated its ability to work together and its profitability.

Good accounting procedures are recognized as critical to the success of any business and FEDEV not only provides training in this area but occasionally pays a small stipend to the bookkeeper during the initial period of operation until the cost can be assumed by the group. When necessary, FEDEV also provides start-up capital for tools and equipment and purchases some supplies in bulk for distribution to the groups at cost. Assistance with marketing the groups' products also is provided.

Each *monitrice* stays in close contact with all pre-cooperatives in her area, sometimes visiting each one several times a month. Through its training and support services, FEDEV expects that over a period of a few years each group will be able to:

• achieve financial viability;
• develop a sound organizational structure; and
• establish a marketing system for its products.

At this point the groups should be able to qualify for legal recognition as cooperatives within Mali which will allow them to receive consultation and training from the Cooperative Section of the Ministry of Rural Development.

Government officials in Mali have shown increasing interest in FEDEV activities. They are invited to visit the groups to see for themselves what the women are doing. One visitor to Markala was quite surprised at the quality of soap being made by the cooperative. Such exposure helps planners appreciate the importance of women's economic roles and the cost-effectiveness of rural extension services, thus justifying continuing governmental support.

Based on the success of the FEDEV project, the AFSC has initiated a similar project in Guinea-Bissau.

II

ASIA

3

The Working Women's Forum: Organizing for Credit and Change in Madras, India

Marty Chen

Most of the women who live in the slums of Madras, a large city in southern India, work as small-scale traders and vendors to provide for the needs of their families. Their economic contributions, however, generally have been dismissed by politicians and planners as insignificant or merely supplemental to the earnings of male family members. In fact, these women entrepreneurs provide, on the average, one-half of the entire family income.

For years these women went about their work virtually unnoticed. Then, in 1978, a group of politically and socially active women became disenchanted with traditional approaches to meeting poor women's needs. They began to talk directly to the slum women and soon discovered that most were in business for themselves and that their main concerns were not social problems, but credit—getting money to maintain and expand their businesses.

In response to this need, the Working Women's Forum was created. This chapter tells the story of how the forum came into being and how it has brought together more than thirteen thousand poor urban women around the issue of credit. It also describes how the forum not only has provided its members with access to funds, but has expanded to include support services such as child care, education, health care, and family planning. It also demonstrates how the sense of strength and purpose that has grown up among the members is helping them to tackle the political and social problems that affect their lives.

Except for the update section, this chapter was originally published as the pamphlet *The Working Women's Forum: Organizing for Credit and Change* in 1983 by the Seeds Publication Project.

The Beginnings

The city of Madras has been called a "rural metropolis." Capital of a large state in southern India, Madras (with a population of 2.3 million) is the fourth largest city in India. Because it has grown by swallowing up surrounding hamlets, most of its slums are actually villages made up of thatched huts rather than multi-storied tenements. Yet the economy of these areas is no longer rural. Residents work as day laborers or in petty trade, catering as best they can to the demands of the metropolis for goods and services.

Typically, men of the slum households work as casual laborers three or four days a week. The women generally work at what are termed "other services," such as petty vending and hawking. They usually work every day of the week. On the average, these women earn about $20 per month, an amount that often accounts for half of the entire family income. When the fluctuations in income of casually employed men are taken into account, along with their typically frequent outlays for tobacco and liquor, slum families are heavily dependent on the earnings of women for survival. In addition, approximately one woman out of ten is the sole wage earner for her family.

In November 1977, Jaya Arunachalam, a well-known political and social worker, was engaged in flood relief work in Madras. As she went through the affected areas talking to women, she became acutely aware that they were not interested in flood relief or politics. Their main preoccupation was their capacity to earn, and the main problem they faced in trying to earn was lack of credit. In words of one of Jaya's co-workers (now a vice president of the Working Women's Forum):

> Jaya and I went on a fact-finding trip around Madras between October 1977 and February 1978. We found out we were doing wrong by calling women to political rallies. . . . We offered nothing in return. By meeting the women in small groups we found out that each and every woman is engaged in some occupation and indebted to the money lenders. We decided to organize women around economic concerns.

During this period, Jaya took the opportunity of a speech to Bank of India officials to challenge them with the question: "Why aren't you helping poor women?" The banks of India were nationalized in 1969 with a mandate to extend credit to the poor. Yet little, if any, credit had reached poor urban women. The local bank manager, an unusually progressive man, took up the challenge and agreed to meet with and fund credit-worthy groups of low income women.

So, with Jaya's encouragement, thirty petty traders in one slum area organized themselves into a group, met the bank manager, and received loans of 300 rupees ($33) each. The group elected a leader and every day she collected money from the members to repay the Bank of India. Within a matter of months it was clear to everyone that the system was working. The repayment rate was 95 percent. By April 1978, 800 women had been organized into forty groups and had received loans. The Working Women's Forum (WWF) was born.

While credit was the focal point around which the forum was founded, its leaders recognized the wider social and political forces that limit women's economic opportunities. They therefore outlined broad objectives for the WWF:

- To create an association of women employed in the unorganized or informal sector;
- To identify and address the critical needs of working women;
- To mobilize working women for joint economic and social action by exerting group pressure to demand their social and political rights;
- To improve the entrepreneurial skills of working women through training, credit, and extension (outreach) services; and
- To organize support for social services necessary for working women and their families, specifically: child care, education, health, and family planning.

Moreover, in recognition of the potentially divisive factors of caste, religion and politics within Indian society, the forum's founders adopted certain strong ideological positions. The forum would be:

- **Pro-Women:** exclusive mobilization of women, who provide the backbone of family income and welfare.
- **Anti-caste and Pro-secularism:** support of cross-caste and cross-religious groupings of women, inter-caste weddings, and religious tolerance.
- **Anti-politics:** strict avoidance of involvement in party politics, yet mobilization of women around issues affecting women and the poor.
- **Anti-dowry:** organization of mass demonstrations against dowry, rape, and divorce.

The Women

According to a 1971 census, there were at least 23,000 women in the Madras slums working in "other services." However, it wasn't until the

Vegetable Vending	*Lungi* (loincloth)	Cycle Shop Owner
Sari/Cut Cloth Trader	Trader	Rice Trader
Fruit Seller	Waste Paper Shop	Meat Shop Owner
Junksmith	Owner	Junk Shop Owner
Greens Seller	*Bidi* (cigarette) Roller	Scrap Iron Shop
Ready-made Garment	Biscuit Maker	Owner
Sales	Carpenter	Bead Stringer
Fish Vendor	Sari Block-Printer	Wood Box Maker
Firewood Seller	Goldsmith	Bangles Seller
Aluminum Utensil	Stationery Shop	Mat Weaver
Sales	Owner	Chili Powder Seller
Incense Maker	Brush Maker	Leaves Stitcher
Silk Trader	Groceries Seller	Gold-Threads Garland
Pandal (ornament)	"Idly" (snack food)	Maker
Maker	Shop	Sweet Stall Owner
Plastic Flower Maker	Flower Seller	Egg Seller
Tea Stall Owner	Wire Bag Maker	Wood Utensil Maker
Pottery Stall Owner	Tailoress	Toy Maker
Hay Seller	Cart Loader	Gunny Bag Seller
Snack Shop Owner	Peanut Vendor	Footwear Shop
Toothpowder Maker	Sweet Shop Owner	Owner
Lime Seller	Mobile Ironer	Coffee Powder Seller
Salt Vendor	Snack Food Maker	Cardboard Box Maker

WWF began that much was known about the economic activities of these women. The forum has identified more than sixty-five petty businesses and trades operated by its members. The majority fall into four occupational categories: vegetable vending, managing "idly" (snack food) stalls, trading cut cloth, and flower and fruit selling.

Within the various occupations there are subtle differences. Some women work at home while some work at a fixed site; others remain mobile. Some women buy wholesale while others buy retail. Some pay cash; some buy on credit. Some women sell within their neighborhoods; others trade at local markets. Some women work part-time while some work long hours or travel great distances to ply their trades each day. Almost all, however, encounter tremendous difficulties in their work, difficulties that almost always revolve around low productivity, low income, and perpetual debt.

The factors confining women to the lowest levels of trade and business

A mat maker spinning fiber
(Marty Chen)

A young forum member
(Marty Chen)

are varied and complex. The structure of the economy and the marketplace favor men, who monopolize wholesale markets and the supply of goods and credit. Women frequently are harassed and inhibited at wholesale markets, where they are considered high credit risks due to the low volume of their trade. Since expansion of a business requires access to greater supplies and credit, it is obvious why the women's ventures remain small. In addition, social customs restrict the mobility of many women and prevent them from engaging in more profitable activities. Others have limits on the amount of time they can devote to their businesses because of their heavy domestic responsibilities.

Joining the Forum

The main reason women join the forum is to gain access to credit. The loans provided through the forum offer women access to larger sums of money than have been available to them previously from moneylenders and at a reasonable rate of interest. Access to credit has made a big difference in the lives of the more than seven thousand women who, so far, have received loans from the forum.

For example, Kamala runs a small snack food business from her front yard. She sells steamed rice and lentil cakes in the morning and fried rice cakes in the afternoon. Every week she buys rice and lentils and every night she grinds these staples into flour and prepares the dough which must ferment overnight. Previously, Kamala had to buy her supplies on credit with a daily interest charge. After paying back what she owed with interest, she earned about 50¢ per day. After receiving a loan through Working Women's Forum, Kamala now is able to purchase supplies in bulk, without high interest, and she is earning $1 per day.

In Kamala's neighborhood there are at least 100 women who operate similar snack food businesses. Countless other women are vendors of vegetables or kerosene, or they work at tasks such as mercerizing thread (treating with caustic alkali solution to strengthen and make it more receptive to dyes) or rolling charcoal and dung balls used as cooking fuel. Some slum women work piece-rate for large traders while others work as wage laborers. In some households, both husband and wife work at the same business. In the majority of cases, however, the women have their own, independent sources of income.

How the Forum Operates

Despite its large membership, the forum's organization is fairly simple. Perhaps its most noteworthy aspect is that, with the exception of Jaya

A forum member making paper bags
out of used paper *(Marty Chen)*

A forum member and her children
on their way to fetch water
(Marty Chen)

57

Arunachalam, its founder-president, all the executive and administrative staff have been recruited from the forum's membership, which is comprised of poor, often illiterate women from slum neighborhoods. These women have been selected either because of previous organizing experience with political parties or on the basis of demonstrated organizing potential. Generally, staff are not given any formal leadership or management training but learn on the job, through experience. The basic structure of the organization was developed around the requirements of the credit program.

The principles of political organizing were applied by WWF staff in developing their organization. The grassroots approach is emphasized. There is at least one local organizer for every thousand people, working right within the community. And there is continual emphasis on organizing new groups and developing new leaders so that the source of the forum's direction is always its grassroots membership.

The Credit Program—How It Works

When the government of India nationalized the banks, it prescribed a differential interest rate (DIR) of 4 percent per annum for the "weaker section of society." This program is commonly referred to as the "small borrower" scheme. Although in theory the working women of Madras were entitled to receive the DIR, they in fact rarely if ever were able to obtain credit from banks. Moneylenders or next of kin were the only sources available to them, generally at 120 percent per annum! When Jaya Arunachalam challenged the bankers to do something to help poor women, they had to admit that they only had thought of the DIR scheme as applying to poor men.

The women themselves said that the banks were reluctant to extend credit to them because they did not recognize the women's petty trading activities as legitimate businesses and they did not like to finance a large number of very small loans. Banks also require male co-signers on loans to individual women. In addition, the women were reluctant to approach banks because they found them very formal and impersonal, rarely willing to assist illiterate borrowers with the large number of forms that must be completed to secure a loan.

In order to circumvent these problems, the forum's founders decided to organize the potential borrowers into mutual-guarantee loan groups. These groups could use an efficient administrative process to link the borrowers to the nationalized banks.

Neighborhood Loan Groups. The key element in the forum structure is the neighborhood loan group. Anyone interested in joining the

A vegetable vendor *(Marty Chen)*

forum must become a member of one of these groups. Each group is made up of ten to twenty members, all women from the same neighborhood. Most groups are formed by word of mouth. Forum members and staff continually hold group meetings and discussions to acquaint women with the program. A usual pattern is for a potential leader to approach a forum staff member. She then is told to bring together a group of ten to twenty women and explain to them how the forum works. When a sufficient number have committed themselves, they elect a group leader. On some occasions, forum staff will approach a woman and encourage her to put together a group.

Once a neighborhood group is organized, it is registered with the forum. Each member then files an individual application form and pays a membership fee. A woman may become either a full member or an associate member. Full members pay an annual fee of 12 rupees ($1.33), which entitles them to participate in the credit program. Most women become full members. Associate members pay half the annual fee and participate only in the forum's noncredit activities (described below).

The membership requirements are simple: a member must attend group meetings regularly, repay loans consistently, and act as a mutual guarantor for the loans of all group members.

The Working Women's Forum _____ 59

Loan Procedures. Once registered, group members may apply for loans. All members apply together at one time. The group may apply for a second round of loans only after the first loans have been repaid in full. The following steps are involved in applying for a loan:

• Review of Credit Worthiness:

1. The group leader assesses the need, capacity, and productivity of individual members before recommending them to the WWF area organizer for loans.
2. Group members review each other's ability to earn before offering their mutual guarantee or security.

• Loan Application:

1. The group leader refers the member-applicants to the area organizers.
2. The group leader, member-applicants, and WWF area organizer go to the forum's office to file the application.
3. The member-applicants fill out a loan application (a simple, one-page form) at the forum's office, with the assistance of the group leader, area organizer, general secretary and loan officer.
4. The general secretary and loan officer sort the applications and submit them to the respective local bank branches. (At present, the forum is working through eight local branches of the Bank of India.)
5. The general secretary and loan officer tell the area organizers which local branch has received the individual applications.

• Loan Disbursement:

1. The area organizers contact the respective local branch to determine the date on which the individual loans will be disbursed.
2. The area organizer takes the members to the bank on the stipulated date.
3. The members fill out two forms at the bank under the supervision of a bank official; the bank official in turn fills out additional forms. At least half a day goes into processing and receiving loans for each group.

• Loan Repayment:

1. The loans are taken at a 4 percent DIR interest rate.
2. Loans are taken on a ten-month repayment schedule. (Ten monthly installments were preferred to twelve in the interest of keeping the mathematics simple.)

Member at large at a forum meeting
(Marty Chen)

3. The group leader is responsible for collecting and depositing the monthly repayments. She collects on a daily or weekly basis, depending on the preference of each individual member.
4. The group leader must deposit the repayments before a stipulated date each month.
5. The area organizer is called in to help collect repayments only in the case of default.

A Woman's Perspective on Credit

The nationalized banks stipulate that loans should be invested only in what they call "productive" purposes (commercial or business investments) and most of the money the women borrow does go directly into their businesses. However, a majority also divert some portion of their loans to meet critical consumption needs (food, clothes, utensils, or household repairs) or to repay debts. As the intermediary between the working women and the banks, the forum has been able to develop a flexible repayment system that takes into account the realities of poor women's lives.

For example, the forum has developed a broader definition of productive and economic activities that includes housework and childcare. It also has recognized the need to borrow to purchase staple items or to meet health expenses. In addition, it recognizes social consumption patterns that reflect vital elements in the Indian culture, such as marriage or religious festivities, which are perceived by the women to be social and economic investments. The forum also recognizes the importance of repaying debts to moneylenders and suppliers, since this eventually will enable a woman to make more money available to her business. It also will keep her on good terms with the moneylender, who still remains a reliable source of funds in an emergency.

It is the forum's loan officer who ultimately decides who gets a loan or who may default or adjust a repayment schedule. A number of reasons for rescheduling might be viewed as highly unusual within the banking community, but are very realistic in terms of the lives of poor women. These include:

- Unusual or unforeseen fluctuations in supply or price of goods. For instance, severe monsoon rains sometimes flood streets and houses and affect the supply and prices of perishable goods, transportation, and communication.
- Marriages. In reality this is an economic transaction since the bride's family must invest a suitable amount to secure a good marriage and both families must invest considerable time, energy, and cash in preparing for the various wedding ceremonies.
- Childbirth. Although women return to work within days (even hours) of delivery, there are still costs (for the midwife, for example) and loss of time (breast feeding, child care) to be taken into account.
- Medical Procedures. When women must visit a health facility for an extended period because of a major illness, sterilization, or other reason, or have a very sick child or family member, time is lost from work.
- Accidents and Disasters. Fire and floods are frequent calamities affecting slum dwellers and can wipe out a woman's entire stock and savings.
- Festivals. Religious rituals are an important part of the women's lives. They not only provide a source of inspiration and hope, but are often their only opportunities for recreation.

When a member has a "good reason" she can postpone one or two of her payments. Most "good reasons" have a seasonal pattern and a flexible program such as the forum is able to take these into account. In the case of death, the banks will recognize the default as legitimate. However, if an elderly woman wants to join the credit program, she must have an heir guarantee her loan.

Of course, there are always a few who default for no good reason.

When the WWF first began, some defaulters would try shifting to another group to try to get a second loan. Now, the forum returns the defaulter's fee and terminates her membership. Only those who are judged to be genuine self-reformers are given a second chance at membership. Occasionally a dishonest group leader will attempt to divert the repayments of others to her own use. However, once the default notice from the bank comes to the group's attention, they can bring pressure on the leader to make the proper payment. The whole system works on the basis of peer pressure. The group exerts pressure on individual members to repay loans because their own credit worthiness rests on the group's repayment record. Likewise, they can exert pressure on the leader to carry out her responsibilities honestly and efficiently.

Results of the Credit Program

The loan program has had a very tangible impact on the women's businesses and on the welfare of their families. An estimated 2,800 new jobs or businesses have resulted from the program and earnings have increased an average of 50 percent in existing enterprises. It also has assisted many women to expand and diversify their economic activities.

For example, Ramanji was a vegetable vendor. She used her first loan from the forum (Rs. 100 or $11) to reinvest in her business. She used her second loan (Rs. 200) to cancel the debts she had accumulated in the vegetable business. With her third loan (Rs. 300) and Rs. 500 borrowed from another source she invested in a new business: the manufacture of cloth brushes used to polish metal. She now employs four other women in this business and has given up vegetable vending to devote full time to brush making. She now wants to take out another loan of Rs. 1000 to purchase a sewing machine.

Ramanji's husband is a semipermanent painter. Her three sons are unemployed. Only Ramanji brings in a steady, daily income.

Still other women, through the credit program and moral support provided by the forum, have started businesses for the first time.

> Before joining our forum I used to work as a coolie (day laborer) at building sites. At that time I met Pattammal (a WWF leader). She inquired about me and I told her all my difficulties. Then she suggested I enroll myself as a member of the forum and that she would get me a loan to start a small business. I enrolled, got the loan, and started a cloth goods sales business.
>
> Murugammal, General Member

The women themselves report that the most basic indicator of the success of the program is that they are eating better; families that often

Members attending one of the regular group meetings *(Marty Chen)*

had to get by on one meal a day now can eat twice and are consuming a better quality and variety of foods. Hilde Jeffers's study, *Organizing Women Petty Traders and Producers: A Case Study of the Working Women's Forum* (Madras: WWF), looked at how 300 loan recipients invested their extra earnings. The study revealed the following priority of expenditures: food, clothing, savings, avoidance of the moneylender, household durables, medicines, improved male education, household repair, improved female education, and jewelry. (For Indian women, investment in jewelry is not a matter of vanity but a primary means of saving for future security.)

Most women report an increased feeling of economic security since joining the WWF. For the first time, their economic activities are on record with an established financial institution and they are being recognized for their work. It is also the first time poor women have been able to get bank loans without a male guarantor or signatory. "We have totally eliminated male members of the family as guarantors. Women have taken on full economic roles," says Jaya Arunachalam.

In Support of Women's Economic Roles

The credit program is seen by the WWF staff as one stage in a larger strategy for social change, a strategy that shifts gradually from addressing basic economic needs to tackling the related and often more complex social and political problems of working women. Now that neighborhood credit groups exist, it is possible to move on to other activities and programs.

Support Services. A number of social service projects have been developed. Many have been initiated by general members. In some slum communities, several loan groups have joined together to set up programs such as:

- Day Care Centers. The forum considers day care to be an essential service for working women. Ten day care centers have been opened by forum groups. Literate general members are selected and paid to serve as teachers. They are supervised by the group. A typical day care center is described by one of the teachers:

  Thirty-six children between the ages two and five attend. They stay at the center from 9:00 A.M. until 3:00 P.M. One maid (paid by the forum) and one mother (on rotation) help me clean, oil, and comb the hair of the children. After prayers and attendance taking, I teach the children Tamil (the local language), English, and math. We feed them a nutritious, low cost lunch consisting of lentils, vegetables and rice or greens, tomatoes and rice, plus biscuits and snacks. The mothers help cook the midday meal. The children sleep after lunch.

  Often these centers are no more than a modest thatched shed. Finding space for more centers has been difficult and is the main reason why this activity hasn't been expanded further. In addition to finding more space, the forum recognizes the need to develop a higher quality of care and instruction and the need to provide more toys and other equipment.
- Night Classes. Twenty-two evening classes for primary and middle school children (thirty-five to fifty boys and girls per class) have been opened. Again, literate general members are hired as teachers. They are paid and supervised by the group. The classes are designed to improve the children's academic performance and prevent them from dropping out of school. The teachers help children with homework assignments from their regular school and coach them in weak subject areas. There has been a considerable improvement in the school performance of children attending these night classes.
- Skills Training. The forum has started ten training centers to expand and upgrade members' skills. These centers focus on the unemployed

and those engaged in extremely low paying work. Upon completion of the training course, women who wish to seek jobs in local industries (particularly the ready-made garment industry) are given certificates of completion. In the future, the forum hopes to organize graduates into cooperative production units.

Health and Family Planning. In 1980, the WWF launched an experimental management training program in health and family planning. The goal not only was to improve health within the community but also to develop the leadership and management skills of a cadre of forum members who could then assume greater responsibility within the organization.

Sixty women have been trained thus far as field workers. They disseminate information on health, nutrition and family planning to families living in their own communities. All trainees must have at least minimal literacy in order to record data. They are given a special training course and earn $18 per month for their work.

The forum considers the family planning program to be an essential component in improving both the health and economic status of the community. To quote one staff member: "The family planning program was an outcome of the realization that income generation and large families do not go together. Many of the loanees face serious difficulties in raising the quality of life for their families due to their sheer size."

The health and family planning program has had an important impact on the community. One trainee describes the situation in her neighborhood:

> The slum dwellers here never know to talk to others. But after joining in WWF, I have come to know many things. Previously the slum children were not shown [were hidden] when the corporation [public health] people came for vaccination. After our training each of us were given 100 houses to take care of. Now that we ourselves have explained the advantages of vaccination, they bring out the children and have the benefit.
>
> Marayammal, Health and Family Planning Worker

Social Action. Organization and mobilization are the essence of the Working Women's Forum. The forum has utilized the strength of the local loan groups to unite the women on issues that traditionally might have divided them (caste, religion, party politics). As a group they also feel more confident to confront political forces that might be threatening to them as individuals (civic authorities, police, middlemen, moneylenders, wholesalers). Some activities undertaken by the forum to help strengthen the cohesiveness of the local groups include:

- Inter-Caste, No Dowry Marriages. Although discrimination on the basis of caste is illegal in India, centuries-old customs die hard. For women of low caste, this is an added burden to bear besides poverty. One member describes her own situation.

I never used to talk to anybody in my school days and others used to say that I was a Harijan* and low caste. . . . I even used to tell my father and cry, saying: "Some people differentiate and talk low of me." My father used to say: "We have more love and affection, they only have money." After joining this forum, we do not have caste differences that much.

Another old custom that has been illegal for decades but still persists is dowry. The WWF has been able to strike a blow against both of these debilitating customs through the promotion of inter-caste marriages. Some three hundred WWF members have been married in mass ceremonies conducted without dowry and at low cost. Many of the marriages simply serve to legitimize long-term common law unions. They therefore provide both legal security and social status for the women. The mass weddings are attended by government officials and provide the WWF with an excellent opportunity to publicize its anti-caste and anti-dowry position and to put pressure on the government to institute the economic incentives for inter-caste marriages that it has promised.
- Lobby for Public Goods and Services. The forum has assisted members in lobbying (and on occasion fighting) city officials on vital issues such as: protected pavement or stall space for women vendors; construction of thatched sheds in markets for women vendors; construction of toilets for women in markets and other public places; building and repair of roads, latrines, and houses in slum areas; and protection from police harassment.

Impact

The mobilization of the women around social and political issues as well as credit has resulted in perceptible changes in their attitudes on matters ranging from caste to family planning. Today, the majority of general members oppose dowry and favor inter-caste marriages and they are even more strongly convinced that women should play active economic roles. Most favor women working outside the home. There also is a

---

*Harijan means "children of God" and is the name Gandhi gave to those of the lowest social class, who had generally been called "untouchables," as an attempt to improve their status.

growing realization that it is possible to have some control over their lives, including their fertility.

Most WWF members report that they have gained greater respect, power, and decision-making authority not only within their own homes but within their communities as well. They recognize that their capacity to bargain and to bring pressure for their rights increases as the degree of their solidarity increases.

> Many of the women are illiterate; some are educated but most are very poor. Through the organization they have gained some status—new respect—in the community. . . . Through the discipline of the organization, we have seen a great advancement for women.
>
> Kala, Family Planning Supervisor

The neighborhood loan groups have become more than a mutual guarantee system for credit. They also provide a social network for the members. Often, the group is the first opportunity women have had to establish relationships outside their families. It offers women a base where they can air problems and seek solutions. Through these groups the forum has been able to tap and develop a vast reserve of dormant "woman power."

New Developments

Through the WWF, the nationalized banks to date have disbursed over 7,000 loans to poor women. The banks now view the group guarantee loan system as highly favorable and, with a repayment rate of over 90 percent, are expanding the program. However, the forum still experiences some chronic difficulties in working with the nationalized banks:

- Delays in receiving loans due to the high volume of very small loans often means that some women must continue to rely on moneylenders while waiting for their loans;
- Inflexibility in disbursement and repayment schedules; the forum has been able to introduce the flexible repayment procedures noted earlier only by absorbing the cost itself.

The forum therefore decided to build on its own experience managing the initial credit-referral program and open its own bank. It opened the Women's Cooperative Credit and Social Service Society in 1981. Selected forum staff were given special banking training and the borrowers with the best credit ratings from among the general membership (5,000 out of the 13,205 members) were invited to become shareholders at the cost of 20 rupees ($2.30) per share. Each shareholder is entitled to a credit line ten times the value of the shares she holds. In time, the forum hopes the Society will provide not only credit but technical and marketing assistance to shareholders as well.

National Union of Women Workers. In 1980, the forum began to work with rural as well as urban women. With the assistance of a government program called Lab-to-Land, forum staff organized a scheme designed to disseminate technological know-how to women in rural areas. WWF helped 400 landless women to acquire livestock and receive training in animal husbandry. The forum also helped organize and negotiate credit facilities for rural fisherwomen and lace makers.

As a result of their work, WWF staff recognized the potential power of organizing women along occupational lines (not only on the basis of neighborhood ties) to increase their negotiating power. They therefore inaugurated the National Union of Women Workers in May 1982, to provide a legal umbrella for expanding the unionizing work of the forum and to publicize the need to unionize women who work in the informal sector, outside the factories and workshops.

Future Directions

When asked to reflect on the future directions of the WWF, Jaya Arunachalam had many thoughts and plans. In terms of general strategies, Jaya sees a need for:

- Additional social services to provide women the necessary backup and support for their economic endeavors;
- More complete and competent technical services to increase the efficiency and productivity of women's enterprises;
- Alternative marketing systems to transform women's petty trading businesses to higher commercial status;
- Increasing bargaining power and strengthening pressure groups to demand greater access to and control over government goods and services.

In terms of specific activities, Jaya and her staff already have proposed the following:

- Cooperative production units to provide more secure and productive employment, especially for unemployed women and those engaged in extremely low-paying work;
- Wholesale marketing depots to supply trade items (saris, cloth goods, ready-made garments) and raw materials to women at the lowest possible wholesale prices; and

- A wholesale marketing network to link the marginal and landless farmers within a 25-mile radius of Madras to women traders within the city and, thereby, to eliminate the middlemerchants.

Update

In 1983, the Working Women's Forum was half the age and barely one-fourth the size it is today. Not only has the forum matured and grown, it has also changed its character in several significant ways. The WWF now has a membership of more than sixty thousand women and has extended loans totalling more than 13 million Indian rupees [approximately 1 million dollars].

The most striking change, beyond the significant increase in members and loans, is that the WWF can no longer be characterized as an urban project. By 1983, the forum had initiated three pilot rural projects for women engaged in animal husbandry, fishing, and lace making. Since 1983, each of these pilot projects has developed into a viable branch of the forum, with significant numbers of members. Two branches have more than four thousand members, the other has more than thirteen thousand. Also since 1983, the WWF has opened a fourth rural branch and a second urban branch, which work, respectively, with women who roll hand-made cigarettes and incense makers. Of the forum's total current membership, more than half are rural women.

The forum has continued its efforts to unionize women in a number of areas of the WWF. The establishment of the National Union of Women Workers provided not only a legal identity, but also marked a strategic shift in the organizing work of the forum. In its credit operations and preliminary stages of organizing, the forum had built on neighborhood ties; with the creation of the union it began increasingly to organize women along trade lines and to analyze the trade-specific constraints faced by women workers.

Two other program directions of the forum have been strengthened since 1983. The experimental health and family planning program initiated in 1980 has developed in both size and significance. WWF founder, Jaya Arunachalam, now describes the activities of the forum as "a balanced program of health/family planning and credit/employment using parallel local cadre and neighborhood mechanisms for delivery." And the Women's Cooperative Credit and Social Service Society, opened in 1981, has also matured. Although the forum began as a credit-referral operation, brokering credit from the nationalized banks for its members, in recent years it has extended more loan capital through its own Credit Society than it has leveraged from the banks. Of the more than 13 million Indian rupees in loans made up to March 1987, more than half were extended through the Credit Society.

_____ Lessons _____

1. **Very small loans (as low as $10) can be made to large numbers of women borrowers by commercial banks at a repayment rate of better than 90 percent.** To do so does not necessarily require high levels of overhead, supervision, or technical assistance.
2. **A loan program can be created and expanded quickly if built around small groups of ten to twenty-five women who share neighborhood, occupational, or other ties.** When a loan program is linked to formal financial institutions, loan procedures need to be reworked so that the review of creditworthiness is undertaken by peers and the women's micro-enterprises can serve as collateral. Repayment also should be structured around peer pressure.
3. **It is preferable to begin a program by supporting women's existing economic enterprises rather than attempting to train them and create new jobs.** Technical assistance, skills training, and enterprise development can be added later.
4. **A project to help poor women should begin with activities that produce quick, tangible results.** It is best to address their most immediate and concrete problems first. Additional activities then can be sequenced, moving from basic economic needs to more complex social and political constraints. Only those issues most often discussed and most adequately analyzed by the women themselves should be addressed.
5. **Program planning should not follow any definite blueprint.** Requirements for staffing and financing should develop out of an evolving program.
6. **A program for women is more likely to succeed if it adopts at least two elements: (a) a strong, pro-women ideology** to instill a spirit of solidarity and self-confidence in the women, **and (b) a commitment to grassroots leadership** as a means of strengthening and nourishing the dormant power of poor women.
7. **It is preferable to make use of existing government programs whenever possible.** Whether they exist in actual fact or only on paper they can be activated to serve the needs of poor women. The WWF proved this by implementing the "small borrowers" scheme and thus institutionalizing its benefits for a broader audience. In principle, existing programs should not be duplicated. However, there are times

when it may be necessary to create parallel delivery systems to guarantee that established programs reach poor women.

8. **An organization wanting to reach and benefit large numbers of poor women need not have a lot of money, educated staff, or technical expertise.** The success of the forum is due primarily to four factors: (a) selection of one critical issue (credit), (b) utilization of local leadership, (c) organization of women around existing neighborhood ties, and (d) decentralized, participatory management. With this structure, the WWF has not had problems in communicating messages or receiving feedback from its members.

4

Developing Non-Craft Employment for Women in Bangladesh

Marty Chen

Too often when development planners or practitioners plan income-generating schemes for women they consider only handicrafts. While in some situations craft production may provide a secure source of income for women, in many cases it results in poor returns and proves more complicated an undertaking than expected. Therefore, those interested in developing income-generating schemes for women should first survey women's existing skills and then ask: "Are there any non-craft activities based on women's skills that would provide a better source of income?"

The Bangladesh Rural Advancement Committee (internationally known as BRAC) is one agency that has developed a successful program of non-craft employment opportunities for women. Some ten thousand poor women have been engaged by BRAC in viable economic schemes, and of these nine thousand have been in non-craft production. This chapter reviews BRAC's experience in developing non-craft employment opportunities and participatory associations for rural women.

The Setting

The world of women in Bangladesh is largely determined by the custom of *purdah*, which literally means "veil" but figuratively extends to in-

This chapter, excluding the update section, was originally published as a pamphlet with the same title by the Seeds Publication Project in 1984.

clude the veiled seclusion of women. Under the norms of *purdah* in Bangladesh, women generally are excluded from the public sphere—fields, markets, roads, towns—and remain secluded in the private sphere—homestead and village, from which they emerge only at pre-scribed times and for prescribed reasons. So much so that under the traditional division of labor in Bangladesh, women are excluded from economic activities in the fields or outside the village and are confined to economic activities in and around their homestead or village.

Like women elsewhere, village women in Bangladesh work long and strenuous days. They raise and tend the animals; thresh, parboil, dry, winnow, and husk the grain; grow fruits and vegetables; clean and main-tain the huts and homestead; give birth to and raise children; and, oc-casionally, produce crafts for sale or home use. However, unlike women in other areas of intensive rice cultivation who are actively involved in transplanting, weeding, and harvesting, village women's work in Ban-gladesh is confined almost exclusively to the postharvest activities of threshing, winnowing, drying, husking, milling, and storing grains. Therefore, the only wage labor traditionally available to women in rural Bangladesh is postharvest work or domestic work in other households. Moreover, unlike other countries where women play very important roles in trade, rural women in Bangladesh seldom leave their villages for the markets either to buy or sell. As a result, the few Bangladeshi women who engage in trade do so only at the lowest levels—as petty hawkers within their own villages. But some women, especially the poor, have begun to break through these traditional barriers in search of work. BRAC's women's program was designed to support such women in their efforts.

BRAC's Approach to Development

The Bangladesh Rural Advancement Committee is a private, non-governmental, rural development institution founded and run by Ban-gladeshis. Begun as a relief and rehabilitation effort in the aftermath of the Bangladesh War of Liberation in early 1972, BRAC today is an established, comprehensive, multi-faceted development institution em-ploying more than fifteen hundred full-time staff. BRAC field activities, with programming and administrative support from a central office, have spread to more than one thousand villages in several rural locations. In addition, BRAC disseminates and communicates the experience gained in its field operations through its rural training center, its educational materials, its development journal, and its research and evaluation pub-lications.

Adult literacy is a
central focus of BRAC's
organizing strategy.
(Marty Chen)

Early in 1973, after a year of relief work, BRAC launched an integrated rural development program with activities in the following areas: agriculture and horticulture, fisheries, adult education, health and family planning, vocational and other training programs. BRAC's approach at the time was much like earlier community development movements. All that really was required to get programs underway, or so BRAC's staff members believed, was to motivate the village community through demonstration. However, very soon a number of inherent weaknesses in this approach became clear. First, motivation, education, and training alone cannot address major structural problems within a society. Second, in assuming that the village was a community, BRAC had not understood the innate conflicts between the rich and the poor within the village.

Over time, on the basis of its experience, BRAC completely reassessed its basic assumptions about rural poverty and development. Currently it operates on the assumptions that: (1) programs designed for the whole community deliver most of their benefits to the rich and tend to by-pass the very poor; and (2) programs designed for the poor must challenge the rural power structure, which keeps not only power but also resources in the hands of the few. Today, BRAC seeks to organize the poor and powerless (both men and women) in the villages into cooperative groups who then plan and manage their own group activities. The groups receive support from BRAC in the form of training, extension, credit, and logistics assistance as needed.

The Women's Program

The women's program began as conventionally as BRAC's general program. In villages where it was working, all women were to receive health and family planning services. Interested women were to attend functional education classes and one sub-group of widows or deserted women, whom BRAC staff called the "destitutes," were to receive vocational training in tailoring.

Underlying this plan were the traditional myths that women play no active economic role and that tailoring is women's work and requires, therefore, only a low level of training and investment. It wasn't long before these myths were proven untrue. Commercial tailoring, for example, requires specialized skills, intensive training, and a steady market. So the vocational training program was abandoned.

In the area of adult education, however, BRAC was more on target. It designed a curriculum of lessons that were functionally related to the skills and problems of villagers, both men and women, and recruited village men and women as volunteer teachers.

Functional education, as developed by BRAC, revolves around village problems and a problem-solving dialogue. A specific problem is presented, discussed, and analyzed during each class. Towards the end of each class, the words (broken down into syllables and letters) and numbers pertaining to that problem are taught. The curriculum and materials—a set of sixty lessons with charts and a teacher's manual—were developed by BRAC staff.

In addition, BRAC recruited and trained other village women to deliver low-cost health and family planning services. These programs proved to be successful. The failure of the vocational training program and the success of functional education and of training village women as community workers pointed the direction for the future development of a program for women.

In addition, research into what being a woman in various economic classes in Bangladesh actually meant revealed that rural households can be distinguished easily by the degree to which women's income or production is required to meet the daily needs of the family. Generally, the more dependent a household is on the income and production of women, the poorer the household. No one struggles harder to feed, clothe, and house the members of poor households than women. And no one faces greater constraints or receives less support than these women. Therefore it was decided to work only with women from the poorest households whose main problem is that of day-to-day survival.

Organizing Groups

The philosophy underlying BRAC's women's programs is not to seek women's economic development or social independence as ends in and of themselves, but to encourage the organization of poor women as part of the larger struggle to organize the poor, both men and women. BRAC therefore insists that all economic and social action be undertaken collectively.

Currently BRAC organizes the poor into groups of twenty to twenty-five. These groups are identified from among those attending the functional education classes. Each group chooses two members to receive training in group management and leadership and one family planning helper. The group plans and undertakes a series of joint economic activities based on traditional or new skills and a series of collective social actions to demand higher wages, settle marital disputes, and demand rights and services.

The task of organizing rests with BRAC's field staff, each of whom is responsible for working with the poor in five or six villages. The field staff live as teams in simple office-dormitory complexes and walk or bicycle twice a day to one or another of the villages in their areas. In the morning they hold discussions and supervise activities; in the evening they attend meetings and classes. They visit each of their respective villages at least once a week.

When they first start to work in a village, the staff members walk around the village talking to individuals, observing neighborhoods and households, and establishing contacts with the poorer members of the community. Prior to initiating work, field staff invariably conduct, if not a formal socioeconomic survey, at least an informal survey of the area. Information gathered includes local skills and occupations, village institutions, and physical infrastructure.

Functional Education Classes. After a few weeks, once they feel familiar enough with the village to know which of the poor could be drawn into a group, the field workers suggest that a meeting be held at someone's house. At that first meeting, the field staff briefly introduce themselves and BRAC. Those attending the meeting are encouraged to talk about themselves and their problems.

At some point during the discussion the field staff ask: ''How many of you would be interested in attending an adult education class? We

Attending a women's group meeting *(Marty Chen)*

will provide the lessons, blackboards, notebooks, and pencils. Would you be able to locate a volunteer teacher? Where could we hold classes?'' If the group is interested and is able to identify a volunteer teacher with a modest education from that group or village, that teacher is trained at the BRAC field office for one week in the functional education curriculum and methodology.

Separate classes for men and women meet in village homes. Village men and women are recruited on a part-time voluntary basis as teacher-helpers. By observing and supervising the functional education classes, BRAC field staff begin to learn about village problems and their underlying causes and to identify groups with like interests that could be organized into cooperative groups.

Group Projects. Towards the end of the functional education course, the groups begin to discuss future activities. Most typically, the groups discuss a joint economic activity. A group may decide to undertake collective farming or fish culture or a rural industry. The field staff, together with the group, talk over all the details and potential problems in such a scheme. Meanwhile, group members are encouraged to accumulate savings as a sign of their intention to work together and to build and maintain a group fund.

No set rules for financial and production transactions exist. Each group decides on its individual production and financial plans. The field staff help them by reviewing their plans in terms of cost-effectiveness and feasibility. Each group member must purchase a small share (averaging $1) per year and is encouraged to save a minimum (average 5¢) per week. The accumulated savings and shares constitute the group fund.

These funds are used on a rotation basis to finance either small loans to individual members, who otherwise are forced to take loans from moneylenders at exorbitant rates of interest, or group capital for small-scale, joint productive schemes. Whatever supplemental credit, support services, or other inputs are needed to back the productive activities are provided by BRAC; BRAC loans carry an interest rate of 12 percent per annum, equal to bank interest rates. Generally, each member is required to repay a minimum (average 15¢) per week from earnings against the group loan. (The average annual per capita income in Bangladesh is less than $100 per year or $1.92 per week. In addition, the women participating in BRAC projects are from the poorest households where the average income is even lower.)

Groups often discuss and undertake collective social action as well. They may decide to use their group funds or pool their labor or assist each other or other poor people in the village, in cases of illness, death, or property loss. Or they may decide to negotiate the terms and conditions of labor, such as demanding minimum wages or contesting maltreatment by employers. Or they may decide to lobby for public goods or services from local authorities, such as power pumps, public lands, medical services, or rations. Another common group activity is to circumvent the local moneylender by building up group funds for use in financing small individual loans.

When the groups carry out their activities they are regularly confronted by the village "establishment" of the rich, elders, religious leaders, and/or local politicians. Much of the skill required in group organization, and much of the cohesion within the groups stems from and relates to devising tactics to deal with these conflicts and obstacles. On principle, mass confrontation and violent tactics are avoided, but small-scale conflicts are the everyday fare of the groups and their organizers. Of course, internal conflict within groups also is not uncommon. However, resolution of such conflict, if skillfully handled by group members and the field staff, can actually serve to strengthen a group.

In terms of internal organization, a minimum of two members of each group receive training in cost-accounting and group management. These individuals then remain the informal leaders who perform key functions within the group. The group is formalized, with an election of officers and adoption of a constitution and by-laws, only if and when the function of the group necessitates it. For instance, groups must be formally registered to be eligible for certain types of government assistance or to receive training from certain agencies.

Subsequently, active and strong groups are chosen to organize other groups in their own or neighboring villages. Not surprisingly, there is a

Women's group member and
child *(Marty Chen)*

significant spread-effect as non-group poor observe the activities of a
group in their area. Gradually, all groups are linked together into a federation, first at the village level and then at the field project level. The
groups have chosen the name Working People's Force for this federation.
(The Bengali original for "working people" literally translates as "those
who live off their own labor.") Exclusively female groups are called
Working Women's Groups; male groups are called Working Men's Groups.

The Working Women's Groups

After its initial failure with vocational training, BRAC launched a search
for existing skills and potentially viable income-earning schemes for
women. They discussed feasible schemes with staff of other programs
and agencies, read case materials on successful schemes elsewhere,
toured other projects, including those in other countries, and came up
with a long list of possibilities. But most importantly, they conducted
surveys, interviews, and discussions with village women in Bangladesh.

In their search, the staff was willing to look at any or all skills and
schemes. But in their programming, they had to be more selective and
systematic. First, they had to look beyond schemes which might employ
thirty women here or another fifty there. They needed to help thousands
of women in hundreds of villages. Second, it would be up to each group
of women to decide which scheme or schemes they wanted to undertake,
depending on their needs, skills, and requirements. Such decisions would
be based on factors such as long-term versus short-term returns, year-

round versus seasonal employment, and the need for partial versus total sources of income. Third, BRAC staff wanted to evolve a framework to expedite economic planning.

As a first step in developing this framework, they asked themselves which skills and schemes potentially were major sources of employment for women in Bangladesh. They came up with the following classifications of skills or occupations:

- Traditionally female occupations that are or have been major sources of employment for women in Bangladesh: postharvest agricultural activities (husking, milling); animal husbandry; poultry rearing; tree, vine, vegetable cultivation; pre- and postfishing processes (net making, drying and storing fish); preweaving processes.
- Traditionally male skills and occupations that potentially could be major sources of employment for women: agricultural field operations (planting, transplanting, harvesting); construction work; weaving.
- Traditionally female skills that potentially are major sources of employment for women: quilt-making; craft manufacture.
- Traditional skills from other countries with a potential for women in Bangladesh; silk culture; block printing.

As a second step in developing a framework, BRAC staff asked what needed to be done to transform these skills and occupations into major sources of income and employment for women. In some areas, what was needed was the type of support given by the government and development agencies to traditionally male agricultural activities (provision of supplies such as fertilizer and seed, technologies, credit, subsidy, price supports, markets). In other areas, what was needed was the type of "job creation" done in industry (skills training, provision of fixed and working capital management). It was decided, given these two broad types of requirements, to classify all potential schemes either as: (a) those which enhance the productivity of what women already do; or (b) those which expand employment beyond what women already do.

Production Enhancement Schemes. In order to enhance the productivity of what women already do, BRAC undertook schemes which aim:

- to transform subsistence production into commercial production by providing small amounts of working capital;
- to increase output and efficiency by providing the same package of extension services offered to men, namely credit, commodities, technology, and training;
- to protect women's labor from displacement by machines; and

- to improve the terms and conditions of production, the reasoning being that if women gained control over their own labor, they would be able to demand higher wages, greater employment opportunities, and access to land.

Employment Expansion Schemes. In Bangladesh, women have been bound by tradition to certain skills and to certain work. Moreover, women's skills and products have not been diversified or improved over time. In order for women's opportunities for paid work and production to expand, these trends need to be reversed.

Therefore, BRAC staff undertook schemes which aim:

- to commercialize traditional skills by creating new markets;
- to revive and adapt traditional skills and designs to new lines of useful, marketable items;
- to train women in new or nontraditional skills; and
- to mobilize demand for women's labor by lobbying for women's participation in public employment schemes and in agriculture.

Between 1976 and 1984, BRAC's employment expansion schemes have been able to engage the largest number of women in rice processing (3,810), animal husbandry (2,344), horticulture (843), and poultry (800). And significantly for Bangladesh, it has encouraged more than 200 women each year to undertake collective agricultural production on leased land.

What follows is a discussion of some of these schemes. Each scheme is discussed in terms of the requirements for training, management, and organization. The purpose of these descriptions is to provide a sense of process; that is, how the problems faced in developing each scheme were confronted and overcome.

The Schemes

Horticulture. In Bangladesh, vegetable and fruit production is the preserve of women. Therefore, early on BRAC launched a scheme to provide assistance to women working in horticulture. New as well as traditional varieties of vegetable seeds were distributed each year to thousands of families and to local primary and secondary schools. Field staff provided instructions on seedbed preparation, transplanting, and care of plants. They also encouraged the growing of fruit trees and regularly distributed thousands of seedlings and saplings of coconut, banana, mango, papaya, and guava trees. All of these supplies were sold at cost to interested households.

Currently, BRAC has targeted these horticultural services to more directly reach and benefit poor women. Those who do not possess much land, or who want to pool their labor, are encouraged to take up collective fruit and vegetable cultivation on leased or sharecropped plots of land. One group of women, by way of example, has planted sixty lemon trees at a cost of 3 taka each; a total investment of 180 taka (15 taka then equalled $1; therefore this represented an investment of $12). They can harvest roughly 30 taka worth of lemons per tree per year, for an annual return of 1800 taka ($120) or ten times their investment. Women are also being organized to plant and rear seedlings and saplings for sale. By December 1982, more than eight hundred women were engaged in horticulture projects.

Animal Husbandry. In Bangladesh, animal husbandry is also the preserve of women. After some initial collaboration with a government dairy farm, BRAC abandoned the idea of providing veterinary services for cattle, which are most often owned by richer households, and decided to focus on calf and goat rearing schemes for poorer women.

Currently, BRAC provides credit to groups of women who possess few if any animals and who wish to rear animals cooperatively. Many of the women's groups, with loans from BRAC, buy young animals which they rear and sell for a profit ten to twelve months later. A calf purchased for 500 taka ($33.33) will sell ten months later for 1,000 taka; a profit of 50 taka per month with little cost or labor.

By way of example, a group of fifteen women borrowed 7,500 taka ($500) in January 1978. They purchased fifteen calves. Each member of the group was responsible for rearing one calf. The rearing costs were negligible and involved no cash outlay. After one year, fourteen calves were sold (one calf had not been properly tended so that particular women continued to rear it to an optimum size for sale).

Purchase price for fourteen calves:	7,000 taka
Sale price for fourteen cows:	14,814 taka

The women repaid their loan a few months behind schedule, but only because they waited for a high market price for their cows. BRAC charged an interest rate of 15 percent per annum on the loan, so the total interest came to 1,050 taka.

Sale price for fourteen cows:	14,814 taka
Purchase price plus interest:	−8,050 taka
Net income:	6,764 taka

Fifty percent of the income was distributed equally among the fourteen members of the group, an individual profit of 242 taka ($16) per woman. The other fifty percent of the net income was deposited in the group fund.

Some groups prefer to take smaller loans and purchase only a few animals. They then decide which members have the space and feed to rear the animals. The initial investment is made by the group and the rearing costs are borne by the individual. On the sale of the animals the individual woman realizes half of the profit and the other half is put into the group fund. If a loss is incurred, that loss is borne by the group. Therefore the group puts pressure on individual women to rear the animals properly. As of December 1982, more than two thousand women were rearing cows or goats.

It should be noted that these animal husbandry schemes for the poor are designed more to maximize a profit from rearing rather than to enhance production. No veterinary services have been offered and little cost or effort needs to be invested by the women. The only supports required from BRAC are credit and field staff supervision. In the future, however, BRAC plans to provide training and additional services (vaccines, improved feed) to enhance the production of those women who are able to purchase their own goats and cows.

Poultry Rearing. In Bangladesh, most women keep a few chickens or ducks, depending on the terrain, to scavenge around the homestead. In 1976 BRAC initiated a poultry program designed to expand the free-ranging/scavenging system of rearing and to improve the quality of poultry through introducing improved breeds, mass vaccination, and training in the areas of improved breeds, feed, housing, and disease control. Early on they decided to centralize the training and technical support of the program at BRAC's Training and Resource Center (TARC), a training campus with hostels, classrooms, and a demonstration farm located fifteen miles from Dacca. Poultry houses were constructed on the TARC campus, stocked with foreign cocks and local hens, and cross-bred chick and egg production was begun.

Initially, BRAC relied on outside expertise from donor agencies for technical training and assistance, but soon it hired its own poultry trainers. These technical trainers were expected to conduct feasibility studies, provide training, and coordinate the supply of vaccines, eggs, and chicks. More recently, another cadre of workers has been introduced to support the poultry program: poultry ''paravets''—high school graduates who, after training from TARC, are posted to the field projects. They provide on-the-spot supervision, with technical backup from TARC. Currently, the paravets are supplying cross-breed eggs from TARC to individual village women. In turn, the women assist the paravets in regular poultry vaccination campaigns.

Ultimately BRAC has learned that there are several critical elements to a successful poultry program: upgrading the domestic flock, centralized breeding, systematic culling of local cocks, regular supply and delivery of vaccines, village-level supervision and management. Their poultry program now includes all these elements.

Fish Farming. In Bangladesh, only richer households own ponds but they often allow their ponds to erode and dry up. Therefore BRAC decided that groups of poor villagers could be organized and supported to lease, re-excavate, and stock such ponds. In theory, a one-third acre pond can yield 10,000 taka ($666) worth of fish per annum.

Most typically, the government and other agencies engage men in fish culture. However, BRAC considered fish culture a potential scheme for both men and women because in fishing communities women perform major functions, such as net making and fish processing, and in many communities young women and girls do harvest fish from village ponds. Also, experience has shown that women can provide the heavy labor required during pond excavation and in the cultivating, harvesting, and marketing of fish. Staff discussed the potential for women in fish culture with a UNICEF fishery expert, and in January 1978 they jointly arranged the first national training for women in fish culture. Since then, women have been regularly engaged in fish culture by BRAC, UNICEF, and other agencies.

Aurangabad village offers a good example. With BRAC support, twenty-four members of a men's group and fifteen members of a women's group leased a pond which had been neglected for fifteen years. They re-excavated the pond in early 1978. Group members donated 20 percent of their labor and BRAC paid wages to cover the remaining 80 percent. The members of the groups started the scheme with capital they raised: each member was asked to put in 2 taka per month to a group fund for roughly a year. They invested the following amounts into the pond scheme:

small fish (3,000)	469 taka
rice husks (2 maunds)	125 taka
lime (300 seers)	60 taka
oil cake (1 maund)	83 taka
chemical fertilizer	20 taka

(A maund equals 82 pounds; a seer equals approximately 2 pounds.) They also supplied some cow dung from their own stocks.

Poor women of all ages participate in BRAC's women's groups. *(Marty Chen)*

In the first year they realized a profit of roughly 4,000 taka; an average investment by each of the thirty-nine members of 19.50 taka ($1.30) yielded an average return of 103 taka ($6.80).

As with poultry, BRAC soon found it worthwhile to hire its own fish culture experts to provide training and technical support through TARC. In 1978, one large and two small ponds were re-excavated at TARC's rural campus and stocked with fast-growing varieties of fish. Now, TARC technical trainers can give regular training in fish culture and in the design and construction of fish ponds and TARC can supply small fish or fingerlings. The actual management of the fish pond schemes are handled by the field staff.

All schemes encounter problems and fish culture is no exception. First are the terms and conditions under which the ponds are leased. Some of the early leases were not court-certified. These contracts eventually fell through, groups became disheartened, and the schemes were discontinued. Now all leases are certified.

Second, various technical problems arise. For example, there is an optimal depth to which ponds should be excavated in order to prevent seepage and allow for maximum cultivation.

Third, there are the human and organizational problems involved in pooling labor and sharing a profit. Marketing, however, presents few problems as the fish are sold at the traditional fish markets. And some groups, depending on the size of the pond and the condition of its banks, grow banana, papaya, and other fruit trees around the pond to prevent erosion and to bring in additional income.

Rice Processing. Postharvest processing of grain, mainly rice in Bangladesh, is also the preserve of women. The following postharvest work is carried out exclusively by women and most of it is very time-consuming:

- Parboiling. This is the process of boiling rice in large drums over slow fires.
- Drying. Before grain is set out to dry, a drying surface must be prepared (plastered with mud), dried, and swept. Drying grain must be turned at regular intervals and protected at all times from poultry and wild birds.
- Husking. Most typically rice is husked first and then polished in a foot-operated, hammer-action implement known as the *dekhi.*
- Winnowing. Like drying and cleaning, it is done at several intervals: postthreshing, postparboiling, and posthusking. Women manufacture their own bamboo winnowers.
- Storage. Domestic and market stocks of grain and seed are also stored by women who prepare the storage bins and supervise the activity. It is women who judge the quality and moisture level of grain and seed before and during storage.

About 70 percent of all rice in Bangladesh is processed by rural women and over 50 percent of all paid work available to women is from processing rice (Harris 1978, 2; Cain and Khanam 1979, 34–35). Rice processing provides, therefore, the critical margin of survival to millions of poor women and their families. It is estimated that over 40 percent of rural households, the poorest households, survive because of women's income from rice processing (BRAC 1979, 75–77).

Thus it was evident that assisting women who wanted to undertake rice husking on a commercial scale had several economic advantages: it is based on existing skills, equipment, and markets; it brings a quick return (within two days); it carries few risks; and it has traditionally been operated as a small business by some women. The only real constraint is lack of working capital to buy the rice.

Groups of women interested in undertaking rice husking can borrow funds from BRAC through their group, work as individuals or in teams, and market the rice through male members of their families. The group serves as an umbrella to receive loans and the group members work as mutual guarantors one to another. Initially, BRAC provided enough credit to each woman to purchase one maund of unprocessed rice. Later, having recognized the cost-effectiveness of processing a greater volume at one time, each woman was given enough credit to purchase two maunds of unprocessed rice (180 taka or $12). A small amount of credit goes a long way. With that amount, women begin to earn between 36 and 56 taka ($2.40 and $2.73) per week. As of December 1982, nearly four thousand women were engaged in commercial rice husking.

In order to insure women's control over this source of income, there are plans to convert some women's rice-husking cooperatives into owner-manager cooperatives of small-scale, custom mills. In Bangladesh, mechanical and automatic mills, encouraged by the cheap capital provided by the nationalized banks and by subsidized electricity, have been gradually taking over rice processing and thereby displacing women's labor. Increasing the scale of women's rice processing and strengthening their control may prevent or reverse the displacement of women from this critical set of operations. If large, automatic mills are prohibited, and if only small-scale custom mills licensed, women could be organized to own and manage these mills. BRAC and other agencies that have considerable experience in organizing women could provide the managerial back-up to women's custom-mill cooperatives. In this way women would not lose their major traditional source of income as the country adopts capital-intensive techniques of production.

Silk Culture. Since the mid-1970's, the Bangladesh Government's silk board and several voluntary agencies, including BRAC, have looked into the potential of different types of silk culture to generate a natural fiber for the nation's handloom sector and to generate an income for village women. Initially, emphasis was put on the cultivation of a variety of silk worm which feeds off castor bush leaves and spins a variety of silk known locally as *endi*. *Endi* silk was reputed to be stronger than cotton, less expensive than mulberry silk, and to involve a labor-intensive technology (hand spinning) rather than a capital-intensive technology (machine reeling). The cultivation and spinning of *endi* silk promised to provide a steady income for a limited investment of capital ($6.33 for a spinning wheel and $5.00 for racks and other implements) and little training (the skills required in cultivating, rearing, and spinning *endi* silk transfer more quickly and easily than those required for mulberry silk).

BRAC was able to arrange for training for three levels of personnel at the government's silk farms and through other voluntary agencies. Successive groups of village women were given intensive training in

Spinning silk *(Marty Chen)*

castor silk cultivation and management in order to work for BRAC as full-time silk para-technicians. And the field staff responsible for developing BRAC's silk industry were trained in the stages of production, technical and support systems, pricing, and marketing.

After a trial phase, systems of production, management, and extension were developed based on three critical decisions. First, all stages of production (from cultivation of the plants and rearing of cocoons to spinning of thread) should be undertaken by each woman to ensure her sufficient income and incentive. Second, only worms (not eggs) should be supplied to the women for rearing. Supplying worms reduces the extra care required for young worms and ensures only quality worms are reared, since diseased or small worms can be weeded out at BRAC's service centers. Third, the service centers would supply all worms and seeds/seedlings and serve as collection depots on set days each week to purchase spun thread. On that day, each woman receives payment for her thread, repays a small amount of the loan for her spinning wheel, and collects worms for rearing. The district government nursery supplies the "parent stock" of eggs and seeds/seedlings, technical back-up, and a market for the silk thread. BRAC purchases damaged thread or low-quality thread at a low price for experimental weaving.

Given the success with castor silk, it was decided to branch out into the cultivation and rearing of mulberry silk. The service centers and silk para-technicians are now equipped to provide the greater care required by the mulberry plant and worm. As of December 1982, more than eight hundred women were rearing and spinning castor silk and another fifty mulberry silk. More recently, block printing and hand embroidery of silk fabric have been introduced and women are being trained to weave silk.

BRAC has found that silk rearing and spinning can provide a primary income to women who engage in silk spinning for eight hours a day or a supplemental income to those who work fewer hours. It believes that silk culture can provide a year-round income, despite the seasonal availability of the plants, and that silk culture has the potential for large-scale employment for many women in Bangladesh.

Agriculture. In Bangladesh, agricultural field operations are the single largest employer of rural labor, but traditionally only men, not women, were involved. BRAC decided to train women in agricultural field work so that they not only would earn an income, but also gain access to the rural labor market. They reasoned that if women were seen working in the fields, they might then be hired by others as agricultural laborers.

As a first step, BRAC decided to support groups of women who wished to lease or sharecrop land to cultivate their own crops. It helps them plan and manage their cultivation and provides loans for the inputs required.

What are the necessary steps in a successful agricultural scheme? How have the women undertaken these steps? And have the women acquired the requisite ''male'' skills?

- Land Leasing or Sharecropping. With loans and advice from BRAC, women lease or sharecrop land. Initially, the women were not good at judging what quality or quantity of land to seek. After training and experience, the women gained this vital expertise.
- Land Preparation and Ploughing. Women do not undertake ploughing but contract men (on a daily wage basis) to perform this function.
- Cultivation. Previously, women did not have the skills of transplanting/ planting, weeding, and so forth. Initially, they contracted men to work alongside them and to train them in these operations. Within the first season, the women had acquired all the necessary skills.
- Harvesting. As with cultivation, the women have been able to acquire the necessary skills with relative ease.
- Marketing. Markets remain the one corner of the male domain that women have not yet penetrated. Currently, women market their produce either through male members of their family, BRAC field staff, or a middlemerchant. Some groups have been cheated by the middles, and thus have had to learn to negotiate for adequate terms and prices.

The Impact on the Women

The BRAC experience has significant implications for those who wish to design programs to increase the incomes of rural women. Before analyzing the lessons, let us turn to the women for whom the program was intended. What has been the impact of BRAC's economic and social programming on these women? What has begun to happen in their lives and in their villages?

In the ten years since it first began rural development work, more than twenty thousand women have been organized by BRAC into more than eight hundred active groups and ten thousand of these women are involved in viable economic activities. Some of the benefits of a group to its members are highly visible and quantifiable, some less so. Some women's lives have changed a great deal, others less so. But no woman's life is ever quite the same after joining a group.

BRAC field staff can describe visible changes in the huts and home-steads of the women. Some homesteads have been cleared and culti-vated. Porches, sheds, and tin roofs have been added to many huts. There are more hens, goats, and even cows to be seen. There are also visible changes in the women themselves. Many women have lost their veneer of shyness and become assertive and outgoing. In the words of one staff member, some of the women are "sophisticated 100 times."

It is the women themselves, however, who have the most to say; they can describe concrete changes in their lives. Before, they had little access to or control over cash incomes; now they are earning personal incomes. Most women spend their first earnings on the most immediate need of their families—food; then they spend for shelter and clothing. Once they are able to meet these minimum requirements of their fam-ilies, they take several steps to ensure the security of their family: they begin to repay debts, they redeem mortgaged goods, or they repair their homes. Once they have saved a little, the women invest their earnings in certain assets, such as poultry, a goat, a cow (in that order) or an addition to their huts or an agricultural implement. Only then, and only very rarely, will the women spend a little of their personal income on themselves.

On the strength of earning some income, combined with the strength of belonging to a group, the women have begun to negotiate new roles and opportunities for themselves. The women describe these less visible and less concrete changes in these ways:

• They have greater opportunities to meet and socialize and, as a result, have developed new loyalties and affections: "If another person does something bad to me, another member of the group will come forward to protest it. . . . I was alone, but now with me there are ten other members. They give support to me."

- They begin to earn more affection and respect within their own families: "Now my husband does not beat me. Our friendliness is increasing. My husband is taking lessons from me. Before he did not know how to write his name. Now he can write his name."

- They are able to avoid being deserted or divorced or, in some cases of desertion, they are reunited with their husbands: "There is another girl who was abandoned by her husband for three years. We asked him to take his wife back home. This year we asked him: 'Tell us whether you are taking your wife back or not.' He said: 'Well, as you are asking, I will take her.' Then he constructed a house and took her back."

- They are able to reduce their dependence on the rich and powerful of the village for advice, loans, and work opportunities: "Everybody used to badmouth against me. I did not listen to them. They are the rich. Why should we listen to the rich? They walked on our bodies. We should not listen to them. They should listen to us. I was very poor. I could not eat properly and buy any clothing. We started studying in the [functional] education classes. We discussed our problems. . . . Now, everything seems good to me."

- They are now able to participate in local judicials (informal courts), initiate legal proceedings, even call for retrials: "We will not allow that. Already he has got a wife, so why should he marry again? The way we will punish him, he will give up notions of marrying again. We will call a *shalish* [informal court]." *But aren't shalish convened by the men?* "A women's *shalish* will be convened by women. And from now on, we will hold our own *shalish.*"

- They have begun to exercise their right to vote or withhold votes in their own interest: "I do not cast any vote. Why should I cast my vote? I understand everyone has the right to cast a vote. Before the election they call us *Mia-bhai* [affectionate title]. After the election they forget us. They come and say: 'We will give you rice and wheat.' They offer us betlenuts. After they win the election and we say: *'Mia-bhai,* please give us a ration slip so we can buy cloth.' They say 'Not now, come later on' or 'I do not have time now, come at night.' We go at night for the slip. 'I work the whole day and at night. And, you all come for a slip.' This is how they win the election and how they behave. That is why I do not cast my vote for him. We will select a poor person and vote for him."

- They have begun to demand their right to public goods and services: "This year we have gotten ration cards. The ration dealer gives us half the allotment of rice, flour, and salt. If we say anything the ration dealer says: 'I only have this much. Wheat is coming.' Before, we could not even ask about the wheat. If all the group members go to the local government officer and complain to him about the [ration] dealer, then what will happen to him?"
- The women also describe significant changes within themselves. They speak of new-found wisdom and confidence: "Before we were blind, although we had eyes. We used to work in other people's houses, but we did not get the correct wages. Now we rear poultry, plant trees, and cultivate other people's land on a sharecropping basis. We grow paddy, jute, wheat, onions, and potatoes. We make a profit from this cultivation. We do not go to work in other people's houses anymore. Whatever we know how to do, we do that sitting in our own houses. I had no such courage before joining the group. I know what is right and wrong now. Now, if anyone says anything wrong I answer back, before I used to keep quiet. Where did I get my courage? From my self-confidence and wisdom. If there is a quarrel with the men in our village and if we, the members of the group, go there, they will not be able to face us. We are ninety members and we have a strength."

Update

Since 1984, the Bangladesh Rural Advancement Committee has expanded, diversified, and modified its women's program. BRAC's integrated field projects, including functional education, group organization, and economic action, have now reached more than ten thousand women and as many men. Moreover, its rural credit program has provided loans and other subsidies to more than sixty thousand women, which means that a total of more than seventy thousand women are supported in primarily non-craft production.

BRAC continues to promote the types of non-craft employment schemes described here, but with some interesting differences. In the area of animal husbandry, BRAC decided to provide veterinary services by training village women to be paraveterinarians. These paravets provide private village services and also conduct public vaccination campaigns for cattle. In the area of poultry rearing, BRAC now identifies and trains women who have proven successful to assume some of the service roles previously provided by BRAC's poultry paravets, who generally had been an educated, non-village cadre.

In the area of rice processing, BRAC has initiated pilot efforts with one or two women's groups who own and operate small-scale rice mills. Moreover, and very significantly in a male-dominated rural society, BRAC has been able to motivate and support some forty women to begin regular trade of their own and others' produce in local village markets. BRAC has also organized both men's and women's groups to undertake a few large-scale collective activities. The most notable of these has been the leasing of a village market (local markets are contracted out for management to groups who can raise the necessary capital) and the ownership and operation of a brick factory.

As described above, BRAC's approach to development is based on the organization of separate village-level groups of men and women. These groups in turn eventually federate with other village groups, both male and female. In the past few years, BRAC has further refined this model by adding a third tier to the federation process: while primary village groups continue to meet weekly (men and women separately) and to undertake group activities, they are now meeting regularly with other primary groups within their own villages to increase solidarity before being federated beyond village and gender boundaries.

―――――――――――――――――― Lessons ――――――――――――――――――

BRAC developed its current approach to building rural institutions and rural employment for poor women through several years of experimentation. Others who wish to create similar employment opportunities and institutions for poor rural women can learn a number of useful lessons from BRAC's experience:

1. **A project to help poor women should begin with activities that produce quick, tangible results.** It is best to address women's most immediate needs and concrete activities first. Additional activities can then be sequenced, moving from addressing basic economic needs to more complex social and political constraints.

2. **In societies where the class hierarchy (or differences between women) is pronounced, it is better to organize women into economically homogeneous groups.** In such societies, the constraints and needs of women will most likely differ by class. Organizing women across classes often may not reflect the priority needs of, or even reach, the poorest women.

3. **Before undertaking economic programs for women, study the overall economic situation, women's traditional skills and occupations, available resources and raw materials, and existing and/ or potential markets.** With each group of women, their particular

circumstances, their daily and seasonal work schedules, their skills, and their priority needs and problems should be assessed.

4. **Schemes that build on women's traditional skills and occupations have a greater chance of proving viable than those that require training in new skills.** When creating new jobs for women by training them in new skills, a wide range of assistance is required: management, skills training, technology and equipment, and marketing. Those schemes that build on women's traditional skills and are geared to local markets generally prove less complicated to manage.

5. **Before providing skills training to women, establish systems for refresher training and technical and managerial support systems.** Generally, skills training is the simplest component and a minor element in the success of a program. Far more critical to the success of a program are the systems that are developed for technical and managerial support. The critical elements of such systems include: raw material supply, technical back-up and supervision, production planning, cost accounting, design, and marketing research.

6. **It is important to subsidize the experimental phase of many schemes, the phase that includes skills training and test production.** In order to benefit the poorest women, the ones who cannot afford to lose their daily wages to attend training or to engage in experimental production, some subsidy may be necessary. Although groups of poor women can pool individual savings to generate a group fund, few groups of poor women will be able to mobilize enough funds to finance any but the smallest economic schemes.

7. **To develop viable economic schemes, technical expertise often found outside existing staff resources is required.** More is required by way of staff capabilities than just the general promotional skills of community development workers. Specialized technical and managerial expertise are also needed. In the initial phase of any economic scheme, arrangements should be made for appropriate technical assistance. Once a scheme proves viable, the technical capacities of field staff and of the women themselves should be built up. Generally, appropriate technologies exist and need only be identified, whereas too few appropriate *technologists* exist and more must be trained and developed.

8. **Payments should be calculated on a piece-rate basis and should be paid in cash on delivery.** Too often with profit sharing systems, efficiency and quality of production can slacken and internal conflicts can arise such as workers accusing each other of being lazy.

During test production, unless the women are paid at least a small amount, their interest will drop. Moreover, in the early stages of commercial production, when efficiency is generally low, the women may need to be paid slightly more for their labor (as an incentive to production) than they will receive once their efficiency is up. While subsidizing test production and providing incentives for women's work, the women should be trained in cost accounting and be told that their wages are tied not only to output but to competition in the open market.

9. **Small amounts of working capital, taken on loan with formal terms of interest and repayment, can launch many economic schemes.** Lack of working capital is typically the major constraint to production in rural areas. Some schemes require larger loans for fixed capital expenses and recurring costs. But the amount required is seldom very large. BRAC-financed individual production schemes averaged only $20 each. BRAC-financed collective production schemes averaged $200 each.

10. **Because women seldom own property or collateral in their own right, group guarantee credit schemes are recommended.** Under such schemes, the group serves as the umbrella for outside support and the group members guarantee each others' loans. If one woman defaults then the whole group suffers. Initially, the loans can be funded through project funds but ideally, once the group guarantee system is working, the women should be linked up to formal credit institutions.

11. **Individual economic or social schemes for women should not be carried out in isolation but in the context of broader policies and plans.** It is important to link women with support services beyond those offered by any specific project, especially government services which should be made more accountable to the needs of women. Similarly, it is important not simply to work with women in one location but to lobby for policies that will guarantee women's overall access to credit, technical and support services, protective legislation, adequate wages, raw materials, and so forth.

Further Information

A Quiet Revolution: Women in Transition in Rural Bangladesh by Marty Chen outlines in further detail the BRAC experience in designing projects to assist low-income women in Bangladesh. It is available from Schenkman Publishing Company, P. O. Box 349, Cambridge, MA 02139 U.S.A.

Works Cited

BRAC. 1979. *Who Gets What and Why.* Dhaka.

Cain, Mead and S. R. Khanam. 1979. "Class, Patriarchy, and the Structure of Women's Work in Rural Bangladesh." *Population and Development Review,* Vol. 5, no. 3.

Harris, Barbara. 1978. *Post Harvest Rice Processing System in Rural Bangladesh.* Dhaka: Bangladesh Research Council.

5

Forest Conservation in Nepal: Encouraging Women's Participation

Augusta Molnar

For the hill woman of Nepal, the forest is the source of products vital to the household economy: firewood for cooking and heating and leaves for animal fodder and fertilizer. In addition to competing for these products with men and with the commercial interests that use the trees for lumber, the situation has been made worse by the ever-increasing pressure of population on limited land resources, which has resulted in increasing deforestation. The delicate ecological balance in the geologically young and unstable Himalayan mountains has been upset, increasing the erosion and the number of landslides. Deforestation is leading to increasing levels of silt in river beds, shifts in the course of rivers, and flooding in the southern plains. The impact of deforestation has profound effects on the lives of Nepalese women. At the same time, women's roles as users and preservers of forest areas are crucial to the success of any program aimed at forest conservation.

This chapter focuses on ways in which women have been involved in a government forest conservation and restoration program. As is common with many large-scale projects with a general impact, women were not a direct focus of the project's original design. As activities got underway, however, both the Nepalese staff and their colleagues from outside Nepal quickly realized that the direct involvement of women was crucial to the success of the project. Over

Except for the update section, this chapter was originally published as a pamphlet with the same title by the Seeds Publication Project in 1987.

Women and children must travel long distances to get the wood they need for cooking. *(FAO: Florita Botta)*

the initial five years, 1980 to 1985, a number of approaches to addressing women's needs and generating their participation have been tried.

The Importance of the Forest to Life in the Nepalese Hills

With 96 percent of its population concentrated in rural areas, Nepal is one of the world's least developed countries. The majority of rural households depend for their livelihood upon a subsistence economy of agriculture and animal husbandry. The World Bank reported per capita income for the country as a whole at $140 in 1980. For much of the population the figure is lower, sometimes as low as $24 per year. The infant mortality rate is reported at 135 per 1000 live births and life expectancy is only forty-seven years for men and forty-six for women. Sixty percent of Nepal's population lives in the hilly section of the country south of the Himalayan range that spans the country from east to west. Here, in scattered villages, each household's subsistence is intricately adapted to the varied and complex ecological conditions.

While the Nepalese hill farmer is aware of the value of forest cover and the negative effects of widespread flooding and erosion, the immediate need for more agricultural land and forest products limits a household's ability to consider deforestation in its own planning. While Nepalese farmers have developed a sophisticated system of land preparation and terracing to limit land degradation, this system cannot resolve the problem of erosion on the marginal and steep slopes that increasingly have come under cultivation.

Deforestation also threatens the supply of forest products, particularly fuel. Eighty-seven percent of the country's energy consumption is in the form of wood, and it is estimated that 95 percent of all wood taken from the forest for home consumption is used for fuel. Fuel needs differ according to a community's altitude, climate, and use of agricultural residue. Households in the lower hills, where cooking is the main use of fuel, have been estimated to consume 3,198 kg. of wood per annum. In the colder, higher areas, where room heating is necessary, the figure is much higher (Thompson and Warburton 1985, 115–35; Campbell and Bhattarai 1983, 25; Campbell 1983).

At present there are no economically viable substitutes for the use of wood for cooking purposes. In the southern plains, where wood is more scarce, families burn cow dung mixed with agricultural residue, a common practice in India as well. Use of such a wood substitute in the hills, however, would be disastrous because of the importance of cow dung for the production of local fertilizers.

Women's Roles in Forest Use

Women's lives are the most seriously affected by environmental damage and the shortage of forest products. Women, together with their children, are the main collectors of fuel and other forest products such as animal fodder and leaf compost. They also take primary responsibility for herding the family's cattle, sheep, or goats. Women's roles in the collection of forest products must be seen in the context of their other household responsibilities.

While women are not as active in the cash economy as men (and are therefore underrepresented in the national statistics on participation in the labor force), recent studies employing data on family time-allocation have resulted in some realistic estimates of rural women's overall contribution to the household economy. In a study carried out in eight villages, women's total in-village work was found to be approximately eleven hours daily, as compared to approximately eight hours for men. Looking at both wage earnings and household subsistence production, women contributed 50 percent of total household income with boys and girls contributing 6 percent and adult males 44 percent (Acharya and Bennet 1985).

Several factors explain the difference between male and female workloads. First, in addition to agricultural and animal husbandry responsibilities, women have primary responsibility for food processing, fuel and fodder collection, and domestic chores, including cooking and child care. Second, in many households men have migrated to other parts of Nepal or to India in search of wage labor and temporary employment to supplement household income. The women then must assume a greater proportion of the agricultural tasks as well.

As forest products become scarce, the burden on the woman and her family becomes even greater. Krishna Devi, a hill woman of the Magar ethnic group, must spend a full day travelling to and from the forest to get fuel and fodder. When she was young, the forest adjoining her village provided plentiful supplies of wood and grazing land. Now the increasing animal and human population of the village has depleted the supply and she and the other villagers must travel much further for these products.

> By law we villagers are only allowed to collect whatever has fallen on the ground in the forest. The trees are used for timber for building for those lucky enough to be sold a permit by the forest officers. Women are left with the leaves, branches, and twigs. Once, it wasn't too difficult to find wood on the ground. But now there is not even enough left over to fill one headload, unless you walk for miles and miles. And no fodder unless you cut the branches.
>
> Even when I travel a long way into the forest, I still have to cut branches illegally to get a large enough headload to cook for my family. If I'm caught by a forest guard, he takes my cutting tool or tells me I have to pay a stiff fine. But what can I do? As it is now, I must bring my daughter with me to help collect fuel and fodder, so she often skips school to help me. I would rather that she got a good education so she would have a good chance in life. But I have no choice. There are too many other chores to complete. I now go to the forest every day that I have no work in the fields or grain to thrash or grind. And one headload (about 35 pounds) lasts only a few days. If fuel gets even more scarce, I will have to take my daughter out of school completely so she can help me with my other tasks.
>
> The better woods are getting much scarcer. I must collect other species that burn very poorly. Sometimes a headload lasts hardly two days when it is made up of only soft wood and shrubbery. And the smoke that those woods create is awful. Some woods make my eyes burn and give the rice a bitter taste my husband can hardly stand.—Krishna Devi

Women care for livestock and must transport their fodder from the forest, as well as wood for fuel. *(CFAD Nepal)*

The Project

Between 1957 and 1977, as a result of the Nationalization Act of 1957, all forest land in Nepal had been considered to belong to the government and was administered by forest department officers through the Ministry of Forests. Each local forest was under the jurisdiction of a forest guard attached to a district forest office and usage rights were strictly limited. Villagers could only collect fallen produce and had to apply to the district forest office for permits to cut timber for construction. After twenty years of government administration, however, the results of the Nationalization Act were mixed. So in 1977 the government amended the Act by introducing two new pieces of legislation. One allowed the legal transfer of tracts of degraded forest land to communities via village administrative units, known as *panchayats,* for replanting and long-term maintenance. The other allowed the legal transfer of limited amounts of good forest land to adjacent *panchayats,* to be protected and managed by the community in the manner most suitable for their own needs. *(Panchayat* is a South Asian term referring to government by a small group of chosen village representatives. In Nepal, however, a *panchayat* is a unit of nine villages or wards administered by a group of 11 elected council members, one of whom serves as the council head, or *Pradhan Panch.)*

A new forestry scheme was designed on the basis of these legislative policies. It is being implemented primarily through a five-year project that tests comprehensive, community-oriented strategies for reforestation and resource utilization. The project began in 1980 and now operates in twenty-nine of the country's hill districts, drawing upon assistance and expertise from the World Bank and from the United Nations Development Programme and the Food and Agricultural Organization. The goals of the scheme are to check deforestation, improve the forest cover, and increase the amount of fuel, fodder, timber, and other forest products available for subsistence needs. It innovatively shifts responsibility for village forest resources from the government to the local villages. Its objectives include:

- Creation of a new forest division within the Forest Ministry, called the Community Forestry and Afforestation Division;
- Development of new forest officer training programs and new training facilities;
- Transfer of forest lands to local communities in accordance with the new legislation;
- Planting of degraded areas handed over to *panchayats* and creation of

Planting seedlings *(FAO: Asse Wolsted)*

community management plans for all forest land reverting to community control;
- Establishment of community nurseries to raise seedlings for private and community tree planting;
- Research on locally viable fuel, fodder, timber and multipurpose tree species, particularly those species that grow quickly; and
- Dissemination of improved, wood-burning cookstoves.

These various project objectives involve many support activities. District forest offices now have trained forest extension workers (Community Forest Assistants, or CFAs) to work with local communities. Nurseries have been started and are staffed by villagers, who are selected by the community and trained by the project. Since the project is the first to make use of the new forest legislation, it has had to work out the management, administrative, and legal details affecting land transfer. Extension materials have been developed for all aspects of the project. In particular, considerable extension work has been necessary among communities to make villagers aware that the planned activities and new legislation are designed for their benefit.

Many villagers fear that the government may change its mind and renationalize the new plantations. There is also frequent distrust of the *panchayat* leaders, particularly in communities made up of several distinct, ethnically varied villages that are administered by a single *panchayat*. A single *panchayat* may contain a variety of Hindu caste groups and one or more distinct ethnic groups of Mongolian origin. While the *panchayat* is the most convenient administrative level at which to establish community-based activities, its leadership does not always represent the interests of the entire community.

Resistance has also been strong in the Forest Ministry itself, where traditional forest department staff fear losing control over "their" forests and thereby losing their prestige. Orientation courses for all foresters, therefore, are an important support activity aimed at convincing these officers of the value of community management and helping them assume new roles as technical advisors and management consultants, rather than policemen and village adversaries.

Women and the Forestry Project

The original project design document did not specifically refer to women or to particular strategies to involve women in planned activities, apart from the inclusion of an improved wood-burning stove program. The planners considered that since activities were directed to general household needs, the project would therefore benefit both sexes equally. Once the project began, however, the staff quickly recognized that success would require actively involving women as well as men. However, two factors would make it difficult to encourage such involvement: women's traditional position in Nepalese society and the absence of female staff in the Forest Department at the time the project began.

While Nepalese society is not as restrictive as in some parts of South Asia, women traditionally are not active in public or political affairs, although participation varies greatly among Nepal's numerous ethnic groups. In general, women do not attend *panchayat* or village meetings and their movements in the village are confined to those required by domestic and agricultural duties and to visiting female friends and relatives. They do not spend much time in public places, such as the ubiquitous tea shops where men typically hold many informal discussions. While women go to market towns and areas on shopping excursions, they do not converse with strange men except for business, nor do they stay in the market longer than necessary. This is particularly true for younger women, both married and unmarried.

Yet it quickly became apparent that women are as involved, if not more involved, in the use of the forests than men, and that women's active participation was necessary in many activities, such as planting.

When degraded forests are replanted, they must be closed to animal and human intervention for the first few years while the seedlings become established. Since women generally graze the animals, they *must* be committed to and involved in protection of these newly planted areas. If they do not understand or accept the replanting, they may feel that it has taken away grazing land and they will oppose the closure. Also, since closure of local forest areas requires women to change their livestock feeding practices from grazing to stall feeding, which requires them to spend hours each day cutting grass, they may allow their animals to enter the closed areas. Therefore, the project has devoted considerable time to extension work with women to gain their support.

Forest department staff were initially quite surprised to find that men were ill-informed about the amount of fuel and fodder required by village households and its availability in the surrounding forests. "Ask my wife," was a common reply to such questions, which were usually directed by a male extension worker to the male head of the household.

Men and women also have preferences for different species of trees. As Krishna Devi's testimony makes clear, women seek types of wood with specific qualities for burning, not just those that grow quickly and easily adapt to soil and climate conditions. Men and women differ in their emphasis on end products too: men are more often concerned with timber production, women with fuel and fodder. The particular mix of fuel, fodder, and timber-producing trees, and the amount of wood that should be cut over a single season to meet household needs, are issues that men and women treat very differently. Therefore, it is only logical that women be consulted in drawing up workable forest management plans: if the plan does not provide for adequate fuel and fodder, the women inevitably will break its rules.

Involving Women

From the project's experience, women can be reached in three basic ways:

- Analyzing women's needs and roles, ideally at the design stage, and then as the program is implemented, in order to ensure that women can benefit;
- Targeting extension information to women; and
- Directly involving women as project staff, village workers, and decision makers.

So far, the project has been stronger in tackling the first two strategies than the last. Had women been a specific focus in the design phase of the project, it is likely that more progress would have been made in fielding female staff from the beginning. The areas in which women have been a strong focus are development and dissemination of extension and training materials and systematic data collection on the progress and problems experienced by field staff in extending women's participation. In addition, women have been actively involved in the stove program and recently have been emerging as staff workers and active members of community forestry committees.

The difficulties faced in reaching women also have been compounded by the complexity and broad coverage of the overall project and its innovativeness, both in terms of activities and the build-up of administrative support. Orientation of forest department staff and creation of the monitoring and evaluation units, research units, and so forth, have all been time-consuming and problematic and have detracted attention from getting women involved.

Male Forest Extension Workers and Village Women

Forest extension workers, known as CFAs, are attached to each district office, and have been recruited for the project and trained in a two-year program in the southern Terai forestry school. Most of the recruits have been drawn from the Terai area itself—only recently have hill people become aware that these positions are open. To date, all CFAs have been men, since there are no facilities at the Terai school for female students. The project has built a forestry school in the hills, at the town of Pokhara, with facilities for women, but the school has not yet produced any graduates.

The CFAs have found it difficult to reach village women with extension advice. There are many reasons for this. First, they have been slow to develop effective extension skills because the department had no prior experience in this area and extension materials have only recently been developed. Second, those CFAs from the Terai region come from a cultural tradition that restricts women's behavior much more than is the case among the hill populations. Not surprisingly, these CFAs tended to avoid women in the villages where they were posted.

Ram Kumar is a male CFA who has worked for the project since its start and who comes from the Terai.

When I was first posted to the hills with the project, I never talked to village women because that sort of behavior would have angered village men in my home district. Women also were hard to find; they never attend group discussions with men and usually are busy with household work. We employed women as nursery workers to plant seedlings, but I

oversaw their work rather than giving them extension advice. I also had my hands full when I first arrived. The information we were given in training was not always applicable to the planting and nursery problems I actually found in the villages. Some patches were so eroded that it was a miracle if even the hardiest pine species grew. Local farmers also knew more than I did sometimes, and I was afraid they would laugh at my advice. I had enough trouble without trying to talk to women.

I never realized how important women were for the project until I was transferred to another district with a really exceptional district officer. He made me realize that the women provided a different perspective on species preferences and forest usage. We also lost many seedlings in private homesteads because only men came to the nurseries. They planted the trees at home, but since their wives never knew they had been planted, the trees were trampled by cattle or children.

When we organized forest committees in participating villages to select village staff, allocate land for planting or protection, and decide on forest management strategies, we were told to be sure at least one woman was elected to the committee. But the women selected seldom said anything in committee meetings. And I had no idea who the influential or dynamic women were in the village so I could suggest that a different woman join the committee. Supervising planting, allocation of forest land, running the nurseries, and planning project activities take most of my time anyway. I oversee four villages, and they are each about a three hour's hard walk. It is hard for me to do enough extension work with the men, much less the women. Maybe if there were some special courses for us during the two-year training, I could have done a better job.

Women's Involvement in Training and Extension

Training programs for project staff and village-level workers (both almost exclusively male) and development of extension materials and their use by local communities have offered ways to involve village women and raise the awareness of women's importance in forestry efforts. All levels of field staff receive training—the forestry extension workers who are attached to the district offices and cover up to five *panchayats* apiece (CFAs), locally recruited nursery foremen, female stove promoters, male stove installers, and locally recruited forest watchers, who protect the legally transferred forest lands. The forestry extension workers provide village-level training.

Extension efforts have included use of pamphlets about the legal rights of communities to newly planted and newly transferred forest areas, posters, slide shows, and leaflets about project activities that include such subjects as the qualities of various species of trees, planting techniques, and stall feeding. The extension materials—developed by the project in cooperation with the Thailand-based Development Training and Communication Project (DTCP), an agency specializing in grassroots communication—discuss women's central role in forestry. All materials use simple Nepalese languages and numerous pictures, including depictions of women planting trees and engaging in other forestry operations.

Slide shows and films shown at village presentations have been particularly successful. If scheduled in the evenings, when women are free from their chores and can attend, these are popular and effective. One slide show, "The Buffalo Must Eat Everyday," uses a female villager as the main character to discuss the importance of stall feeding. The documentary film on Nepal's environmental crisis, *The Fragile Mountain,* by Sandra Nichols, which was shown on U.S. public television's NOVA series, has been translated into Nepali for these showings. It is ideal for extension work with village women because it allows them to talk about how *they* perceive the problems and solutions. In these showings, the women will chat with one another while the commentator speaks, but are always silent when a villager is being interviewed in the film. There is also a regularly broadcast radio program that includes sessions devoted to women's participation in the project.

Nursery worker, wearing a
sweater with the project logo,
watering seed beds
(CFAD Nepal)

Women as Forestry Staff

The main employment of women under the project has been as nursery labor, filling seedling containers, watering seed beds, and planting. This work neither increases women's participation in decision making nor increases the awareness of other village women about project activities. To date only 5 of the 240 nursery supervisors have been women. In two cases these women took responsibility after the death of a male relative, demonstrating that village men do not always shun the employment of women. But their presence has not had the desired impact in reaching other women, nor has it led more women to visit the nursery. In fact, some staff have complained that these women are less effective than men because they are more shy when discussing the project with men yet do not actively seek out village women. In part, this may be a problem of their accidental selection as opposed to being specifically selected and appropriately trained for the position. A few women have been effectively employed as forest watchers, who watch over new plantations and educate villagers who violate the closure rules about the advantages of the project. This is a position that increasingly should be filled by women, particularly because it is women who most frequently go to the forest for fuel and fodder.

A number of non-Nepalese foresters have been employed by the project, recruited under volunteer programs (Peace Corps, British VSOs, Japanese volunteers, and from an FAO program of Associate Experts) to assist at the district headquarters and to work with local CFAs and villagers. Some of these foresters are women, and they have had a positive role in identifying some of the problems and constraints in reaching women, suggesting ways to increase women's involvement, and providing a strong role model to villagers and staff by demonstrating the value of trained women in forestry. Because they are foreigners, these women are able to move freely in the field with little criticism from villagers about the suitability of their role.

The recruitment of women as CFAs is an important issue for the project, particularly because its plans call for extension of the project into a second five-year phase. Some women are presently enrolled in a course in Natural Renewable Resources in the university in Pokhara. Although some of these women could be recruited to serve as CFAs until women begin to graduate from the new forestry school, simply recruiting women as CFAs alone will not address all the problems of women and extension work. Female CFAs may not be as effective as males in working with men in the *panchayats,* given the present social status of women, nor would the presence of a female CFA carrying out the identical set of duties now required of male CFAs necessarily guarantee that more extension work would reach women. Indeed, one serious complaint of present CFAs is that oversight of several villages requires so much travel that they have little time left to talk to individual farmers.

The project must find a solution that effectively uses women as extension workers. If the experience with women's programs in Nepal and elsewhere is indicative, this will require special tailoring of training, job descriptions, supervision, and support systems. For example, the women will need help to establish initial contacts in their client villages. It has been learned from family planning services that when lone women are required to travel and to stay overnight in strange households, they may be the subject of gossip. CFAs who already have contacts with individual women in all the villages where they intend to work and have respectable places to stay are more easily accepted by the local society.

Experience with Women as Decision Makers

Female leaders have begun to emerge as the project's activities have expanded to more villages. Initially, some emerged spontaneously, but there were no formal means to incorporate them into the project. One example of a woman acting on her own initiative involves a woman resident of Ilam *panchayat* in eastern Nepal, who became interested in forestry after attending an election meeting held by a female candidate to the General Assembly. During the meeting, attended by women from a number of government-supported women's organizations, some time was devoted to explaining the new forestry program. This woman was so enthusiastic about what she heard that she began making visits to different households in town explaining the advantages of private tree planting and encouraging families to take seedlings from the nursery. Since her activities coincided with the onset of the planting season, the district forest officer hired her for a few months with funds from his budget for daily laborers. He then tried to incorporate her more formally into the project at the end of the season, but there was no opening for a nursery manager or forest watcher, the only two paid positions in the project budget, and there was no separate fund from which to pay her.

Another similarly motivated member of a local women's organization came forward in a far western district, Dandeldhura. She approached both the district office and project staff to request support for carrying out extension work with women in the area. Again, local staff were unable to hire her, given the inflexibility of the budget categories for local workers. She had no desire to tend a nursery—the only position open—but wanted to concentrate on extension work. She still hopes to get support in the form of extension materials and help from local staff in organizing meetings with women about private planting. She is particularly concerned by the lack of female participation in this program and believes extension work that more clearly specifies the benefits of the program to women (along with better coordination of the stocking of the nursery with multipurpose fuel/fodder/fruit species) could greatly increase the number of women taking seedlings.

Thus far, no formal means has been found to incorporate such women into project activities. Since the project is intended to provide a replicable model for forestry development throughout Nepal, central staff do not feel that arbitrarily creating a single post for such "exceptional women" presents a viable solution. What is needed is a mechanism for routinely employing such women, or at least covering their expenses. One possible mechanism is the project-initiated village forest committees. In two instances, women have formed such committees on their own. In Kaski district in central Nepal, where many villagers traditionally have maintained forest lands as a sub-unit of the *panchayat,* the project successfully sought modification of forest legislation allowing sub-units to take control of forest management rather than the larger, less homogeneous *panchayat.* Their committee is formed on this sub-unit level and was organized by a bright, assertive woman who had just graduated from high school and was training to be a teacher. She decided that community forestry had great relevance to village needs and felt a female forest committee could be an effective vehicle for needed social action.

Another committee is made up of eleven members. Its original organizer has been appointed treasurer and its president is the wife of a village leader. The women chose the leader's wife as committee head because she is middle-aged, experienced, and by virtue of her position in the community has access to important information about local political affairs. The committee already has overseen the planting of thirty-five hundred seedlings in one degraded area of their village and has instituted a policy of charging a minimal fee for permits to use existing sections of forest. This fee provides revenue for future planting efforts and other planned community improvements, such as piped water and new school facilities.

An interesting aspect of the two committees is that both were started completely at the instigation of local village women, although they have since received encouragement from district staff. Furthermore, the committees are highly regarded by the men in the village—and the men are happy to abide by their decisions regarding village forest resources. Participation by women in decision making regarding management of village-controlled forests is certainly a crucial step in the direction of long-term community forestry.

The Fuel Saving Smokeless Cookstove

Women have served as successful extension workers in the stove component of the project. Almost all Nepalese families cook on wood-burning stoves. Kerosene and bottled gas are limited to urban areas because of their expense and unavailability. Many women and children suffer from respiratory infections and eye problems caused by exposure to the smoke from the traditional wood stoves. Recent studies estimate that the smoke pollution inside a Nepalese house produces the same amount of one harmful hydrocarbon as is produced by smoking twenty packs of cigarettes a day.

To combat health problems and at the same time improve the fuel efficiency of cookstoves, the forestry division collaborated with a Nepalese research institute and several international appropriate technology groups to develop a series of prototype stoves that were similar to the ones traditionally used in Nepal. From these, one model was selected that had two prefabricated ceramic bowls and a prefabricated ceramic chimney that could be installed in a traditional mud stove housing.

Development of an improved cookstove (as seen being installed above) is an important component of the forestry project. *(CFAD Nepal)*

The model was fuel efficient because the prefabricated pieces ensured that the inside of the stove was correctly proportioned, and it was inexpensive because the ceramic pieces could be made locally by Nepalese potters after they received training from the project. Since it used the mud housing, members of traditional Hindu castes could use the stove because they could build their own structure around it: they would have rejected a stove constructed by members of an "unacceptable" caste if it came directly in contact with their food. In addition, the stove has no dampers to regulate air flow (as do many improved South Asian cookstoves), thereby avoiding the need to teach women how to use the dampers properly.

The plan was to install an initial fifteen thousand stoves on a promotional basis, in the hope that families would then be willing to pay for replacements as the stoves wore out. The initial distribution also served as a test of stove reception, manufacture, supply, and logistics, and provided guidance towards future marketing strategies.

To disseminate the stoves, nine female stove promoters and twenty-four male stove installers were hired, with plans to expand these numbers to thirty and sixty, respectively, as the areas covered by stove construction increased. Stoves initially were introduced in the Kathmandu valley where the first potters were trained and follow-up was easiest. Other hill districts have since been added and the Kathmandu potters have trained the potters in these new districts.

The first stove promoters were young home economists. They were given training both in stove promotion and in community forestry, so they could tell women about forestry activities as well as fuel conservation. One woman of the Newar ethnic group from Kathmandu, Chandra Devi, has been a very successful and enthusiastic stove promoter.

At first it was difficult to get women interested in the new stoves. They were very reluctant to try them. One thing that did interest them, however, was the chimney. Nepali households are really uncomfortable to sit in when a woman is cooking.

The response to the stoves has been really positive. Of course, we have had a lot of problems, but many have been resolved. And the women are willing to work with us to find solutions. Some of the earlier stoves did not have enough clay in the mud housing and the housing cracked between the two stove pieces after only a few months. The designers did more tests and we changed the mud mixture. The worst problem was with the chimney. The installers often had to put the chimney closer to the outside wall than specified so that it wouldn't break. But then the wind forced the smoke back into the room. Several families were so keen on keeping the stove that they rigged up a kerosene can on top of the chimney to keep the wind away. We still have to find a more permanent solution to this problem.

There are less people in the original sample now than during the first year due to breakage and other problems, but many women use the new stove exclusively. Our follow-up visits have made a big difference. For one, we never would have noticed a lot of the problems, and many women had problems adjusting to the new stoves. My visits gave them a chance to ask questions. Sometimes they were upset that the stoves don't create as hot a fire on the front burner, so I show them different ways of cooking the various dishes in a meal so that the new stove will actually be faster. And I can be sure they know how to clean out the chimney regularly. I also talk to them about the planting program. Quite a few stove users have gotten trees from the nursery as a result of my visits.

So far the model stove seems to be a good one for saving fuel. A study of families using the stoves found an average wood savings of 28 percent, with a 40 percent savings reported in one region. However, breakage and other problems have led to a drop-off in stove acceptance. Initial feedback obtained in 1983 showed that 70 percent of all stoves installed were in use; one year later the rate had dropped to 60 percent.

Now that the stoves are being distributed in hill areas outside Kathmandu, continued research and development is increasingly important. Since the stoves are still being distributed free, it is not known whether families eventually will be willing to purchase them. The largest market initially will be in urban areas where firewood must be purchased; it is estimated that a viable stove can save 500–800 kg. of fuel per year and can pay for itself in three months in an urban area. In rural areas users may not see the savings as readily, but the stove should also prove a popular purchase where women must travel long distances to collect fuel, if initially in smaller numbers.

Future Directions

The project is attempting to develop the infrastructure for a program of community forestry that will benefit all Nepalese people, including women. To date, activities of particular value to women have included training and development of extension materials, the management plan system enabling the community to plan how their local resources will be used, development of an improved stove program, and collection of information and experiences on the problems and possible future ways of actively involving women both as staff and decision makers.

If women are to become as actively involved in the project as men, project staff must continue to monitor activities in this regard and to explore how to:

• more directly involve women at various levels and more specifically orient male project staff in the skills required to reach women;
• increase involvement of women in forest committees; and
• find means to incorporate village women enthusiastic about forestry into the project.

These are important challenges that could have a far-reaching effect by making women a more integral part of the project.

In terms of the stove component of the project, when the stoves are distributed on a wider scale, it will be necessary to consider such issues as quality control of commercially produced stove pieces and maintenance of an adequate local supply. The biggest issue currently facing the stove program is the length of time it should be overseen by the Forest Department. Many foresters feel it falls outside their area of expertise and think the stove program should be relocated or disbanded as soon as stoves are being sold rather than given away. Others feel that fuel conservation is as important to forestry as tree planting and that no other government agency will show as much interest in such a program.

Update

As of early 1989, the Nepal Forestry Project is about to go into a new phase. If the government agrees to implement the proposed plan, it will result in a change in legislation that will allow user groups, made up of individual villages and ethnic groups, to manage forest land instead of the *panchayats*. There will also be the addition of a one-year training consultant who will develop training components, including extension materials, that will include a focus on women in forestry. Training will also become decentralized, so that there will be a training capacity built up in each region rather than only at the national level.

_____ Lessons _____

1. **The key to involvement of women in a forestry project is an awareness of the central roles that women play in forest utilization and maintenance.** This ideally should be reflected in the initial design of the program. Staff must continually monitor the project to be certain that planned activities are meeting women's needs.
2. **Extension efforts should be tailored specifically to women and their interests.** This can be done by using media that women understand, whether literate or not, and by scheduling presentations at times when women can attend. Materials directed to men also should explain the importance of women's involvement in the project.
3. **Women will support a project when they can see tangible results.** Since it takes a long time for trees to mature, early positive results such as increased grass production or village nurseries stocked with tree species of known value for farm planting will help elicit women's support.
4. **Women need to be involved in decision making regarding community forestry management plans if these plans are to be effective.** Aspects requiring their involvement include: types of species to be grown; desired forest products; how much produce to distribute, when, and to whom; methods of harvesting; and revitalization of protected forest areas.
5. **While project staff are aware of the value of more direct involvement of women, they also recognize the complexity of the problem of women's participation, particularly in a broad sector project like community forestry.** Successful experiences involving women in other endeavors elsewhere in Nepal and South Asia mainly have been implemented on a small scale within a limited geographic

area, and have depended upon intensive local planning and strong support and supervision by female staff. Simply creating a cadre of female workers to undertake extension work with women is not enough. Sufficient staff support and resources to identify suitable recruits and supervise their activities are also necessary.

6. **Employing female forestry staff will increase the involvement of women and better address their particular needs.** However, unless women's and men's duties are tailored to meet these objectives, women's needs may still be overlooked, even if a large proportion of staff are female.

7. **The fielding of female extension staff requires overcoming specific obstacles to their recruitment, posting, and supervision.** The problems that female extension staff will face within a particular cultural setting must be specifically addressed in the design of their duties, in the recruitment of candidates, in helping them establish themselves in client villages, and backing them up with adequate supervision.

8. **Since an important component in controlling environmental destruction is conservation, project planners need to look closely into how resources are used.** Since so much wood is used by women for cooking, development of an improved stove program represents a positive effort in fuel conservation that complements preservation and restoration of forest lands. In addition, the stove component provides staff with an important way to reach women that can be used for discussion of broader environmental concerns.

9. **A mass stove-distribution program will succeed only if attention is paid to developing a long-term, self-supporting program.** A stove program should not be grafted onto a forestry project with the expectation that forestry staff, busy concentrating on other activities, will have the expertise, the time, or the willingness to devote to such a program. The provision to hire additional staff, or to train and redefine assignments of existing staff, must be made prior to launching a program in the field.

10. **Female extension workers have proved to be an integral part of an improved stove distribution program.** In Nepal, women have been helpful in training women to use the new stoves properly, in gathering information about women's attitudes towards the stoves, and in informing women about other aspects of wood conservation.

11. **The stove program has been very successful largely because of its emphasis on long-term research and development of models that eventually can be disseminated through the private sector.** The experiences of similar stove programs around the world increas-

ingly stress the importance of (a) developing a product with the actual user's needs in mind; (b) testing acceptability and cost effectiveness in a real life setting; (c) carrying out long-term research and follow-up to resolve design and durability problems; (d) teaching women to modify their cooking and fuel preparation habits to make optimal use of new stoves; and (e) establishing the commercial marketability of the stoves in the local economy.

Further Information

Information about this project and the community forestry experience can be obtained from:

The Community Forestry and Afforestation Division, Ministry of Forests, Kathmandu, Nepal. (Various project papers are available.)

The CARE/Kenya Agroforestry Project, P.O. Box 43864, Nairobi, Kenya.

Food and Agriculture Organization of the United Nations (FAO), Via delle Terme di Caracalla, Rome 00100, Italy.

World Bank, South Asia Projects Division, 1818 H Street, N.W., Washington, D.C., 20433.

The film *The Fragile Mountain* is available in 16 mm. and Beta or VHS video cassettes. For purchase, contact: Sandra Nichols Productions, Ltd., 6420 Goldleaf Drive, Bethesda, MD, 20817 U.S.A. For rental information contact: Sandra Nichols Film Library, P. O. Box 315, Franklin Lakes, NJ, 07417 U.S.A.

Works Cited

Acharya, M. and L. Bennett. 1985. "Women and the Subsistence Sector: Economic Participation and Household Decision Making in Nepal." Washington, D.C.: World Bank Working Paper No. 526.

Campbell, J. G. 1983. "People and Forests in Hill Nepal." Project Paper No. 10. Kathmandu: FAO Project Documents.

Campbell, J. G. and T. N. Bhattarai. 1983. "Preliminary Evaluation of Project Effects: Results of Key Indicator Surveys." Kathmandu, Nepal: FAO Project Documents.

Thompson, M. and Michael Warburton. 1985. "Uncertainty on a Himalayan Scale." *Mountain Research and Development*, vol. 5, no. 2.

III

LATIN AMERICA AND THE CARIBBEAN

6

Market Women's Cooperatives: Giving Women Credit in Nicaragua

Judith Bruce

As in most countries, women in Central America are economically active, especially in subsistence farming and petty trade. Yet, like women elsewhere, their contributions to the economies of the household, the community, and the nation generally have been disregarded by financial and political institutions. The market women of Nicaragua play a critical role in the lives of a large segment of the country's population by providing goods at low cost, in convenient locations, and with the personal touch of familiarity developed through daily contact. In order for the market women to operate, like any other business, they often need access to cash. However, because they have been considered to be outside the mainstream of economic activity, they have found it very difficult to get credit.

In 1972, the Nicaraguan Foundation for Development (Fundación Nicaraguense de Desarrollo or FUNDE)—one of two programs sponsored by the Nicaraguan Institute of Development (INDE)—became aware of the market women's need for credit. What follows is a description of FUNDE's experience in developing savings and loan cooperatives to meet this need. This summary stresses the human aspects of the process as much as the financial and technical ones. The project has been successful because the cooperatives have built upon the existing market women's culture, using all the subtle and complex interpersonal relationships established over the years. In essence, what the cooperatives have done is to teach women to use to their own best advantage

---

This chapter was originally published in 1982 by the Seeds Publication Project as the pamphlet *Market Women's Cooperatives: Giving Women Credit.*

123

what they already possess, and to provide them with information, experience, and encouragement.

======

The Learning Process

Market women need cash to buy the produce and small manufactured goods they sell, to pay for transportation, to rent stalls in the market, to pay for water, electricity, and *cargadores* who carry goods in the market district, and to use the public toilets. It costs approximately 100 to 1,000 cordobas ($10–100) per day to operate a medium-sized retail stall in the capital city, Managua. Smaller operations in smaller towns may cost less, but these women also need cash. Since market women's incomes are usually small, they seldom have money saved and tend to operate on a day-to-day basis. This means that very often they are forced to borrow money in order to keep their businesses going. They also need to borrow money if they want to expand and compete with supermarkets and other modern marketing systems.

In theory, market women have three potential avenues of credit: banks or credit unions, friends and family, or moneylenders known as *prestamistas*. Bank loans and credit are difficult to obtain because most local banks do not want to administer the small loans the women request, nor are they usually willing to consider the women's enterprises as collateral. Moreover, a cosigner or guarantor is required. The assumption is that only men—preferably husbands—can be guarantors. The credit system, therefore, perpetuates the myth that women are dependent upon men for money, even when they are the primary or sole support of their households. As for friends and family, most have little if any cash to lend.

This leaves only one real source of cash—the *prestamistas*. *Prestamistas* typically give short-term loans (thirty to sixty days) at 10 percent interest per month, or 120 percent or 240 percent per year.

FUNDE was aware that the market women needed loans at more reasonable rates of interest and believed that they could be of assistance. The best way to provide credit, however, only emerged through trial and error. Their first attempt failed.

FUNDE opened a loan office in the Central Market to provide the many traders operating there with credit at a reasonable rate, 1 percent per month, or 12 percent per year. Yet, despite the presence of the office, many market women continued to secure loans from the *prestamistas* at rates ten times higher than FUNDE's. To find out what they were doing wrong, FUNDE hired two of the moneylenders. They identified several reasons why the market women were reluctant to come to FUNDE for

A typical market scene in Nicaragua *(Victoria Schultz)*

loans: FUNDE's office was too formal; the FUNDE operation seemed strange and impersonal to the women; and, to quote one of the *prestamistas,* "After a long day in the market, a woman might catch cold here," a reference to the office's air conditioning. In contrast to FUNDE, the *prestamistas* can speak very informally and intimately with their clients because they know them and their situations well. The moneylender's daily presence in the market conveniently allows the women to pay back loans daily. And the *prestamistas* can usually be found at odd hours if there is an emergency need for cash.

To compete effectively with the *prestimistas,* FUNDE clearly had to develop a new approach. Drawing upon the lessons learned in their first attempt to provide credit to market women and their previous experience establishing cooperatives for low income people, FUNDE decided to try a scheme that would involve the women in building their own, community-level credit institutions that they eventually would run themselves: a market women's savings and loan cooperative. Since market women generally have low social status and rarely participate in formal "institutions," credit cooperatives they run themselves would not only assist economic expansion and diversification, eliminate debt, and encourage savings, but would also enhance the women's social status.

Establishing a Cooperative

FUNDE's long-range objective is to provide all market women in Nicaragua with an opportunity to join a local savings and loan cooperative. To begin they chose market towns with more than twenty-five hundred people. They already had some experience working in such towns and were relatively well known. Based on their past experience and the process of trial and error, FUNDE followed several steps in getting a cooperative started.

The first group contacted in a market town is the community leaders. If they accept the idea of further meetings, a core group of five to thirty prospective members is jointly called together by the community leaders and FUNDE's field staff. In these meetings the meaning, structure, functions, and benefits of cooperatives are discussed. Field staff point out that cooperatives are not simply a means to get credit. Members must first save before they can borrow (loans are usually made for as much as three times the amount saved and no sooner than forty-five days after opening an account). Though it is a less tangible benefit, some emphasis is put on a cooperative's role in using collective action to solve economic problems.

These first meetings are about two hours long. They usually are held near the market place and continue over ten days, by which time as many as one hundred people may have come to listen and talk. Initially, the reaction of most market women is curiosity. Usually the first women to come forward are slightly better off than the other market women, but still are deeply in debt to the *prestamistas*. Strong enthusiasm on the part of these prospective members will then carry the others towards acceptance. Repeated meetings are necessary to attract sufficient people to establish credibility and to insure that the information is fully absorbed. FUNDE staff and the core group explain over and over again how a cooperative works. This is important if the cooperative is to gain people's trust. Acceptance of the idea of a cooperative is slower in communities where previous cooperatives have failed, and where the *prestamistas* spread rumors that the cooperative will steal the members' money.

Once thirty or more women agree to form a cooperative, FUNDE helps them handle the formalities of legal incorporation. It is essential for the cooperatives to have legal standing so they can receive and dispense funds independently, establish relationships with other institutions (including banks), function as a pressure group, and ultimately separate entirely from FUNDE. Since many of the women are not literate, and since most of the women have no experience with legal or governmental systems, each step in the formation process is carefully explained and discussed.

A cooperative is established when legal documents have been signed, eleven directors have been elected by the participants, and when each member has purchased a share in the cooperative at a cost of 10 cordobas and paid an additional 10 cordobas for administration and 2 cordobas for a passbook. The necessary legal process takes two to three months.

At the same time the legal steps are being taken, an office is rented in a convenient location, usually near the market. It looks like any other local office, with simple furniture and often outside toilet facilities. FUNDE makes a grant of furniture and equipment: a file cabinet, typewriter, desk, chair, and adding machine, all of which are symbolically very important to the young cooperative.

FUNDE then makes a general loan of $10,000 at 12 percent annual interest to get the loan process started. They also make an essential loan for management and organization to cover eighteen months rent and the salary of a manager (22,248 cordobas or roughly $3,000). This loan is interest free. In studying causes of failure in cooperatives, either financial failure or failure to attract and hold members, FUNDE found that lack of skilled management early in the cooperative process was often the biggest mistake. Therefore a manager is hired and trained at once. The manager is jointly selected by the cooperative directors and FUNDE on the basis of interviews and a skills test. Frequently the candidates are young women with a secondary school degree. The pay is equal to or greater than that which would be paid for supervisory factory or office work. One unique aspect of the manager's role in the cooperative is that she reports directly to the members, not to FUNDE.

Another factor in the previous cooperative failures was a lack of competent, sustained training. FUNDE's key contribution to a new cooperative is not money—that is repaid—but technical assistance and training to give the skills necessary to enable the cooperative to become self-sufficient. Two types of training are given, one for directors and managers, and another for members. Directors and managers are usually trained in Managua to give the training more prestige and to minimize distractions. Members are trained near the cooperative site.

Two kinds of training techniques are used: the case study method and a review of documents. In the case study method, small groups are presented with situations likely to be encountered in the operation of a cooperative. The group determines a problem and its causes and then decides how it should be solved. Each group then presents its assessment to the general class where comments are made and conclusions drawn. In the document review stage, papers describing different cooperatives

QUE ES UNA COOPERATIVA?

UNA COOPERATIVA ES LA UNION DE UN GRUPO DE PERSONAS QUE TIENEN LOS MISMOS PROBLEMAS Y QUE SE ORGANIZAN VOLUNTARIAMENTE PARA SERVIRSE A SI MISMO O A LA COMUNIDAD.

COMO SE FORMA UNA COOPERATIVA?

SE FORMA POR LA VOLUNTAD PROPIA DE UN GRUPO DE PERSONAS.

To explain the concept of a cooperative, FUNDE published a simple pamphlet. The first page, reproduced here, says, "What is a cooperative? A cooperative is a union of a group of people who have the same problems and who organize themselves voluntarily to serve themselves and the community. How is a cooperative formed? It is formed by a group of people of their own free will."

are distributed. Members learn the facts presented through individual study and through group discussion. Now that cooperatives are becoming more common, a third method is being used in some training: the idea of "model cooperatives." Directors, managers, and members are taken to efficient, well-run cooperatives to observe and learn.

At present, managers and directors are required to be literate. But since many members cannot read and write, training materials include pictures that convey basic concepts and encourage discussion. Pictures and charts are used to help members answer such questions as, "What shall the cooperative's goal be this year?" If the aim is three hundred new members, a picture of three hundred new associates is prominently displayed. Similarly, pictures of how the markets once were and of how they can be with help from a well-functioning cooperative help the members learn about the benefits of cooperative organization.

Training methods build on familiar ideas and concepts. For example, the Roman Catholic concept of the Trinity (three in one) is used to explain that a cooperative is one whole made up of three different groups—owners, workers, and associates—and that each member is at the same time all three.

Training sessions run from three to six days, a short enough time that women with families are able to participate. But training is never a one-time affair. Directors, managers, and selected members frequently are given additional training, building step by step to self-sufficiency. The process of learning new roles and self-concepts takes time.

Once the cooperative is legally established, it begins operation. Membership usually starts at thirty to fifty people and reaches two to three hundred over several years. Most cooperatives welcome anyone who wants to join, but increased participation usually comes as members bring in new people. This tends to happen in groups, with a new group joining after one of their associates has been a member and is satisfied with the cooperative.

An active member is defined as anyone holding savings or a loan. Members do not have to attend cooperative meetings or the annual assembly of members to be considered active. Members are of all ages, 18–80, with the directors usually being 30–50 years old.

The eleven directors, selected by the members, divide themselves into three committees: five for administration, three for the credit committee, and three for monitoring the accuracy and honesty of the other two.

During the first months of operation, general meetings are held every week and a FUNDE staff person is usually present. The meetings are open to everyone in order to demonstrate the democratic nature of the cooperative and to provide information to the community.

Picture books describing the cooperative's functions, structure, and the process for obtaining loans are distributed to all members to be kept and used for reference. These also are distributed to nonmembers in the community as a means of interesting them in joining the cooperative. Visual aids are also used in the day-to-day operations of the cooperative, including wall posters showing the number of members, the amount of savings and the amount of loans. Charts are maintained on a weekly basis and are a tangible measure of the cooperative's progress. Because they can be understood by both literate and nonliterate members, the charts help to bridge the gap between these two groups, which is critical in maintaining the cohesiveness of the cooperative.

A cooperative usually begins slowly, with an organizational period of one to three months. The first loan request occurs within three to six months; then, when the system and the way it works has been demonstrated and is widely understood, the demand for loans increases substantially. The demand eventually levels off, fluctuating in a predictable pattern. Typically, a period of saving is followed by a period of borrowing.

Loan Procedure

When a cooperative member wants a loan, she speaks to the manager, who fills out a request stating the amount, purpose, proposed payback timetable, and applicant's current savings. This information is reviewed by the credit committee, which meets at least once a week and sometimes daily. A "soundness analysis" is made which includes the committee's knowledge of the member's character, the kind of work she does, her pattern of work, and the rate at which she earns. Credit committee members are supposed to make judgements based on their own perceptions, not the manager's or anyone else's. A good credit review studies each request, defers decision when there is a controversy, considers a loan as a right and not a privilege, and does not extend credit beyond a member's means.

The credit committee plays a very important role, especially in the early stages of the cooperative. Committee membership rotates to minimize favoritism; there are always three people. Since credit committee members generally belong to the same community as those requesting loans, they are in a good position to know who is a good or bad risk. This familiarity also exerts a kind of pressure to insure that borrowers repay their loans.

The formal conditions for obtaining loans are as follows:

• Members must have retained savings for at least six weeks before taking their first loan.

- Members requesting loans must repay any previous loan.
- Members may not receive loans of more than three times the amount of their savings.
- Loans of more than 3,000 cordobas must be paid within one year; loans less than 3,000 cordobas must be paid back within eight months (there are exceptions).
- No one is permitted to request more than 8,000 cordobas.
- Interest is incurred at 1 percent per month.
- The guarantor of a loan must be either another cooperative member or a third party with sufficient financial resources to cover the loan.
- No member can be a co-signer or guarantor of more than two loans at the same time.
- Any member wishing to withdraw from the cooperative must give thirty days notice so that all transactions (outstanding loans) can be settled and the member's savings returned. If a member defaults on a loan after repeated requests to repay, she is asked to leave.

About 3 percent of all loans are never repaid. About 10-15 percent of all loans require rescheduling. Terms of repayment are set to take individual needs into account. While differences in repayment schedules can create uncertainties among members, it is important that cooperatives remain flexible. Repayment terms must be those the women can handle. *Prestamistas* receive daily payments; banks, on the other hand, find the paperwork and management time required by daily repayment too troublesome. The cooperatives accept daily repayments because many members do not like to hold cash since they may be put under pressure by the family to spend it.

During a typical day, a cooperative may have between five and thirty members stopping in to take out or repay loans or to deposit savings. Offices are generally open between 9:00 A.M. and close of the market at 4:00 or 5:00 P.M. Everyone knows where the manager lives so members can find her in case of an emergency. The manager does her accounts and record keeping between members' visits.

Once the cooperative is fully operational, meetings of the three cooperative committees (credit, administration, oversight) are held at least once a week and meetings of the entire membership are held monthly, called by the manager. There is an annual general assembly where the cooperative's finances are reviewed and written reports issued by each committee. These reports are mimeographed and distributed to the membership. They are an important means of communication for the cooperative because, in addition to providing specific information, they help reinforce trust. They also become part of the cooperative's legal record. Preparation of reports is a learning experience for the manager and the directors. Each cooperative decides how to publish its annual report, but must follow the same budget format.

In the early months of operation, FUNDE staff make weekly visits to the cooperative to meet with members and to supplement the manager's training. Over time, contact between FUNDE and the cooperative declines. Every visit by a FUNDE staff member concludes with the manager making out a receipt that describes the services provided. This receipt has a symbolic as well as practical value. In addition to being a good management tool for FUNDE to keep track of its own staff time and performance, it gives the cooperative a certain power: it allows the cooperative to describe and evaluate the service it has received, thereby reinforcing its right to good service. This is important in building independence and self-sufficiency.

FUNDE generally limits assistance to a cooperative to three years, but expects it to be almost self-sufficient after two. FUNDE will not grant more than $10,000 to a cooperative during its first year of operation, a limitation which has less to do with the cooperative's ability to use the funds than with FUNDE's own lack of access to more money. But FUNDE does not seek to be a source of funding; rather it tries to broker support for loans to cooperatives from commercial banks by serving as a guarantor. This has already occurred with a number of the better established groups. When a cooperative does become financially self-sufficient, it can begin to purchase FUNDE's services, such as training, rather than accepting them free of charge. In general the stages of cooperative development are:

- Two years: the cooperative has repaid its initial loans from FUNDE and can pay its manager out of its own funds.
- Four years: the cooperative can make loans with money received from regular financial institutions, guaranteed by FUNDE.
- Five years: the cooperative can buy auditing services and technical assistance from FUNDE; loans from FUNDE can now be used for diversification.
- Seven years: the cooperative can function entirely independent of FUNDE.

Results

In the seven years since its first loan-giving experience, FUNDE has assisted in the establishment of fifty-eight cooperatives. Fifteen of these are the market women's cooperatives discussed here and 90 percent of

Market women at work
(United Nations)

their members are women. The majority of the remaining forty-three cooperatives, some in central market areas and some in towns, involve farmers or small retail or manufacturing enterprises. Between 50 percent and 80 percent of the members of these groups are women. FUNDE also supports cooperatives that focus on agriculture and other development projects. These generally have a larger percentage of male members.

Between 1975 and 1979, total savings of the fifty-eight cooperatives grew from $74,556 to $1,640,500. The amount of loans given by FUNDE to the cooperative movement in 1979 was $1,273,700. Total assets increased from $126,056 in 1975 to $623,000 in 1979.

The value of the cooperatives to their members is reflected by increased participation—from 283 members in 1972, to 12,522 in 1979. Among the fifteen market women's cooperatives, membership increased from 210 in 1972 to 5,530 in 1979.

The availability of credit has helped women maintain and expand their existing businesses and has reduced the cost of some aspects of commercial marketing. For example, women with little cash had to make frequent trips to suppliers to buy small quantities of goods. With more cash, the women make fewer trips and buy greater quantities at lower prices. These savings are then passed on to their customers. The cooperatives have helped members reduce their debts, increased their ability to make investments for short- and long-term purposes, and promoted saving. Increasingly, credit is being used for long-term investments such as education, purchase of homes, and upgrading of living conditions. This diversification in the use of loans turns a market cooperative into a multi-purpose savings and loan association.

The first women to join the cooperatives worked in the commercial sector and had some experience in managing money. Many of the newer members, however, are marketing through their homes rather than through organized structures. Access to credit has enabled these women to engage in income-generating activities and to become part of the economic development of their country.

The cooperatives have also affected relationships between formal financial institutions and the community. Most well established cooperatives have by now received loans directly from local banks. These loans are often the first involvement of financial institutions with low-income, community-level organizations. Even though the banks get regular commercial interest on these loans, in a sense they are an investment in the community's poorer members as they indirectly promote a better distribution of income. Loans to women, for example, help equalize the great income disparities between men and women.

The establishment of the cooperatives has also brought about an accumulation of information about the need for and use of money, and about changing patterns of money's use. Such information previously was scattered among the *prestamistas* and, to a lesser degree, the banks. Now this information is concentrated in a structure that is trusted by the community, has legal standing vis-à-vis other administrative structures, and exercises some peer group pressure over those engaged in commerce. This makes it possible for the members to analyze their own economic situation as well as that of their community and thus plan and carry out broader political and social action programs.

Cooperatives are in a position to identify and carry out community projects which usually would not be undertaken by either the government or outside private agencies. Some examples:

• A cooperative is working to establish a central marketing structure in a community now dependent on Managua.
• The cooperative at Chichigalpa operates two day care centers for preschool children, benefiting not only the mothers but also the children by keeping them healthier and preparing them for the content and discipline of school.
• The cooperative in Granada runs a health clinic, where local physicians contribute their time several mornings a week. Supplies from a dispensary are available free of charge.

A strong cooperative can, in other words, develop broader social and political power and legitimacy from an economic base.

Some of the benefits of a cooperative to its members are less visible or quantifiable. The meaning to individual women may, however, be captured in these accounts:

• A woman, thirty years old, married with four children and a cooperative member for several years, makes clothes for local sale. Her original loan of 500 cordobas was used to travel to Panama where she bought fabrics of greater variety and at lower cost than those she could find in Nicaragua. Currently she has loans totalling 6,000 cordobas and an annual income that exceeds her debt. She now travels not only to Panama, but also to Mexico to get materials.
• A widow, seventy years old and a member of a cooperative for several years, suffered a cerebral hemorrhage. She took out a loan from the cooperative to cover her medical expenses. Without the loan, she would have gone out of business. She does not understand much about money, but she pays her loan on time and trusts the cooperative.

- A twenty-year-old cooperative manager, who used to supervise three hundred persons in a clothing factory, prefers working with the cooperatives because she is not on her feet all the time and likes to manage and to be of service to other people. She enjoys introducing women to the cooperative and showing them how it works. She would like to train other women to be cooperative managers.

One of the objectives of the market women's savings and loan cooperatives was to raise these women's status in the community as well as improve their economic outlook. Women describe their new roles, opportunities and responsibilities in these ways:

- They have more control over what happens to them.
- They have greater influence over decisions in the household.
- They have a stronger sense of their right to services and support from the community.
- Many women who formerly carried baskets of goods now rent stalls and have their own space.
- They have the resources to invest in their children's education.
- With increasing pride in their occupation, they encourage their daughters to become market women.
- They see ways to improve their community and help it become a good place for their children to grow up.

One reason for opening access to credit and investment to women is to give them a voice in the community. Market women's cooperatives express the women's point of view in a very important way, and most of the community projects they have undertaken support and assist women's roles in the domestic sphere, such as day care, health, or potable water for the school. From their strong economic base, the market women can work to insure that their priority needs are met. It is questionable whether men's cooperatives would have done the same things.

_____ Lessons _____

Savings and loan cooperatives do not work in all settings. The particular model developed by FUNDE was a second attempt after initial failure. The second attempt succeeded because it applied several lessons:

1. **The size of the capital share members of the cooperative must purchase was small enough so that very low income women could participate.** Even poor women can save initially—if not cash, then a commodity that can later be sold for cash (for example, rice that is

put aside). It is important for a cooperative to be flexible in the amounts they accept from low income women. If the small units poor women can save are not treated seriously, these women will not get involved. FUNDE learned that the market women liked to take loans from the traditional moneylenders because they could repay loans daily, in small amounts. Frequent small installment payments tend to increase repayment rates since they eliminate pressure to spend the money elsewhere. A successful savings and loan and credit-giving program should be flexible in repayment schedules and collection procedures.

2. **A cooperative credit program should have a constituency—such as the market women—who are in immediate need of its service.** Many women in agriculture and petty trade are already seeking credit. They often become a cooperative's first members and leaders and are responsible for drawing in a wider circle of women. Before poorer, less economically active women become involved, they need to see a more visible group of women's needs being met.

3. **Review of creditworthiness should be undertaken by peers— women in the same kind of work and from the same community who are in a position to evaluate the reliability of the person receiving a loan. In this way repayment rates without collateral can be high.** Traditional loan procedures through community financial institutions or even traditional money lenders often require collateral. This discriminates against those who are quite ready to repay a loan but who have no material assets to put aside as a guarantee. The procedures FUNDE has adopted in its cooperatives increase the sense of community responsibility for a high repayment rate. More importantly, they provide a way for low income people to make money without already having money.

4. **The organization initiating the formation of a savings and loan cooperative need not have a lot of money (perhaps $10,000 annually: $5,000 in funds to contribute and $5,000 to loan) but it must be able and willing to make a long-term commitment to the development of low income women's leadership.** Organizations must commit the time necessary to develop the program slowly (one to four years). They should develop proficiency in training the women to manage money and should provide technical assistance as well as practical and moral support during the first few years. Some organizations that now are undertaking social welfare programs might consider using their staff as cooperative promoters and their funds as seed money for savings and loan projects. If the FUNDE project

provides any example, most cooperatives will repay their loans in two to three years, and there are very few development projects where an agency can expect to see its investment repaid.

5. **The process of establishing a cooperative is in essence a process of building a social contract among members and developing the confidence of individuals.** Presenting the idea of a cooperative takes time and must be done with support, discussion, and visual aids so both literate and illiterate women understand the importance of their role in the cooperative and that the success of the cooperative depends on them.

6. **The cooperative must produce rapid, tangible results.** For example, FUNDE legally establishes cooperatives and sets up an office within three months; members are permitted to save as soon as it is legally established; the first loans are granted within six months. All meetings from the beginning are open. Membership cards, wall charts, and annual reports are all tangible evidence of participation, growth, and legality, which builds the credibility of the cooperative.

Further Information

FUNDE has established a research and development office that will be glad to provide additional information on their cooperative program. Please write to: FUNDE, Apartado 2598, Managua, Nicaragua.

7

Community Management of Waste Recycling in Mexico: The SIRDO

Marianne Schmink

At the beginning of 1978, a group of families were awaiting access to low-cost housing in Mérida, a city on Mexico's southeastern coast. Typically, such low-cost, subsidized housing consists of a three-room core unit with water, electricity and drainage. The waiting list for houses with the conventional type of drainage used in the region, consisting of an absorption well and septic tank, was long. There were some units, however, equipped with a new drainage system, called SIRDO (Integrated System for Recycling Organic Wastes). This system cost 20–40 percent less than the conventional one and posed fewer risks of environmental contamination. Families interested in living in the experimental block where the SIRDO was to be installed could be given housing right away. Those who accepted the offer were compelled by an urgent need for housing. Although the drainage system was explained to them, for most it was still very unfamiliar when they moved in. They had no way of knowing then that they were to become leaders in the adoption and dissemination of this new technology.

Three years later, families in another community located in the crowded Valley of Mexico were seeking a solution to growing problems of waste management. Upon learning about SIRDO, they visited the Mérida pilot project and subsequently decided to try the system in their own neighborhood. Despite

Except for the update section, this chapter was published in 1984 by the Seeds Publication Project as the pamphlet *Community Management of Waste Recycling: The SIRDO*. Parts of this description were taken from the project report entitled *Documentación y Evaluación de Experiencias Tradicionales y Alternativas para el Manejo de Residuos Urbanos en Zonas de Bajos Ingresos en el Valle de Mexico* by Fernado Ortiz Monas-

many differences, these two groups have faced similar challenges in learning to manage the technical, economic, and social aspects of a new, community-based technology. Women have played a crucial role in this process and, in so doing, have strengthened their own standing within their families and communities. They also have become the principal managers of a system that both improves sanitary conditions and offers possibilities for community-based, income-earning activities. This is the story of these women and their communities, and the changes brought about through the introduction of this new technology.

The First Setting: Mérida

The city of Mérida is located in the north-western corner of the state of Yucatán, on the peninsula by the same name that juts out from Central America. Mayan Indians occupied the Yucatán Peninsula, the state of Chiapas, and the highlands of Guatemala for centuries before the Spanish conquest, and the region retains strong traces of this heritage. Captured by the Spanish in 1542, by 1600 Mérida had emerged as the region's political, economic, and cultural center. From the colonial period through World War I, the city grew in size and importance, based on the traditional hacienda (large estate) system of agricultural production that grew up around it. From the mid-nineteenth to the early twentieth century, during the boom of the production of henequen (a fiber similar to sissal used for making rope, twine, rugs, etc.), Yucatán was the richest state in Mexico and palatial homes lined Mérida's main boulevard. But a small elite controlled this wealth while the majority of the state's population was subsistence farmers or indentured workers on the haciendas. Beginning in the 1930s, henequen production began to decline and the region's economy entered a long period of depression that forced more and more reliance on government programs.

Today the city continues to depend on the production of foodstuffs by peasants in outlying areas, while the urban economy is based on commerce, tourism, and other services. Industry is dominated by small-scale, informal enterprises that are a legacy of the artisan workshops that grew up to service the henequen-processing industry. Henequen

terio, Josefina Mena, and Angel Parada, October 1983. The report was written for the Mexico City working group entitled *Mujer y Ciudad*, part of the Population Council/ U.S.A.I.D. project on "Women, Low Income Households, and Urban Services in Latin America and the Caribbean," Marianne Schmink, co-manager. For more information on the project, contact: Judith Bruce, The Population Council, One Dag Hammarskjold Plaza, New York, NY, 10017.

Doña Lola: The SIRDO has greatly
improved the productivity of her
kitchen garden. *(Charles Wood)*

production is still the largest single industry, but it continues to decline; most manufacturing is of basic consumer goods such as food, drink, and clothing. Because of the city's weak economic base, and continued rural-to-urban migration, under- and unemployment are growing problems. Mérida's approximately four hundred thousand inhabitants constitute about one-third of the state's population, and this proportion has been steadily growing. Many of these migrants have settled in the poorest, southern zone of the city, where the housing project with the SIRDO is located.

What is the SIRDO?

The SIRDO system has been under development by the Alternative Technology Group (GTA, for Grupo de Tecnologia Alternativa) since 1978. GTA is a small group founded by architect Josefina Mena in order to develop technologies for recycling organic wastes in urban areas. The SIRDO is designed not only to manage urban wastes, but also to include in this process the potential for income- and employment-generating activities. The system is based on intensive labor inputs in all phases of construction, maintenance, and production. Its characteristics enable cooperative community management for day-to-day operation.

Basically the SIRDO system works as follows. Each house is connected to the community system by two pipes that separate the "gray waters" (those containing detergents flowing from bathroom, sink, and laundry) from the "black waters" coming from the toilet. After filtering, 80 percent of the gray waters can be reused for irrigation. The black waters are channelled into a tank where sludge is separated from the water. The sludge is spread out in an aerobic decomposition chamber and is then mixed with household garbage. In this chamber, solar drying evaporates the water and within a year's time the sludge is transformed into a nutrient-rich fertilizer. The treated black waters in the meantime pass into garden beds where vegetables and flowers may be grown; they may also be channelled into ponds to support aquaculture.

The SIRDO system is unique because it requires an amount of careful control at the various stages of the decomposition process that makes it impossible to implement within a large, municipal-level system. On the other hand, it is too costly to be installed on a single-house basis. Therefore it is ideal for community-level management and operation. GTA carefully adapts each SIRDO facility to a specific site and monitors it over time to assure proper functioning.

Introducing the SIRDO in Mérida

Between January and May of 1980, the GTA built the first two SIRDO units in Mérida with financing from a government agency charged with assisting low-income populations in acquiring lots for housing that include basic services. The agency's central office was interested in the new technology, and the regional office in Mérida somewhat reluctantly revised its housing program to accommodate the new drainage system. Apart from offering lots with water and electricity, the agency financed the drainage system and connected it to core houses—the basic three-room unit to which families could later add more rooms. Original plans called for installation of houses and drainage in twenty-eight blocks near the southern edge of the city. In fact, only one block was provided with the SIRDO.

At the end of 1980, the agency granted housing to two dozen families in the experimental block. Little by little they began to occupy their lots. In most of the families the men were employed in services, small-scale commerce, or crafts. The vast majority were self-employed, and more than half earned less than the prevailing minimum wage. Most of the women had no regular employment, but since marital unions are often somewhat unstable, many had worked at some point in their lives, either as primary or supplementary supporters of their families. Those women who did hold jobs generally worked as domestics or in the small-scale

The children of Mérida painted murals that show how to use the SIRDO system.
(Charles Wood)

sale of food and other items. Only one woman worked in a factory. The families had three children on average, and most of the adults were literate but had not continued their education beyond the primary school level.

The GTA presented a series of orientation talks in August 1979 about the SIRDO which the families attended somewhat skeptically. The drainage system began to function, but there were many problems in its initial phase of operation. Users complained of flies, unpleasant odors, and leakage. In addition, changes had to be made in the house-cleaning routine. Acid products could not be used for cleaning because they would damage the chemical balance in the decomposition chamber. The system also required that organic garbage be separated from plastics, glass, and metals, which could not be dumped into the chamber. For these reasons, many community members were resistant to the system despite the assurances they received from GTA as to its advantages. But soon the odors began to disappear and other problems were resolved. Interestingly, the children were the first to begin collaborating with GTA staff. They participated in maintenance tasks such as separation of garbage and dumping of organic wastes into the chamber. They even painted wall murals that showed how to use the system. The children's enthusiasm encouraged many of the women to begin to cooperate as well. In

May of 1981, a few community women started meeting to allocate tasks on a cooperative basis. They also formed a committee to guard the system against vandalism by those opposed to the SIRDO.

Strong opposition to the SIRDO was encountered at both sites where the system was initially introduced. As in many other countries, in Mexico the provision of urban land and services is influenced by political considerations. Typically, community leaders or groups recognize the need for housing sites and services, and they organize residents to make demands to politicians in the ruling party. In response, government agencies seek to establish a ''patron-client'' relationship with these leaders by offering to subsidize urban services in exchange for their political backing. Usually the community receiving the services is required to contribute labor and money to the project as well. Private companies also profit from contracts for these public works projects. Through such ''clientelistic'' politics, all parties stand to gain.

It is perhaps not surprising then that a community-managed system such as the SIRDO initially might be perceived as a challenge by those having an interest in the established way of doing things. Community members with close ties to benefactors worry that their position may be weakened by such community initiatives. Some government officials may be resistant because they think such projects will make the urban population less dependent on state support and thereby increase their political independence. And private firms may resent the loss of profits from large public works contracts. An additional source of resistance by those with vested interests in the status quo is their natural skepticism about the introduction of any new technology, especially one whose environmental benefits can only be demonstrated through an educational program.

There is, however, increasing support among some government officials for new ways to deliver basic services and technologies such as the SIRDO because they stimulate community self-help and are lower in cost than traditional systems. This position has grown stronger in Mexico as the government has become less and less able to afford costly investments such as conventional drainage systems. Furthermore, the SIRDO has generated strong interest because of its role in reducing the risks of environmental contamination and in educating the urban population about these concerns. So, despite some incidents and harassment, the experiment went forward.

In October 1981, to the astonishment of the residents of the experimental block, the first harvest yielded nearly a ton of fertilizer. Community members now needed to organize the labor required to remove

Doña Lucero is a woman in her late twenties who comes from a lower-middle-class background. She is trained in accounting and holds a full-time job. She is articulate and can both write and type (the only cooperative member with this skill). She has two children. Her husband is a carpenter. Because of her leadership abilities and abiding interest in the SIRDO and the cooperative, she has been its president since the beginning.

the fertilizer from the chamber and to process it for use or sale. This increased the workload and required greater organization on the part of the community. Thus the idea of forming a cooperative was born. After seeking information and technical advice from several sources, the residents voted to name their new cooperative "Muchuc-Baex," a Mayan term meaning "let's get together." The fertilizer itself was named *tierra bonita* (pretty earth). By January 1982, the Muchuc-Baex Cooperative was legally constituted with eighteen members, fourteen of them women.

The cooperative's first economic activity was the sale of the fertilizer. This required modest capital to purchase plastic bags, labels, stapler, a scale, and a few other essential tools. The GTA offered several small loans during this initial period to assist the cooperative and was later repaid in fertilizer.

Members set to work extracting the fertilizer from the chamber, mixing it with earth, and putting it into 1-kilo bags for sale. Initially the mocking remarks of neighbors ("crazy women playing with shit") discouraged some women from participating in these tasks. Others, however, persevered and by the end of 1982, the cooperative was selling its fertilizer in two main supermarkets in the city, bringing in a small, but symbolically important income to the group.

By September 1983, the GTA had delegated most of the responsibility for maintenance of the system to the community, the neighborhood's children had written and performed their own play recounting the history of the cooperative, and Muchuc-Baex had reaped four fertilizer harvests. The quality of the fertilizer was evident both in the kitchen gardens of the members and through tests carried out by the local agency of the federal agricultural ministry. To promote its fertilizer, the group used photographs of Doña Lola and the giant cucumber she had produced in her garden.

Doña Lola is the only cooperative member who speaks Maya as a first language. She comes from the henequen-growing zone outside Mérida. Abandoned by her first husband, Doña Lola moved to Mérida with her second husband, Don Alvar, who had been a peasant leader in their place of origin. He works as a garbage collector for the city. Both of them were interested in the SIRDO from the very beginning, attending all the talks given by the GTA before they moved into the experimental block. Don Alvar was interested in waste management because of his job. Doña Lola was interested because she has always cultivated her own kitchen garden to supply the family with vegetables. She saw the system as a way of improving her production and has taken a leading role in experimenting with the fertilizer in her own garden plot. The giant cucumber is but one example of her success.

Operating the System

With technical assistance from the GTA, eight cooperative members operate and maintain the SIRDO. In general, the men carry out the heavier, periodic cleaning jobs for which they receive nominal payment. The tasks associated with day-to-day operation, which are not too time consuming, are taken care of by the majority of the neighborhood's women who do not hold jobs outside the home. The maintenance tasks are periodically rotated among members on a voluntary basis. The technical requirements of the SIRDO are spelled out in the "Biotics Manual" provided by the GTA, which serves as a reference guide for community managers.

While cooperative members are now convinced of the advantages of the SIRDO, they also recognize that some problems exist. Their housing development was not designed with the system in mind, and its piping and treatment sites occupy physical space that is in short supply; nor is there any work area for maintenance operations such as cleaning filters. Other aspects also could be improved: the cement covers for the gray water filters, for example, are so heavy that women generally must rely on men to remove them; and there is a need for equipment, such as gloves and masks, to protect workers from the fine dust raised during the sifting and mixing operations.

Marketing the Fertilizer

To insure its economic feasibility, the cooperative's current need is to widen the market for its fertilizer. Thus far they have produced four harvests of about one ton each—about half the maximum capacity of

Adding organic waste to the
solar collector *(Charles Wood)*

their two units. Most earnings to date have been reinvested in production (for example, purchase of earth for mixing) although small amounts have been distributed to members based on the amount of labor contributed. In the future they hope to improve their enterprise through the purchase of a machine to mix the fertilizer and construction of a warehouse for storage.

At this initial stage, the cooperative is willing to sell below real costs in order to build a market for its product. The good results achieved in their own gardens have given them confidence in their product and the patience to wait for demand to grow in the long run. Currently, most sales are made to middle class urban dwellers who use the fertilizer for gardening. Cooperative members hope they eventually can get it into the hands of farmers to improve the quality of their overworked soil. Fertilizer could even be exchanged for foodstuffs needed by members' families; however, as yet they have not found a mechanism to link them directly to peasant producers in their region.

Doña Betty, her husband Don Tito, and their children are all active in the cooperative. Doña Betty is illiterate and has ten children; she has never held a formal job. Don Tito is a baker. They arrived in the experimental block in November 1981, and began to take a personal interest in the SIRDO when by chance they witnessed an act of sabotage against the system. The people who had closed the valves later threatened them with a beating if they revealed their identities. The incident passed, but the couple afterwards became involved more directly in the cooperative. For a time Don Tito was afraid of his wife's involvement and even forbade her to attend cooperative meetings. Shortly after the first fertilizer harvest, they had a fight over the issue. Doña Betty made a decision to resist her husband. While she had allowed him to prohibit her from other activities in the past, she saw the importance of her participation in the cooperative. "This," she told him, "you cannot take away from me; it is helping me to develop as a person." Now there are four members of the family actively involved in the cooperative.

New Perspectives

Aside from the potential economic return from fertilizer sales, cooperative activities take on a larger meaning for the community. From the beginning, membership has been made up almost entirely of women, although several of their husbands regularly help with specific tasks. In some cases, husbands have tried to impede their wives' participation, but the women recognize the value of their collective activities and continue to participate in the organization.

To these women, the SIRDO provides a basis for community solidarity that surpasses the importance of the future income they hope to generate. The cooperative's president, Doña Lucero, puts it this way:

"Most people [in the cooperative] are not thinking about money. Before, I lived in one place for eleven years without knowing my neighbor's name. After I moved here, I lived for three years without knowing my neighbors. If I don't know my neighbor and there is an emergency in the middle of the night, I can't call on her—nor can she call on me. This is the greatest value of the cooperative. Here we are more sisters than neighbors. If I don't have money to eat, I'm not ashamed to ask Doña Candita for two hundred pesos or for some leftover tortillas [flat corn cakes that are a staple of the Mexican diet]. The drainage system has done this. If it did not exist, I can assure you that I would be here all these years without knowing my neighbors' names."

Community women stress that mutual aid is now a practice that extends to virtually all aspects of their daily lives. Cooperative members work together in other activities as well, including the collection of inorganic garbage for resale and the wholesale buying of vegetables from peasant producers. In 1981 they built a recreational park for their children and convinced the state to donate playground equipment.

The Second Setting: The Valley of Mexico

A more recent pilot SIRDO project in an urban community in the Valley of Mexico has drawn on the lessons learned in Mérida. This zone, including Mexico City and its surroundings, accounted for about 20 percent of the total Mexican population, or roughly 13 million persons, in 1978. While the population of the zone continues to grow at an annual rate of about 5 percent, the volume of wastes produced has grown at the astounding rate of about 30 percent per year. By 1984, this amounted to approximately thirteen thousand tons of waste per day in Mexico City, of which about one third were organic materials. On average, each resident of the city produces one and a half kilos of waste products each day. An estimated 70–80 percent of these wastes are not systematically recycled and pose a threat of contamination to the environment. Approximately ten thousand persons work informally in the city's dumps or in the streets separating wastes according to their resale value, selling items for about 1 peso per kilo ($1 equals about 167 pesos) to middle-merchants who in turn sell to industries for 3 or 4 pesos per kilo. Alternative waste-management systems like the SIRDO therefore appear to be well suited to this environment.

The history of the community where the second SIRDO pilot project is located is distinct from the Mérida neighborhood. Located near the northern margin of the city, the community is managed by a cooperative, begun in 1956, which has more than eighteen hundred low-income families. The cooperative first negotiated the purchase of an area for settlement, then took charge of dividing it into lots, opening streets, and assisting residents to construct houses. Later it oversaw the installation of the community's own water system and electricity and the building of schools, green areas, and other facilities. All this has made the community a desirable neighborhood in comparison to other less organized areas in the Valley of Mexico.

By 1976 the problem of waste disposal had become apparent. The community was inhabited by about eighteen thousand persons who produced about 240 tons of waste per month. About one third of this quan-

Doña Candita was born on the island of Cozumel, off the coast of the Yucatán Peninsula. When her first husband abandoned her, she lived with her mother for a time. A few years later her husband returned and proposed that they be reunited. He took her with him to live in Mérida. But he continued to drink heavily and to beat her on occasion. Finally she decided to separate. She found work preparing snacks such as tamales, antojitos, and empanadas to sell to cafeterias in the city. She would spend the morning making them in her home and then deliver them to her customers in the afternoon. In this way she managed to support her five children, all of whom have been able to finish their schooling. Doña Candita herself can read and write only with difficulty.

Later she married again, but began to have the same problems with her second husband. Finally she told him she no longer wished to live with him. When she moved into the experimental block, she moved alone. This was the beginning of a new, more independent phase in her life. At first she did not become involved in the SIRDO. But as she watched the cooperative take form, she was impressed by the hard work of the other women and of GTA staff. So she plunged in and was elected the cooperative's treasurer. From this position she has become involved in new experiences that have increased her own self-confidence as well as her effectiveness in working with the cooperative.

In February 1982, the GTA arranged for Doña Candita to be invited to a meeting of housing authorities in another state interested in the SIRDO. Two years later, she attended a national level meeting on housing sponsored by federal and state agencies. She described for them the cooperative's experience with the SIRDO. During five days, she was the only community representative at the Mexico City meeting. This experience increased her awareness of the importance of what the cooperative was doing. She returned to Mérida determined to convince local authorities and cooperative members of the need to maintain their commitment to the SIRDO. She has also taken on an active and influential role in cooperative decisions.

In her forties, Doña Candita is the eldest of the cooperative members. Her son, Miguel, is also an active member. His interest stems from his course of study in engineering. The cooperative has relied on his expertise to oversee the system's operation and maintenance.

tity was collected by trucks; the rest was deposited by residents in ravines, green areas, or vacant lots. Open-air drainage also collected in the ravines. As these deposits led to contamination, the community began to explore ways to resolve this growing problem.

The first option was a conventional, water-borne drainage system, the

The SIRDO in the Valley of Mexico *(Charles Wood)*

cost of which had been estimated at 26 million pesos in 1972 (about $1 million). The community was able to raise only 2 percent of this amount over the next eight years. In 1979 a new estimate by the municipality placed the cost of this system at 44 million pesos, without calculating direct costs that would raise the sum to nearly 60 million (more than $2 million). By this time the cooperative had managed to raise 2.5 million pesos, or about 4 percent of the total cost. Given the impossibility of paying for the conventional system, the cooperative began to seek alternative solutions. This is when it came into contact with the GTA in Mérida.

Early in 1982, forty members of the cooperative visited Mérida and attended a meeting of the Muchuc-Baex Cooperative in order to become familiar with the SIRDO. Shortly thereafter, the Valley of Mexico's cooperative members voted in a general assembly to use the money collected for the conventional drainage system to finance installation of a pilot SIRDO, with technical assistance from the GTA and other groups in Mexico City. Community members explored financing for the project's various stages. The pilot system would serve eighty-four families settled on forty lots surrounding a natural pond, as well as a secondary school with about eighty students. Experiments with aquaculture were to be carried out in the lily pond.

Packaging the fertilizer for sale
(Charles Wood)

Introducing the SIRDO: Progress and Conflict

At the outset, only about 20 percent of the population favored the new technology; about half were doubtful or did not understand how it worked. The remainder were opposed. Nonetheless construction went ahead over a period of twenty-seven weeks and the pilot system was inaugurated in December 1982. Twenty-two community members contributed their own labor; the direct costs of construction came to 2.5 million pesos (about $55,000). In order to assist in preparing the community for the new technology, members of the Muchuc-Baex Cooperative developed a seven-lesson course for users, promoters and technicians. Adults and children attended this course.

Immediately after the pilot system began to function, two more sections of the community requested consideration for the next SIRDO. One group formed a committee of twenty-four persons and named a treasurer on each block to collect funds to finance the project. The GTA began to prepare designs for these two areas. A Technical Council consisting of cooperative representatives, technical advisors, and state and municipal government personnel was formed to oversee the new installations.

While these plans were getting underway, however, those opposed to the new system were also organizing. They formed a Council for Municipal Collaboration and tacitly opposed construction of the new SIRDO. They put pressure on the municipality, causing it to withdraw its offer of support for the SIRDO and instead to promise to construct a traditional drainage system at a cost of 300 million pesos (about $3 million). The atmosphere became unpleasant as a director of the local primary school prohibited two teachers from taking their students on a site visit to the SIRDO as a field lesson on the environment, and the dome on the gray waters filter and the grating on the chimneys of the decomposition chamber were broken by vandals. In 1983 the anti-SIRDO group was able to win control of the cooperative's directorship, but the community itself remained divided over the issue.

In contrast to the experience in Mérida, membership in the Valley of Mexico Cooperative averages only about 30 percent women. Since cooperative statutes permit only one member per family, representation is usually by the male head of the household. One woman reported being prohibited from taking her absent husband's place at a cooperative meeting. In contrast, the Muchuc-Baex Cooperative is based on individual membership, which permits women to have a greater voice in collective decisions. As one woman put it: "Sometimes I think one way and my husband thinks differently. But both votes count." Despite the limits to their direct participation in the cooperative, however, the women in the Valley of Mexico have found ways to exert their collective power in matters related to basic community services, including the SIRDO.

The cooperative's new leadership soon felt the women's pressure when the community's water system failed. For weeks the women bore the brunt of hauling water long distances and deteriorating sanitary conditions. A small group of women, who previously had not known each other, called a meeting to discuss solutions to the water problem. Systematically they organized neighbors in each zone within the neighborhood until they succeeded in ousting the cooperative's directorate and calling for new elections. They also succeeded in forming a commission to oversee the work of the cooperative's directorate. Six of the nine commission members are women.

Once the water problem was resolved, the commission turned its attention to other community problems, including road paving, green areas, and drainage. When the municipal authorities showed up and began to dig up the neighborhood streets to put in the promised conventional drainage system, the women resisted. Individual women faced the construction teams saying, "You will not dig in front of my house!" They were backed up by a large group of women who informed the officials that, "If you arrest her, you will have to take all of us."

The installation of the conventional system was stopped. The women then pressed for a paved road which would enhance the installation and operation of the SIRDO.

During the first year following its installation, the SIRDO's primary merit was an improvement in the environmental condition: fewer flies and rats were present once garbage and sewage no longer accumulated in the ravine behind the houses. However since only a small proportion of the neighborhood's houses were connected to the system, other sources of contamination still existed.

As in Mérida, the appearance of the first harvest of fertilizer provided the needed incentive for greater involvement by the users. The fertilizer was tested by the state water and sanitation company after the residents used their ties to advisors to the state governor (who favors the SIRDO) to elicit its assistance. The tests initially showed some harmful bacteria remaining, so the residents corrected this problem by further drying and the addition of more organic matter. By May of 1984, the tests had improved.

In the meantime, the SIRDO users began to organize themselves for the tasks of producing the fertilizer and planning new productive activities. In March 1984, about twenty families connected to the system had formed a more formal user's group called the "Community of SIRDO Users," which began to meet on a weekly basis. One community resident, a medical doctor, also began to train eight young men from the group to maintain the system and collect garbage. Given the large number of users at this site, and the greater distances from the houses to the chamber, this division of labor was more attractive than the communal system used in Mérida. The users agreed to pay these young people a small wage, based on the Mexican minimum wage, for an estimated two to four hours work per week. In order to cover this expense and start-up costs for other activities, members agreed to contribute 500 pesos (about $3) to the group every two weeks.

Soon the user's group decided to adopt a more formal organizational structure with elected officers and six specialized commissions. The general director and secretary are men, the treasurer is a woman, and each of the six commissions is the responsibility of one woman. The group also named three advisors for technical, social, and administrative matters. These are professional people who live in the experimental block.

Each commission began to develop its own set of activities. Commission I is in charge of operation and maintenance of the pilot SIRDO. Its principal task is to supervise the young trainees who operate the system. Commission II is preparing for the production and sale of the fertilizer. They have spent about $50 for a two-color, silk-screened logo which will be printed on the plastic bags containing the fertilizer. The initial

Children help with the SIRDO in many ways, including putting fertilizer in bags. *(Josefina Mena)*

plan is to distribute most of the fertilizer to SIRDO users and to sell the rest to cover production costs. Already the group has been approached by other community residents who want to buy the fertilizer for their own gardens. A market survey is also planned to set an appropriate price for the product.

The other four commissions have more long-term objectives, which are expressed by the group's motto: "For a Self-Sufficient Urban Community." Commission III is in charge of planning productive activities related to the recycling of plastics, metal, and glass. The group hopes to move towards recycling most of the neighborhood's inorganic, as well as organic, wastes. As a first step, commission members consulted an expert in plastics recycling from Mexico's National University who is experimenting with a technology to convert waste plastics into useful products such as the plastic tubing used for plumbing and for construction of SIRDOs.

Commission IV has the task of developing horticulture projects. Its members began by planting a small experimental plot of carrots, radishes, squash, onions, tomatoes, and herbs next to the chamber. Two biologists from the local university have provided advice, as well as seeds, on a voluntary basis. The first garden was planted without the use of fertilizer in order to compare it with later yields. The group now plans to expand the plots to other areas surrounding the SIRDO. They also plan to plant fruit trees nearby, beginning with trees that already have been grown successfully in the area, such as peaches, pears, and avocados. To irrigate these crops, the group is building a large holding tank for recycled gray waters from the SIRDO, with a pump to allow year-round irrigation. The goal is to have 400,000 square meters of land producing food for the community's twenty-three thousand inhabitants on a regular basis.

With assistance from biologists, Commission V is developing plans for future aquaculture projects using treated black waters from the SIRDO. Plans call for creation of four tanks for the various stages of water treatment; six to ten thousand trout will be raised in the fourth tank. Infrastructure and community training necessary to operate such a project is estimated to cost $12,000, which must be raised from outside sources. Initially the fish would be consumed within the community and then the cooperative hopes, with increased production, to sell them for a profit.

Commission VI has the delicate task of overseeing waste management in homes and caring for the environment. These tasks are primarily social and educational. Committee members oversee the composition of garbage dumped into the SIRDO chamber and, when necessary, suggest corrections. Another task of this committee is to contact the twenty-eight families living in the SIRDO area who still are not connected to the system. They encourage these families to clarify their views on the SIRDO and either decide to be connected or waive their rights so that families on nearby blocks, who have expressed an interest in using the system, may do so.

Growth and Change

All these new activities reflect a greater sophistication on the part of the SIRDO users as to the need for effective public relations within the community. SIRDO users also have learned not to be aggressive in their opposition to the conventional drainage system favored by some community members. Instead of proclaiming themselves *sirdistas,* they now advise neighbors to base their decisions on an analysis of the relative merits of the two systems. They are confident that the conventional system will never be completed due to its high cost and that the SIRDO will gradually win over community residents as the income-generating activities take shape and environmental conditions improve. Within the community there are already about two hundred families who wish to have SIRDOs installed on their blocks.

SIRDO users also point out that the system has brought about more unity and communication among residents of the experimental block than had previously existed. Solidarity has been fostered by their everyday communal labor, their work on the commissions, and their weekly meetings. The SIRDO and its related activities have greatly increased women's visibility within the community and their confidence in handling community affairs. While men continue to dominate formal decision-making positions in the community, women have increased their power through informal pressure groups, such as the water commission. Women represent more than half of the membership of the SIRDO users' group; they have the greatest involvement in the day-to-day operation of the system, and they head all the working commissions created by the users' group. While they have not yet reached the level of confidence and independence achieved by the women in Mérida, the women of the Valley of Mexico are emerging as a political force through their involvement with the SIRDO.

Economic Potential

The potential economic return from the SIRDO depends on the development of productive activities by community members. The GTA has calculated that 50 to 80 full-time jobs could be generated at the Valley of Mexico site once fertilizer, aquaculture, and agricultural production are well underway. The cost of producing the fertilizer can be reduced by more than half if maximum use is made of community labor. The Mérida experience has demonstrated that a kilo of fertilizer, which sells for approximately 75¢, can be produced for less than an estimated 5¢ per kilo. Material costs to produce four tons of fertilizer accounted for only $250 per year. Given the demand for low-cost fertilizer in all parts of the world, including Mexico, there is a clear economic incentive to maximize fertilizer production.

Expansion

Six years after the first pilot project in Mérida was installed, the SIRDO has achieved national visibility and credibility in key sectors of the government, the press, and the academic community. The nation's three principal newspapers carried out a support campaign called "Operation SIRDO" beginning in June 1984 that focused on the system as the solution to problems of environmental contamination in Mexico's cities. Scientists from a variety of government and academic institutions have been drawn into activities, such as plastics recycling, aquaculture, horticulture, and testing potential uses for the fertilizer, once GTA's educational effort convinced them that they should apply their technical knowledge to the problems of low-income communities. The GTA has also enlisted the aid of allies within the government in order to neutralize opposition to the system from other official sectors. In Mérida, for example, the new state governor and federal-level housing officials put pressure on regional authorities who were opposed to the system, with the result that the state government agreed to share with the community the costs of some needed repairs to the system.

By 1984 the GTA was building SIRDOs not only for grassroots groups, but also for the government and the private sector. The state oil company, PEMEX, intends to build ten SIRDOs a year in its new developments in order to protect the environment from contamination. The federal urban development and ecology agencies are beginning to work with the GTA in several communities and would like to build as many SIRDOs as possible during the next year. University students will be trained to work with communities where these systems are installed.

With growing acceptance of the SIRDO come new challenges for GTA. Current initiatives include creation of workers' cooperatives to produce parts for the SIRDO, thus providing employment for community people who have participated in construction of the systems. The parts would be sold to both the public and private sectors.

The Changing Role of Technical Assistance

As responsibility for operating and maintaining the systems is gradually handed over to the community, GTA's role becomes that of an outside technical advisor. The process is all part of GTA's goal to design a system that would alter the relationship between user, technology, and the environment in order to foster collective action as an alternative to passive dependence on governments that often lack either the will or the resources to respond to local demands. In both Mérida and the Valley of Mexico, this transfer has entailed periods of tension as community members begin to assert their independence by reaching decisions contrary to the advice of GTA. After these experiences, GTA modified its strategy of technology transfer in order to reduce the potential for technical mistakes. Before introducing the system to a new area, GTA now forms a community Health Committee and a Production Cooperative to be responsible for decisions related to the system's productive activities. A small number of community members are trained to operate and maintain the system within the technical limits established by GTA.

The two pilot experiences in Mérida and the Valley of Mexico demonstrate some of the problems and potential involved in introducing new technologies. Community acceptance of an innovation like the SIRDO involves overcoming technical, social, and political obstacles. Because of their involvement in managing household and community wastes, the priority they give to a safe environment, and their need for new sources of income, women play an important role in promoting the understanding and acceptance of a new technology such as the SIRDO. Their participation in such new activities catalyzes their collective organization. Their effectiveness increases their visibility and defines their voice in community affairs. Finally, the potential of the system to generate income through the sale of fertilizer (and eventually fruits, vegetables, and fish) may offer women a greater opportunity for economic independence as well.

Update

The twenty-four families in Mérida continue partial use of their two SIRDO systems for waste disposal only. Conflicts developed within the group when they began to sell their fertilizer in local markets. The venture proved quite profitable and disputes erupted over division of the income: the old dilemma, whether to distribute equally to each member or according to the amount of work contributed. This issue has stopped the production of fertilizer and related income-generating activities in this community.

The original Mexico City site continues to operate, but the conflicts between the *Sirdistas* and those who seek to operate the system as part of the municipality remain. The latter group currently holds the dominant position. Fertilizer derived from the system is being used to produce various crops.

There has been considerable expansion of the SIRDO technology in Mexico City and surrounding areas. Three urban cooperatives are functioning in the El Molino section of the city with six SIRDOs operational and three more under construction, serving eighteen hundred families. Another twenty thousand families are being served in eleven settlements in Bosques del Pedregal; twenty middle class families in the Residencia Los Duraznos; and seven hundred families in the State of Morelos.

A new "dry" SIRDO system, constructed of a fiberglass reinforced plastic, has been developed and introduced in Mexico City. GTA installed units to provide sanitation to hundreds of victims of the 1985 earthquake. Based on this experience, the Secretary of Urban Development and Ecology (SEDUE) of the national government has decided to adopt the dry SIRDO technology to combat the growing problem of human waste disposal in Mexico City. SEDUE plans to manufacture sixty thousand units to serve 1 million residents of the city. A World Bank loan will allow families to purchase the units for an initial cost of $25, followed by minimum monthly payments of 5 percent of their annual salary over eight years.

The SIRDO technology continues to be refined, but the major problems surrounding the use of the systems continue to be political, social, and administrative rather than technical. Successful implementation will most likely depend upon how these problems are resolved.

_____ Lessons _____

1. **The introduction of a new technology depends on both technical and social processes. This requires the long-term commitment of community members.** Technical aspects of even sophisticated systems can be readily understood if appropriate participatory training methods are used. In the case of the SIRDO technology, the unique ecological features of each site demand the active collaboration of community members to adjust the technology to the local environment. Planning and organizing the productive activities associated with the system are even more complex challenges, which require communities to assess their priorities and the competing demands on their time and resources. It is therefore important that technicians be realistic in their understanding of the delicate process of technology transfer.

2. **The nature of community participation in waste management, or any new technology, is a process that changes over time.** Learning to operate and maintain the system, and educating skeptics about its merits, took place during the first year. The first harvest of fertilizer placed even greater demands on cooperative members, but also provided a tangible incentive for greater involvement. Recognition of these different phases in the process will help communities to prepare for their growing management responsibilities and will help instill the patience to overcome residual skepticism.

3. **Women and the community must see an immediate benefit in adopting a new technology.** The SIRDO's immediate benefit is an improvement in physical sanitation, which is of greatest interest to women. While the system has the potential to be a community-based, income-generating activity, this is not an immediate advantage. Therefore, economic potential should not be overemphasized at the outset. Instead, the environmental advantages should be stressed and mutual cooperation encouraged. Women's participation in the management of critical community services can increase their influence

in community affairs and in relations with outside authorities. In Mérida, the need to operate and maintain the SIRDO, and to handle fertilizer production, gave rise to a new cooperative structure, dominated by women, that developed a strong sense of solidarity among women who previously had not known each other. It also increased their independence and confidence in dealing with husbands and other family members. In the Valley of Mexico, a strong, preexisting cooperative structure, dominated by men, initially impeded women's access to formal, decision-making power. However, the SIRDO stimulated the creation of new, less formal organizations in which women have expanded their community influence. Their growing consciousness of the effectiveness of collective action has spread to other areas of community concern, such as water management.

4. **The cooperative structure enhances the ability of the population to address other community problems and to view them in a longer-term perspective.** Learning to make collective technical decisions builds confidence and analytical abilities among cooperative members. The use of recycled wastes to increase the community's self-sufficiency provides a dramatic lesson about conservation of resources and environmental protection.

5. **New technologies must be modified as the requirements of women's participation in their operation becomes clear.** Since women and young people generally take charge of household waste disposal and sanitation and are less apt to be employed outside the community, they are the ones who are able to devote the necessary time to operating and maintaining a system such as the SIRDO. The system should be adjusted in such a way that they can carry out day-to-day activities without outside assistance. (For example, some parts of the original system had to be reduced in weight so that women and children could handle them.) Children's participation provides a unique educational opportunity; not only do they learn about environmental protection, but they can be trained to carry out tasks such as routine lab testing of fertilizer.

6. **Responsibility for managing the system must gradually be transferred to the community, with sufficient outside technical assistance to insure proper maintenance.** The introduction of a new technology requires a strong initial infusion of help from outside experts while community members are gradually trained to take over operation. As they take on greater responsibility, community members must build sufficient confidence to make decisions independent of, or even contrary to, the advice of outside technicians. Occasional mistakes are a part of the process of learning to collectively evaluate

and discuss decisions. However, outside assistance will still be needed to address new technical problems as they arise.

Further Information

Information about the SIRDO can be obtained from: *Grupo de Technologia Alternativa,* Calle Alamo 8-16 Col. Los Alamos, Jardines de San Mateo, Naucalpan, Edo. de Mexico, 53230 Mexico (Telephone 393-7414).

8

The Kingston Women's Construction Collective: Building for the Future in Jamaica

Ruth Mcleod

The Caribbean island of Jamaica has a population of roughly two million people, over half of whom live in urban areas, the largest being the capital city of Kingston. The island's sophistication is clearly demonstrated by the high-rise buildings that comprise Kingston's financial center and the luxury hotels that dot the island's North Coast. However, other tell-tale signs of rapid urban development are also highly visible: squatter settlements and urban ghettos characterized by high unemployment, political partisanship, and a low standard of living. In these densely populated areas a complexity of social, economic, and political problems confront development planners, particularly those concerned with improving the status of women.

Given that at least one third of the island's households, and one half of those in urban areas, are headed by women, and given that women's unemployment rates are more than twice those for men, it is not surprising that the position of women within Jamaican society and their role in the development process attracted considerable attention during the United Nations Decade for Women (1975–1985).

This chapter focuses on a project developed to integrate low-income women into Jamaica's construction industry. In two years, thirty-four women passed through the project's basic training and skills upgrading courses. More than

This chapter, apart from the update section, was originally published as the pamphlet *The Women's Construction Collective: Building for the Future* by the Seeds Publication Project in 1986.

90 percent of these women have been employed, the majority as masons and carpenters. The story of how this field was identified as a potential source of income for women, and how the project developed and evolved in response to changing circumstances, presents many useful lessons. These should be of particular interest to those seeking to identify employment areas where women's participation is feasible and in helping them prepare women for entry into nontraditional skill areas.

The Urban Working Groups

In July 1981, the Population Council initiated a program entitled, "Women, Low Income Households and Urban Services in Latin America and the Caribbean." Its goal was to bring low-income women's concerns into the existing urban planning and service delivery process through the creation of local working groups in three metropolitan areas: Kingston, Jamaica; Lima, Peru; and Mexico City, Mexico. The working groups were made up of urban planners, researchers and statisticians, development practitioners and social scientists. This encouraged links to grow between government bureaucracies, academia, and community development organizations. Through the working groups, information about the urban poor from a variety of perspectives was brought together and realistic priorities for action were identified. The Kingston Women's Construction Collective is one of the successful projects undertaken by the Kingston Working Group as a part of this overall program.

The Population Council, under a cooperative agreement with, first, the U.S. Agency for International Development's (U.S.A.I.D.) Office of Urban Development and Housing, (a second phase of the project received support from U.S.A.I.D.'s Women in Development office,) provided each working group with a modest fund which could be used to support low budget projects such as documentation of ongoing action projects, experimentation with new service approaches, reanalysis of existing data, and generation of new, primarily qualitative information. The information and policy advice generated by the working groups were then disseminated locally by the groups themselves, internationally through the publication of working papers, and through meetings and seminars coordinated by the Population Council.

Identifying the Need

In May 1983 the Jamaica Working Group, made up of approximately a dozen planners, researchers, and community development specialists, approved a proposal for an experimental project to train and place unemployed women in jobs at the trade level of the Jamaican building and construction industry. Why women in construction? Three factors were behind the group's decision to pursue a project to train and integrate women into the construction industry.

First, in mid-1982 the building industry was booming. According to the Planning Institute of Jamaica, the industry grew by 14.8 percent in 1981–82 and by mid-1983 it was contributing 6.1 percent to the island's Gross Domestic Product while employing thirty-two thousand people. The president of the Masterbuilders, an organization representing construction contractors, had predicted that five thousand new skilled workers would be required annually for the next three years. However, only eight hundred of those thirty-two thousand currently employed workers were women. Of these, only one hundred women were ranked as professionals, six hundred were clerical or service workers and one hundred were unskilled manual workers. Women also were unrepresented in official government statistics as trade workers in the industry.

Second, in effect, women had recently been excluded from entry into the government's building and construction training program at the trade level due to implementation of a new training policy. Before 1983, more than one hundred industrial training centers were in operation throughout the island, offering daytime classes on a coeducational basis. An estimated one thousand women were trained in building skills between 1976 and 1980, though few had found jobs in the industry. In 1983, the government shifted to a policy of utilizing a smaller number of larger training facilities that offered residential training for men only. While theoretically open to women on a day student basis, as of December 1985, not a single woman had been trained in building skills under this new system.

Third, there was particular concern that the high unemployment rate for young women would undermine the National Family Planning Board's attempt to reduce teenage fertility through the provision of free family planning services. A positive correlation had been observed between female unemployment and fertility, particularly in the ghetto areas where the role of "baby mother" (in Jamaica mothers are typically called "baby mothers" while fathers are referred to as "baby fathers") was frequently the only source of status available to young women.

Another major attraction of construction work as a possible employment area was the potentially high wages even at the entry level. For example, entry level masonry and carpentry helpers earned a salary of J$100 per week, while the official weekly minimum wage in Jamaica is J$65 per week and the average pay for a woman doing domestic work is J$50 per week. One collective member began work as an industrial painter at a starting wage of J$500 per week. Generally construction helpers can expect to be earning J$125 per week at the end of one year. Overall the monthly income of Collective members ranges from J$400–2000 per month. (As of January 1986, J$56.00 = US$10.00.)

The Working Group found the proposed project of particular interest because it would address these problems at both the industry and community levels and might offer a way to strengthen links between training and job placement for women. At the same time it would offer an opportunity to document the role of women within a nontraditional skill area. The latter was of high priority since there were no accounts of the women who had received construction training earlier or of the results of their job-seeking efforts. These women thus remained invisible within the statistics and could not serve as a positive example for the construction industry or provide role models for other women. In the absence of such documentation, policy makers developing training programs tended to assume that women either were not interested in the construction area or were unable to find work in this sector.

Laying the Groundwork

The project began with the formation of The Kingston Women's Construction Collective, which would be the vehicle through which a training program, tailored to the specific needs of young, unemployed, low-income women, could be made available. Not only would this training program provide women with skills, it would also help them learn about the realities of the workplace, including men's reactions, and develop strategies to overcome their fears about the practical obstacles involved in working in a male-dominated field.

Initial plans called for ten unemployed women from western Kingston to be selected, put through an intensive training program, placed in jobs, and monitored so that their experiences, over a 15-month period, could be closely documented both with photographs and in writing. The documentation would serve to strengthen the case for opening the government's training program to women.

A number of problems had to be addressed from the outset. One concerned the sixty-six occupational groups recognized in the Jamaican construction industry, many of them with three grade levels. Which group would provide the best opportunities for job placement? These complications were exacerbated by traditional hiring practices. Subcontracting is a major feature of the Jamaican construction industry, with between 70 and 100 percent of all trade work on each site being

Collective member ready for work *(Ruth McLeod)*

carried out by subcontractors on a task basis. The vast majority of subcontractors work through informal trade gangs, the composition of which may change as often as the jobs. Most subcontractors have no known addresses, let alone telephones or secretaries. Entry into these trade gangs occurs through a male network of friends, relatives, and workers met on previous jobs. Clearly this was not going to be an easy network to break into—particularly through formal, let alone female channels.

The balance of building work, however, is carried out on a direct hire, day-rate basis. In this mode, the main contractor normally hires site supervisors, timekeepers, equipment and plant operators, security guards, trade helpers, and casual laborers. Trade helpers often are selected from among the laborers and may be assigned to work with specific trade subcontractors as construction progresses. The planners felt that if women could find employment as trade helpers, this would provide them with access to the subcontractors' network which, in turn, would provide them with on-the-job training opportunities and the chance to upgrade their building skills while earning an income.

Another complication was presented by the extensive influence of territorial political rivalries in the Jamaican construction industry. If a site is located in an area associated with a particular political party, the followers of that party automatically expect exclusive job privileges. These expectations are encouraged by official or semi-official representatives and those affiliated with other political parties enter at their own risk, unless they possess a scarce skill or a strong tie to the main contractor. Early on it was realized that it might be necessary to confront the violence associated with this political territoriality.

An additional problem was how to accurately anticipate the funds required to operate the project. The initial budget provided by the Working Group was $8,000 over a 15-month period. This amount would have to cover facilities and instructors, materials and transportation, and the job placement process, which would require time for research and establishment of appropriate contacts. Any major deviations in planning could require additional fundraising.

The first step in developing the training program was locating a suitable training base. This task was undertaken by the Project Coordinator, who possessed experience in the field and knowledge of agencies able to provide such training. The Construction Resources and Development Center (CRDC) often develops experimental training programs for adult construction workers, frequently in cooperation with the Vocational Training Development Institute (VTDI). VTDI is an agency responsible for training vocational instructors for Jamaica and other Caribbean islands. It also provides short-term courses to upgrade skills in a wide variety of industrial areas. The project benefited from working with both CRDC and VTDI in developing its training program.

The second step was identifying potential trainees. One member of the Working Group, the Community Liaison Officer for the Western Kingston area, agreed to select the participants. All were to be chosen from the Tivoli Gardens section of western Kingston, a community developed as part of an upgrading scheme during the 1960s when the Jamaican Labour Party (JLP) was in power. It consists of one thousand living units, mostly four-storied apartment blocks and terraced units. This community strongly supports Prime Minister Seaga. It is characterized by high rates of female unemployment and teenage pregnancy and a large population of young women with dependent children. Women were chosen to participate in the Kingston Women's Construction Collective on the basis of literacy and numeracy tests as well as input from leaders of the local youth club.

It was decided to select women from a single community as this would provide a strong basis for cohesion among the women in the group. They would know each others' strengths and difficulties and could help each other with practical problems, such as child care. They would also know the Community Liaison Officer, who acted as an important anchor for the project, particularly in the early stages. For example, when a woman had problems with her "baby father," she would talk to both the man and the woman. She also made sure that the community was kept informed about the project.

The majority of the original recruits also belonged to the Tivoli Community's Ultimate Youth Club. This club is managed mainly by men, who fortunately recognized the importance of developing new employment options for women and agreed to support the project from its inception. They provided ongoing assistance in organizing fundraising events and also attended some of the collective's early meetings. The support offered to the women by influential members of the local community was very important. It made their attempt to enter a male-dominated field not only credible but legitimate. People such as the Youth Club leaders and the Community Liaison Officer talked about the project in the community and portrayed the women as pioneers and examples of strength and determination.

Training

Overall, the training aspect of the project can be broken down into four phases:

- October 1983, Phase One begins at VTDI with ten women;
- January 1984, Phase Two begins with five women initiated as part of the CRDC's Building Maintenance Program;
- May 1984, Phase Three begins with fifteen women recruited from newly selected communities; and
- June 1984, four additional women receive training at CRDC.

On the basis of initial research, the experience level of the collective members and the funds available, it was decided that trainees would begin with a five-week masonry and carpentry training program. This would consist of three components: practical tasks, classroom sessions, and instruction by visiting lecturers experienced in the industry. This basic training would then be followed by a wide range of skills-upgrading programs, developed in response to needs.

The ten women who arrived at the VTDI Building Department in Kingston early one morning in the fall of 1983 resembled anything but a potential gang of construction workers. They wore shoes suited only for a dance floor, stockings of the sheerest material and, with a few exceptions, giggled nervously behind their hands as they were asked to introduce themselves to the team of instructors. They were all between

Two members at a building site *(Ruth McLeod)*

seventeen and twenty-five years of age, from Tivoli Gardens, and had completed at least the ninth grade. All were numerate, literate, and physically fit, and most had borne at least one child by the age of seventeen. None had ever considered looking for employment in the building and construction industry. It was difficult to imagine that within five weeks these same women would be prepared to start work as trade helpers on large construction sites. By then they would have developed basic building skills and an understanding of building terminology. And if they were successful in finding a job, they would be guaranteed take-home pay of at least twice the minimum weekly wage and a chance to become skilled tradeswomen.

Getting right to work, the training began with an exercise of the most practical kind: the VTDI Building Department had no bathroom or changing facilities for women. Thus the women's first task was to partition the existing male facilities so that they would have access to their own washing and changing area. During this process a substantial number of stockings were ruined and within a few days the physical appearance of the women began to change. Jeans and sneakers replaced skirts and sandals and work began in earnest.

In addition to hands-on experience, there were classroom sessions on

Pauline dropped out of school two months before graduating, pregnant with her first child. She then tried commercial college, but had to drop out when her baby's father got sick. When he left for the United States, Pauline became fully responsible for her child's support and started looking around for work. She heard about the collective because "all her friends were talking about it," and decided to join with the second group of entrants in Phase Two.

Pauline has spent ten months working on a large construction site, building a new training facility for building-skills trainees. If she were a man, she would be eligible to attend this institution on a residential basis. However, as a woman, she cannot attend.

Asked about her experience in construction, Pauline replies: "It has been real good for me. It has more career possibilities than the sewing I did before. If it wasn't for the collective, I wouldn't have [got involved] in construction because there wasn't anything to involve women in work like this."

---

topics such as accurate measurement, estimation, and correct mixes for mortar and concrete. Each woman had to build a concrete block wall using a trowel, hand hawk, plumb-bob, and spirit level. The wall had to be rendered correctly and finished neatly. In addition, she had to saw wood for making building forms and construct a correctly jointed stool.

Both male and female visiting lecturers spoke to the women on various topics. A woman contractor introduced some of the practicalities of working as women on a building site. Questions about changing facilities, keeping the respect of men, and dealing with menstrual cramps were discussed. This woman operates six of her own companies, ranging from a building and contracting company to a manufacturing plant for gas cylinders. She therefore provided a formidable role model. Since her initial participation as an instructor, she has also sponsored booths for the collective at trade fairs and she supported the training of one member at the College of Arts, Sciences and Technology.

Another lecturer, a prominent male contractor, is also a supporter of the collective. He spoke on career options, which later led to all the members taking a tour of the offices of engineers, quantity surveyors, and builders, and of a building component factory and several building sites.

Halfway through the training, most of the women had completely changed their idea of the building industry. As one woman put it, "I thought it was just laying blocks and digging trenches. I didn't realize there were all these other jobs—I mean even computer work."

During the training the women were expected to work hard. If they were persistently late or absent, or became pregnant, they faced expulsion. They would never survive on a construction site if they were not disciplined and physically tough. No trainee allowances were provided other than lunch and enough money to pay for a bus ride to VTDI and home again each day.

After the first training program for Phase One recruits, the training received by members of the collective took many different forms. The basic objective was always to develop skills of the kind and to the level that the industry could use. The three basic components of the training remained the same, but as women were recruited from other areas, the program was changed to adapt to their needs and to the changing demands of the industry.

Placement

While the first ten women were being trained, an agreement was reached with contractors to place them as trade helpers on a government construction project. This project involved refurbishing several downtown Kingston markets used by vendors (almost all of whom are women) who bring produce from all over the island. The market facilities are extremely old and the upgrading project was aimed at improving sanitation, lighting, ventilation, and stall space. Since the chief architect was a member of the Working Group, and the project was in an area sharing the same political alliances as Tivoli, the women's involvement might not be resisted on political grounds. The contractor had agreed to take the women into the regular labor force, pay them the same rates as male trade helpers, and allocate them work with subcontractors. However three weeks into the training program major budget cuts by the government led to the indefinite postponement of the market project. In terms of placement, the project was back to square one.

Training ended toward the end of November and with the approach of Christmas, arranging job placements became difficult. The collective members agreed to meet on Sundays at the Tivoli Community Center. As December progressed, the mood become more and more depressed. However, the collective soon developed a new strategy for finding placements through "job auditions"—offers to work on-site on a trial basis at no cost to the employer. If the employer was impressed and offered a long-term placement, the auditioner would be paid for the time already worked. If, on the other hand, the auditioner did not perform satisfactorily, the contractor would be under no obligation to pay her.

A number of contractors were contacted and asked if they wished to audition members of the collective. In mid-January, the woman contractor who had participated in the training responded. She offered to hire two women on a trial basis for a housing project in Spanish Town, 12 miles outside Kingston. Two women with excellent technical evaluations from VTDI were there the following Monday, complete with new trowels and measuring tapes provided by the collective. By the end of the week, they had been taken onto the regular work force.

Soon afterwards the male contractor who had addressed the trainees offered to try four women on a site in Kingston, building middle-income housing units. They began regular work almost immediately. At last it seemed the job drought was over. Every woman who auditioned after that got a job.

One problem associated with this strategy is deciding who should be chosen to attend a job audition. At first, with only ten women, the selection could be handled easily on the basis of technical performance during training. As the collective became more diverse, however, a system was needed. Thereafter women without job experience were given first consideration for placement.

Expansion

Soon it became apparent that the rising demand from employers justified expansion of the project. Five more women joined the collective in January, but still there were more jobs available than women to fill them. In February 1984, the collective was asked to provide ten to fifteen women for a factory building project. However, to further expand the collective would require additional human and financial resources. A number of critical decisions needed to be made regarding the Project's further development. For example,

- How would new participants be selected?
- What kind of organizational structure would permit the collective to cope with an increasing membership?
- How could the collective become independent and self-sustaining in the long term?

The collective could have expanded its membership with new recruits from Tivoli. This, however, would have resulted in the collective being clearly identified with the political party to which the community was allied—the Jamaica Labour Party (JLP)—and would make the collective vulnerable to charges of political partisanship, which in turn could threaten its long-term developmental prospects. Another alternative would have been to advertise for new recruits on an open basis. This option was rejected because the experience of the Working Group indicated that a strong community base can greatly increase the ability of women's groups to develop cohesion. A third option was to identify specific new communities for recruitment.

The collective members finally agreed that the best approach would be to identify additional feeder communities with different political affiliations. A proposal outlining this approach was presented to the Canadian International Development Agency (CIDA). In the meantime, a local foundation, the Grace Kennedy Foundation, helped with a short-term grant of J$5,000.

In making the decision to expand the project to other feeder communities, selection criteria had to be spelled out:

• The communities would have to demonstrate high female unemployment rates, particularly among younger women with dependent children.
• They would have to demonstrate identifiable and sympathetic community leadership (formal and informal).
• They would need to have a local meeting place available for use by women joining the collective.
• They would have to be within reasonable distance by bus of the training institution and the areas where construction jobs are available.
• Ideally one of the communities would be as strongly identified with the opposition political party—the People's National Party (PNP)—as Tivoli was with the JLP.

The final decision to expand coincided with the arrival of a new volunteer resource person who offered to assist with the management of the project over the next year. Her major role would be the monitoring of up to nine different construction sites in geographically separate areas.

By May, the funding from CIDA had arrived, the new co-manager was in place and expansion could begin. Two new communities were selected to participate in the collective: Nannyville, a housing settlement built within Kingston city limits in the 1970s by the PNP Government, and Glengoffe, a rural community about 15 miles outside of Kingston. Nannyville met all the criteria, including political allegiance to the PNP. Glengoffe was selected as a result of approaches made by a community worker who was developing a women's horticultural project. This project required that women be trained to construct and maintain plant houses, but did not have funds to design a special training program. The collective therefore decided to include five women from Glengoffe, at least on a temporary basis. (While it was felt that Glengoffe was geographically too remote to make access to work sites easy, the horticulture project

The collective built a wooden house for Ma Lou, one of Jamaica's famous potters. *(Ruth McLeod)*

A member at work using a circular saw *(Ruth McLeod)*

"Before I became a member of the Women's Constructive Collective, I was at home suffering from the frustration of depending on my family for whatever I needed for my use, not able to obtain a job, and thinking of what I could possibly do to make myself independent."

Sharon was twenty-five years old and the mother of two children when she joined the collective. She has always been very close to her grandfather who encouraged her to make little trucks and fix things with his tools. Her father worked in construction too, and used to take her with him to visit building sites. When Sharon first told him about the collective, he laughed, but he is pleased now when she talks about one-by-twos or two-by-fours. "If I had been a boy, I would have been working at the Public Works Department helping to patch roads, but Public Works does not seem to really employ women except as secretaries."

Her baby father "talked against" her joining the collective so, "I told him I was just nailing a few nails and didn't tell him anything about the cement. When I took home the stool I made, he started calling me carpenter and now, when anything wants to fix, they ask me to do it."

Sharon has learned how to put up an entire wooden house and to use electric drills, squares, sledge hammers, saws, and hammers. She laughs when she says, "I never thought of myself hitting down walls and all that, I really enjoy it."

Sharon joined the group in the third phase and comes from Nannyville. She feels strongly about the unity of the collective. "We're supposed to be close to each other as sisters—I don't see where politics comes into our bracket. I don't see where it would help us. I think it's good that we're women from different political areas—all mixed up."

should have absorbed the women's labor. As it turned out, this project was not implemented and these women also ended up in need of job placement.)

There were some political concerns as expansion began about possible violence to PNP supporters entering Tivoli or JLP supporters going to Nannyville. Initially it was assumed that two separate collectives would be required. This division, however, was adamantly opposed not only by the new recruits but by the collective's original members. At the women's insistence the collective remained a single entity. It now holds its monthly meetings on neutral territory at the CRDC offices. As one of the members puts it: "We don't have any business with tribal politics. Let the men have that, we women have had enough."

By June 1984, nearly one year into the project, the members of the collective decided that further expansion of the collective's membership might be unwise as there were clear signs of contraction in the building industry. Housing starts declined by more than 30 percent in 1984, and the Ministry of Housing's budget was cut from thirty million Jamaican dollars to J$100. Instead it was decided to consolidate and focus on further skills development for the women already in the collective. There was still a long way to go before any of the women could really be considered "skilled" and able to work without supervision. However, this approach also would require further resources. Funds needed to carry out the skills upgrading program were secured from the Inter-American Foundation.

Organizational Structure

CRDC served as the parent organization for the Women's Construction Collective, administering the international funding, hiring personnel, and providing office space as well as a structure and legal framework for the collective from 1984 until it became an independent legal entity in 1986.

The process of expansion led to a redefinition of the role of the collective and the creation of a new organizational structure. The challenge was to increase the collective's ability to govern itself and gradually decrease the need to rely on the judgment of the coordinator and the co-manager, thus enhancing the capability of each woman to play a responsible role.

The question of dependency has been a critical issue since the collective's formation. The first group of women spent a considerable amount of time discussing the issue and actually expelled one woman from the group because of her almost total passivity and inability or unwillingness to take responsibility. A good example of this problem was the enormous effort required to open a bank account in the collective's name. After the project had been operating for three months, the coordinator refused to go to the bank to get the necessary forms, arguing that the members should allocate that responsibility among themselves. Several women were eventually selected to deal with the banking matter, but it was two months before they coordinated their efforts sufficiently to open a standard bank account (that could have been opened in ten minutes by the coordinator). By the end of the two months, however, at least a few members had learned how to deal with bank personnel and how to open a standard bank account.

One of the results of the attention focused on dependency was the collective's decision to set selection criteria for new recruits entering Phase Three of the project. The objective was to weed out early those who were not highly motivated. As part of the selection procedure, the members designed two test papers, one in English and one in mathe-

The collective *(Ruth McLeod)*

matics, that every potential recruit would be required to take. The tests included a question asking the applicant why she wanted to be a construction worker as well as specific questions relating to estimation and measurement using building examples.

Initially the women elected a single gang leader, who chaired meetings and acted as the collective's spokeswoman, a secretary, and a public relations officer. In addition, most women working together at a particular construction site would also select a site gang leader to represent them with the employer and to speak for them at monthly meetings. One group developed an informal, revolving system of representation.

By the end of the first year, the collective's gang leader and the secretary were complaining that everything was being left to them and that ''the women are cussing us and giving us a hard time when we ask them to do things.'' The collective as a whole therefore agreed to appoint a formal Executive Committee with clearly defined job responsibilities. As a result, the collective now has an active Executive Committee of five women who meet on a regular basis with the project coordinator.

The transition of the collective as a whole from dependency on outside management to independence is taking place relatively slowly. Initially, the project coordinator made most of the key policy decisions regarding

Millicent is President of the Kingston Women's Construction Collective and is also one of its youngest members. She was only eighteen years old when she joined the first phase. She lives with eleven relatives in a two-bedroom apartment in Tivoli, but spent much of her childhood with an aunt who is a farmer.

When she first heard about the collective, she thought it was a "bit weird," but decided she might as well try it. "Being made gang leader was a real challenge. I knew it would mean a lot of trouble because some of the girls love a 'long argument.' When we started to pay money into the tool fund and put on activities to raise money, there were a lot of problems. Everybody seemed to have an excuse for not doing something. But one of the things I like about the group is that everyone is open and we can talk things out."

Millicent walked 3 miles to get to her first building job. "I was a bit scared at first because the men looked rough, but after talking with them, I felt different as they always wanted to work with us. When the mason men did not come, we helped casting. We filled the first foundation and laid the first set of blocks. When the mason men came the next day, they were amazed and said they did not know women could do it."

participant selection, training content, job placement, and so forth. When the co-manager joined the collective, it was decided to select two members as trainee managers. One woman had been the gang leader and now serves as the collective's president. The other woman had joined the project during the third phase and came from Nannyville.

When the co-manager left the collective after one year, it was agreed that the time had come for the members themselves to take over the day-to-day management of the collective. The trainee managers have now moved into the old co-manager position, taking charge of bookkeeping, placement, site monitoring, and other organizational tasks. They are assisted by other members of the collective's newly appointed Executive Committee.

New Directions

One move to encourage greater independence has been the establishment of the collective's own business: a repair and maintenance business and a carpentry workshop. Women who are not employed with contractors rotate through the business in five to eight-week cycles, either in the workshop building wooden components such as doors, shelves, and windows, or carrying out repair work throughout the Kingston area. The workshop is run by a male carpenter employed by the collective, while the repair work is done "on the road," supervised by a former government building skills instructor.

The repair and maintenance business emerged in response to a clearly identified need for firms able to carry out small-scale domestic repairs such as rehanging or replacing doors, fixing windows, installing shelves, and so on. Also, many female clients tend to feel more secure about letting women into their homes. This project-based training pays for itself out of business fees. Each woman is paid as a trade helper during her training, according to rates established in the industry, and is expected to carry out an individual project such as making an item needed by the collective. The business's earnings go into the collective's fund. The workshop building, for instance, was constructed by the collective with money made when the business built a wooden house for Ma Lou, one of Jamaica's famous potters.

Initial funding for the business came from Inter-American Foundation funds, which allowed for upgrading of training and provided equipment and two vehicles. The latter reduced the dependence of the collective on the one or two people able to drive the CDRC's pick-up truck and has encouraged more women to learn to drive.

Now that the collective is operating on so many levels, the need for effective coordination is becoming much greater. Recently CRDC staff and the Kingston Women's Construction Collective members involved in the workshop, the repair business, and the office agreed to meet on Friday afternoons for an open "rap session" to discuss the previous week's activities and to allocate tasks for the coming week. There is little question that both the organizational structure and the administrative framework of the collective will continue to change and adapt to new developments over the next two or three years, before settling into a permanent form.

Support for the Trainees

The industry focus of the project appears to have been largely responsible for the high placement rates achieved, but the emphasis on community participation and support that accompanied it proved no less important in laying a strong basis for cohesion among collective members. The community support system played a crucial role in helping the women in their transition from unemployment to nontraditional employment in the male-dominated world of construction.

Family support was also needed, but not always forthcoming. This took time and education. As current Collective President, Millicent

Powell, said. "At first my parents were not in favor of me doing construction work because they spent money on me for business study." Other women described how their families thought they were joking and did not take seriously their intention to work as construction workers: "Everybody knew that was a man's job." Some women were even prevented from joining because their baby fathers "did not want two men in the house." Two relationships were broken off as a result of the conflict.

One of the interesting findings of a university student who interviewed members of the collective was that they had received far greater support from female members of their families than from the males. This support also appears to have come from women in church groups. In contrast, one male pastor was totally against the project because it encouraged women to "wear pants."

However, the strongest psychological support system was probably provided by collective membership itself. The members meet one Sunday each month. Not only do the women share their experiences on the job and the reactions they receive at home, but they also organize group events, such as team sports and outings, that increase the collective's cohesion. The collective also initiated a public awareness campaign through local newspapers, on television and radio, and through a video showing the women at work and talking about their experiences, which also describes the training model used by the collective in its early stages.

Women require not only the will to enter a nontraditional field, but also the financial means. It is practically impossible, for instance, to get a job as a carpenter's helper if you do not have a saw. For this reason, the collective runs its own revolving tool fund. Each woman is loaned tools for her job audition. If she gets the job, she keeps the tools, and as she begins to earn income, she repays the cost into the tool fund. She must repay in full in order to be eligible for further loans or for sponsorship in additional training programs. The tools are not so costly when purchased in bulk and the operation of a revolving loan fund in an interest bearing account ensures that new tools can be provided on a credit basis without requiring collateral.

Nowadays a member of the collective who wants to participate in a skills upgrading program can approach the Executive Committee. If they consider that the training will be beneficial both for the women and the collective, and if the necessary loans are available, then the applications for training will be approved.

The collective also provides the women with bus fare to attend monthly meetings and any training for which they are sponsored. This is partic-

Lurl joined the collective in May 1984, having passed through the selection procedures developed by the original members. Her first task as a member was to introduce herself, which she did while giggling and covering her mouth so that much of what she said was inaudible. It finally emerged that she had not completed high school, had two children to support, had never been employed, and had wanted to be a beautician. Failing to find opportunities in that field, she was prepared to try anything that came up. What came up was the Women's Construction Collective. She started training in Phase Three.

When the five week training period was up, there was no job immediately available for Lurl due to delays in implementing a particular building project that was to have employed her. Instead, she started on-site with ten other women who worked unpaid for six weeks to refurbish an old wholesale liquor store that was to become the CRDC and the WCC's center. In the last week of this exercise, the collective was asked to send two women to interview for a maintenance job with one of the large bauxite companies. Lurl was the first to arrive at the interview and started work the next week, earning the highest wage any of the members has ever earned.

Shortly afterward there were rumors, later confirmed, that Lurl had moved out of her community. Lurl had left her baby father. She was one of eight children from a poor rural family. By the time Lurl was fourteen, her mother could hardly cope with the economic burden of supporting her family. The burden was eased by moving Lurl in with a male benefactor who agreed to pay her way through school. By the time Lurl was sixteen, she was pregnant by her "benefactor" and out of school. At eighteen, she was already the mother of two children and being beaten regularly by the man on whom she was economically dependent.

As a result of her experience, Lurl had no hesitation about packing her bags and leaving as soon as she had an independent income. Today she lives in another parish with her two children and a sister. Her work as an industrial painter is stable and her performance has been favorably evaluated by her employers, who are now considering employing other women on their maintenance team.

ularly important for the women who may not be working because they have not been placed or are between jobs. Occasionally the collective fund, which is managed by the Executive Committee, has been used to give loans for health and child care, but this is very unusual and is not encouraged as the collective does not aim to become a welfare system.

Results

Sharon, Millicent, Pauline, and Lurl all had different experiences during their time with the collective. While the long-term impact of the project on them and their families may be difficult to evaluate, other changes have been rapid and dramatic. As they found themselves able to earn their own livings in a male-dominated industry, they developed new confidence in themselves. All four of them have stuck with the project—two of them have turned down a total of five job offers in more traditional areas. Many have become articulate spokeswomen for the collective and all have learned a great deal about individual and group responsibility. In the course of two and one-half years, of those women who have left the collective, four did so because of pregnancy. Two of these women claim to have been made pregnant against their will by their baby fathers who did not want "two men in the house." Neither of these women started work on a construction site and neither returned to the collective.

The impact of the collective on the construction industry appears to be positive. This may be due to the early analysis which determined the needs of the builders at the trade level. The willingness of project participants to job audition, and thus prove themselves, certainly helped with placement. Reported decreases in violence and increases in productivity on sites where collective members are working seems to be directly related to the positive perception of women's roles. Builders and foremen report that men almost automatically behave less abusively and violently in the presence of women. They also feel that both men and women tend to compete with each other on the job—the women working to show that they "could do the job as well as men," and the men trying to "always outdo the women"—a form of competition that almost inevitably boosts productivity. Another interesting achievement has been the ability of the women to move across political boundaries. Women from communities associated with one political party have been placed on sites identified with the opposition party without any serious problems.

As yet the women present no serious threat to male dominance on construction sites. They are few in number and have not reached the skill level where they can compete for jobs as subcontractors. In effect, they are still "bossed" by men and this may account for the absence of any serious resistance to them by their male co-workers. However, as jobs in the industry become more scarce, resistance is likely to increase. One woman recently reported being threatened on-site by a man who declared she was taking away his job because he was a man and came from the "correct" political territory, while she did not. She seemed to think that the politics of the situation were more significant than the gender, at least in this instance.

On the other hand, the publicity that the project has received in the local media has made the concept of women working on construction sites increasingly acceptable both at the work place and in the community. This is demonstrated by the ability of the collective's members to retain jobs and find new placements despite the serious slump in the industry and by the regular requests received for entry into the collective.

While the entry of thirty-four competent women into the construction industry at the trade level may not seem significant, contractors who have employed collective members report they are now employing other women. This may mean that some of the more than one thousand women who received building trades training prior to 1980, along with those who may benefit from the introduction of the new residential training institutions, will now have employment opportunities. The collective has also been excited by the interest shown in its activities by women's groups in other countries, largely as the result of the video tape produced to document the collective's activities.

Overall, in the two and one-half years it has been in operation, the collective has trained thirty-four women and placed more than 90 percent of them in construction jobs in the areas of plumbing, masonry, carpentry, electrical installation, painting, and steelwork. More than fifteen members have also received further skills training ranging from driving a car to reading blueprints. Two women have completed the Construction Technology Course at Jamaica's College of Arts, Sciences and Technology, and two members have taken over day-to-day management of the project. In addition, the collective has refurbished new office space for itself and the CRDC. Funding sources have been expanded and the project has launched its own business in order to develop an independent source of income.

Looking Ahead

The future of the collective will certainly not be easy. Despite all the members' efforts, the effects of a major decline in the construction industry are bound to be felt, especially in terms of direct employment. The general economic recession has left potential clients with less money in their pockets. This has occasioned a search for new markets for the skills the women have developed and for ongoing skills upgrading opportunities. At the moment, it is still too early to say whether this approach will be effective, although it is clear that the experience gained in the workshop business is significantly improving the members' carpentry skills.

So far response to the maintenance business has been extremely positive, but its long-term viability has yet to be established and it is unclear how many women it will be able to absorb. As the business grows, greater formalization of the collective's operations will be necessary. Therefore, as of March 1986, the organization has officially become the Kingston Women's Construction Collective, Ltd.—a legally recognized Jamaican company.

The collective, however, is by no means independent as yet. The project as a whole continues to be supervised by the project coordinator and the CRDC continues to administer major funding, hire staff as needed through its organizational system, and provide office space.

Since its inception, the collective has relied on overseas grant assistance. In May 1986, current funding from these grants will expire. The growth of the business as a significant source of income will be a major determinant of the collective's self-sustainability. The membership feels strongly that the collective should continue not only for the benefit of the women involved, but also because provision of entry-level skills and upgrading of building skills is still not available to women on the same basis that it is for men. As noted above, the government has recently opened a central residential facility for training in building skills, known as the Port More Heart Academy. This institution will, in theory, accept women as day students. However, this in fact limits entry to women living within the immediate area. Ironically, six collective members living outside of the immediate area helped to build this facility. One solution to this problem being considered by the collective is to establish a hostel for women trainees near the institution. Another is the expansion of the collective to include women who have already been trained in building skills but who have not been given access to the support systems that facilitate job placement and skill upgrading. Either option would require additional funding.

In facing these critical challenges, it is hoped that the links between the industry and the communities will continue to provide the flexibility that has been so central to the collective's development.

Update

The collective continues to expand and evolve. Its most significant step was becoming an independent business and moving to its own building. A recent focus has been on providing an environment in which the women can develop their entrepreneurial skills to enter the industry at the level of subcontractors and micro-businesses. They also have restructured their organization so that the training and production components are kept separate. It was decided that the members should not be made to undertake responsibility for developing and overseeing projects. This would ask them to take on too much, too soon. Therefore, professional project managers are being hired instead. Experience has also shown that it is not possible to operate democratically at every step, especially when the goal is to become self-sustaining. In the running of a business, someone must have authority.

Recently, the collective has received government contracts for building facilities such as health centers. These jobs provide an excellent opportunity for on-the-job training. The group has also begun working within low-income communities to assist in areas such as sanitation. This is the collective's first move out of the field of construction.

The Inter-American Foundation produced a film about the collective, which has been shown to members of the United States Congress. (The film is also available in Spanish.) Already the replicability of the concept has been demonstrated in Mexico City, where a similar construction training and internship program is operating through the initiative of the local Working Women's Group.

--------------------------------- Lessons ---------------------------------

1. **A thorough analysis of the industry, particularly if it is one that does not traditionally employ women, is crucial.** The trainees found employment because they had been trained for identified job openings at specific levels.

2. **Women must have access to needed equipment without initial cost outlay in order to start work.** In the case of this project, there would be no jobs available for women without tools. A revolving fund can ensure this access without requiring collateral.

3. **Strong links to feeder communities through a body such as the Working Group provide a good basis for group cohesion.** The Tivoli community worker and local leadership in Nannyville and Glengoffe provided on-going support and motivation for the women, particularly in the early stages. The Working Group provided access to these support systems.

4. **It is extremely useful to have access to individuals or institutions able and willing to provide "customized" training.** A freestanding training program can be exorbitantly expensive and short-term training does not in itself justify expensive outlays for machinery and equipment. The Vocational Training Development

Institute allowed project management to have significant input into training design while offering well-equipped and well-supervised facilities.

5. **When working in politically volatile areas, a project should maintain a neutral political identity.** The political neutrality of project management allowed for entry into the violently opposed political communities and for movement across territorial lines. This, in turn, allowed for cooperation between women from these various communities.

6. **Projects often evolve in directions quite different from those anticipated in proposals to funding agencies. A good relationship with the project officer of the funding agency will allow for flexibility in both program design and use of funds.** For example, after this project began, it expanded far more rapidly than had been envisaged. However, soon after money was mobilized to accommodate this rapid growth, the construction industry went into a slump and the project had to focus on consolidation rather than expansion. Dialogue with the various funding agencies allowed for the necessary changes to be made smoothly and according to decisions made by the collective.

7. **Development cannot be rushed. Women who have been dependent most of their lives need time to adjust to taking on responsibility.** It took eighteen months before any woman found a construction job as a result of her own initiative. It took two months for the collective members to open their own bank account once a decision had been made to do so. If the project staff take the easy way out and do things for the group, a welfare mentality develops that stifles the growth of initiative. It is better to allow the necessary time for participants to work out a way to do things for themselves.

8. **Documentation is worth all the energy and effort it entails.** Detailed written and photographic documentation, together with the ten-minute video, made it easier for the project to approach funding agencies. It also allowed the project to "travel," both inside and outside of Jamaica, and hence widen its impact. The women's own energy, enthusiasm, and involvement is captured much more clearly on video and in photos than is possible in any written or verbal account.

Appendix

SUMMARY OF TRAINING AND PLACEMENT					
	Phase I	**Phase II**	**Phase III**	**Phase IV**	**Total**
Initial Training	5 weeks full time VTDI	12 weeks part time	5 weeks full time plus 6 weeks "live" project	12 weeks part time plus 6 weeks "live" project	
Tivoli Community	10	5	6	1	22
Nannyville Community			4	3	7
Glengoffe Community			5		5
Drop Outs	2	1	1	0	4
Masons	7	3	9		19
Carpenters	1		2		3
Plumbers			1		1
Electricians			1	2	3
Steelworkers		1			1
Painters			1	2	3

TRAINING PROGRAM				
Training Program	**Skills**	**Type of Delivery**	**No. of Women**	**Additional Information**
Basic Training I (VTDI)	Carpentry, masonry	5 days per week for 5 weeks	10	Learned to carry and lay blocks, build complete wall and render it, build simple forms and their own wooden stool.

Training Program	Skills	Type of Delivery	No. of Women	Additional Information
Basic Training II (VTDI)	Carpentry, masonry	5 days per week for 5 weeks	15	As above, but with the addition of basic plumbing and pipe fitting.
General Building Maintenance I (CRDC)	Introduction to plumbing, carpentry, masonry, electrical, painting, and air conditioning maintenance	1 day, 1 evening per week for 12 weeks	5	Not entirely satisfactory as most trainees were men with previous experience. Best compromise in the absence of sufficient funding for alternative.
General Building Maintenance II (CRDC)	As above	As above	4	As above
Live Project CRDC/WCC's offices	Carpentry, masonry, electrical	5 days per week for 6 weeks	12	Proved extremely valuable in placement, especially for women who went into painting.
WCC Carpentry Workshop	Carpentry, painting, estimation	5 days per week ongoing	2 or 3 at any time	Key resource person is a male carpenter. Workshop pays its own way so women also learn some business skills.

Training Program	Skills	Type of Delivery	No. of Women	Additional Information
WCC Repair Business	Carpentry, masonry, steel work, painting, estimation	Depends on the job	Variable 2–7	Kind of work varies from building entire wooden housing units to relatively simple repairs.
Office Practice and Project Management	Bookkeeping, placement	Full time ongoing	2	Training delivery by CRDC staff.
General Building Technology (CAST)	Construction drawing, physics, building technology, math and English	1 day and 2 evenings per week for 1 year	2	Allows access to higher level skills training and building training programs.
Blueprint (CRDC)	Blueprint reading and plan interpretation	1 evening per week for 12 weeks	4	
Driving (individual instruction)	Driving car	Variable	3	Invaluable
Automechanics (individual instruction)	Basic auto mechanics and car maintenance	Saturday afternoons for 8 weeks	3	Aimed at cutting costs of vehicle maintenance.

Training Program	Skills	Type of Delivery	No. of Women	Additional Information
Bookkeeping and Secretarial Skills (Commercial Business College)	Typing, shorthand, English	2 evenings per week for 1 year	1	
Drama (Sistren—Women's Theatre Group)	Explaining issues affecting women by using drama	3 Saturdays	2	
First Aid (Blue Cross)	General first aid	2 evenings per week	7	
On Site	Skill upgrading in trade areas where women are working	Full time, informal	2	Quality very dependent on individual foremen and male gang leaders, but probably the most effective long-term form of training.
Improving the Safety of Wooden Houses (CRDC)	Carpentry, masonry	1 week workshop	2	This was an introductory course. Long-term plans call for using women as instructors in outreach programs.

IV
INTERNATIONAL

9
Women and Handicrafts: Myth and Reality

Jasleen Dhamija

Whenever planners, program developers, and project directors are faced with the question of how to develop viable income-generating activities for women, the first thing that comes to their minds is handicrafts. The myth is that handicrafts are women's work—something they do well, an activity that presumably does not interfere with their domestic responsibilities, and one that requires a low level of investment and short gestation period. Rarely does anyone bother to look at the realities of the situation, either in terms of the handicrafts industry or in terms of the lives of the women the project proposes to serve. Few planners or program staff understand that handicrafts require specialized skills and often years of apprenticeship or that crafts that provide a reasonable income have already become the exclusive province of men.

This chapter reviews handicrafts as a means of providing income to women. In some instances, crafts are a solid source of income and can also provide women with a link to their own cultural heritage. In most instances, however, crafts production concentrates women in an area that is labor intensive and exploitative, providing a meager income for long hours of work. Therefore, people interested in assisting women to earn income should first ask, are there other activities that would provide a better source of income than crafts? All possibilities should be given careful consideration. If handicrafts appear to be a viable option, there are still many additional questions that should be asked before starting a craft project.

This chapter was originally published as a pamphlet with the same title by the Seeds Publication Project in 1981.

What Are Handicrafts?

Handicrafts will be defined here as activities in which available materials, tools, and skills, plus the producer's imagination and creative ability, are used to create objects. In some countries, the term handicrafts is extended to cover all activities where nonmechanized processes are used, including activities such as food processing, making of food specialties, and innumerable other handskills. Here the definition of handicrafts will be confined to objects of utility and decorative value, a definition that is commonly accepted in the developing world.

Feminine Crafts: Sex Roles and Discrimination in Crafts Production

Crafts which give good returns to the craft person, such as bronze casting, metal engraving, jewelry and lapidary skills, glass blowing, and brocade weaving, rarely are practiced by women. The skills are the domain of men and are strictly guarded and passed from father to son. A daughter is rarely taught these skills because it is assumed that she will marry, leave the family, and therefore might impart the skills to her new family. Women usually practice crafts associated with their domestic lives and do so in order to meet their families' needs. Sometimes they are able to sell surplus items in local markets.

Generally, the types of crafts which are introduced among women are euphemized as "feminine crafts" because they are associated with the home. They include stitching, embroidery, crocheting, knitting, weaving, basketry, mat making, and in some parts of the world, pottery. This is also true of tie-dye, batik, and macramé, which have been introduced fairly recently in areas where these skills have not been practiced before.

If we examine these crafts, we will see that their "femininity" lies primarily in the fact that they are essentially time consuming, provide little income, and are not easily upgraded to yield a higher price. These crafts rarely prove to be a stepping stone into a small-scale industry that would offer greater incomes to women. When such activities are commercialized, the more remunerative part of the work generally is taken up by men. Take the case of tailoring: the best paid job is cutting, which requires special skill and 90 percent of the time is done by the men. The more laborious but lower paid work of handstitching, finishing, and stitching buttons is given to women and they are paid the lowest wages.

The situation can be even worse when "feminine" crafts are commercialized. In India one of the big commercial operations in handicrafts is white embroidery done on fine cotton material called "chikanwork." The women who do this work are from the Muslim community and because of social customs are confined to their homes. They receive the work from traders (middlemerchants); for handstitching a shirt and embroidering it they earn about 25¢ for eight to ten hours of work; such wages are exploitative.

Although most societies distinguish men's crafts and women's crafts, there is no universal rationale in this division of labor. What is unacceptable in one society may be common practice in another. For example, blacksmiths are generally thought of as men. But anyone who has travelled by road in northern India has seen female ironsmiths side-by-side with the men, hammering in perfect rhythm the metals that are forged into agricultural implements. In most parts of Asia, pottery is the work of men, but in much of Africa it is taboo for a man to even touch the implements. In many areas of the world, women are the weavers, but in most of Africa it is the men who weave. The delicate and highly lucrative work of the goldsmith generally is the domain of men, but it could be termed a gentler art and women have shown that they can do it just as well. Today, one of the finest Turkoman jewelers in the Caspian area of Iran is a woman.

The truth is that women can do any of the jobs that are done by men provided they have the opportunity and the training. If handicrafts are to provide viable income-generating activities for women, then such distinctions must be overcome.

The Lives of Rural Women

Before developing any type of income-generating program for women, particularly one that involves handicrafts, it is essential to have a solid understanding of the lives of the women to be involved, so that the program is in fact a means of bettering women's lives and not just one more drudgery for an already overburdened woman to bear.

The rural woman generally is the provider of the family's basic needs. Her tasks are many and she is under tremendous pressure. Water must be brought from long distances; fuel must be gathered; and she produces and processes food for the family. Minor repairs to the house are her responsibility and she tries to meet the needs of the household by making containers from available materials and by patching the clothes or skins. Recycling, which has become such a fashionable word today, is her specialty. Worn out clothes are made into patched quilts; waste paper is pulverized and made into simple papier-mâché bowls.

Women sewing in Liberia *(United Nations: S. Wolff)*

Before new activities can be effectively developed to provide cash income so greatly needed by the rural woman, it is necessary to first look at her life in its totality. Are there ways in which her burdens could be lifted and should these problems be tackled first? In some settings, simple innovations of tools and facilities to reduce women's drudgery are necessary to give her the extra time for income-generating activities.

Handicraft Production

Before trying to develop any handicraft program to provide women with an income, it is absolutely essential to look at the existing possibilities open to women based on traditional or easily acquired skills, and to study current demands for these products in the local and extended domestic markets. It is also necessary to consider the prospect for creating and managing the organizational structures which will provide needed support for the project. In some instances, a handicrafts program will be the answer; in other cases, it will not. For example, India, with the majority of its population in the rural areas and a high unemployment rate, has successfully developed its handicrafts by pursuing a policy of protection for many years, and by providing various forms of technical assistance, including a well-developed marketing operation organized by the private and public sectors. Handicrafts, however, may not be an effective strategy for other countries which have a limited population and other possible avenues for employment. In some areas of Africa, where the land is fertile and women traditionally have farmed and marketed their agricultural products with no restriction on their movement, handicrafts are probably not the best answer. Here, improvement of agricultural practices and food processing may be a better means of increasing their incomes.

The Feasibility Study

Before planning a handicrafts program, a comprehensive feasibility study should be undertaken. A first step is to look at the overall economic situation, the work women already do, materials available to them, and existing or potential markets for products. In most cases, this assessment should be done by experts, since many of the facts and judgments required are of a technical nature.

Some questions to ask include:

Location and Socio-economic Situation
• Which groups of women are available for training and production work (age, residence, cultural background, et cetera)?

- What income-earning work are women presently doing? Do they work outside their homes?
- What skills (not just craft skills) do they have that might generate income? (These include skills they currently use and those that have fallen into disuse.)
- Do the women need a primary livelihood or supplementary income?

Technical Data

- What techniques are used for production and what types of technology are available?
- What are the raw materials to be used in the craft and are they locally available? What are their costs?
- What other raw materials are available locally? Are they locally processed? What are their costs?

Marketing

- Where do local people sell their products? How and when? At what prices?
- What are the prevailing prices for similar types of products made by hand and by machine?
- What products are beginning to be demanded by the community which are not yet provided by the local industries?
- How long will it take to develop the new skills needed and to go into production?
- Which markets will be aimed for? The local market? Extended market in the home country? An export market?

In the following case, a feasibility study of this nature was carried out by an expert consultant for a government industry in charge of a rural, non-farm development program. A poor district in Kirman, Iran, was surveyed and it was found that:

- It was an area with marginal agricultural activity dependent on the erratic rains. The slack season was very long and nonfarm job opportunities were very limited, but every family had sheep that gave good quality wool.
- All the women had primitive horizontal carpet looms. The carpets they wove were of very poor quality, but still retained the traditional tribal designs.
- Older, finely woven carpets with the same designs sold at a premium in the antique carpet market.
- The fine quality wool from the sheep was being sold to city merchants, leaving the weavers of Kirman without good raw material.
- Dyeing facilities were not locally available.
- There were a few modern looms in the area belonging to the mer-

chants. Here, men were engaged in the production of fine quality carpets which were in great demand and provided good returns to the weavers. Some of the local men also owned their looms and thus not only earned wages but shared in the profits from the carpet sales.

The investigator also learned that large copper mines would be coming to the area in the next ten years. They would certainly attract many men away from weaving and would also raise incomes in the area, thus expanding the market for carpets. Based on this knowledge and the information from the feasibility study, it was decided that it would be worthwhile to introduce a program to upgrade the carpet-weaving skills of the women of Kirman.

The idea was to help the women to form a cooperative through which wool could be processed locally. The cooperative would increase their production by:

• giving them better quality raw materials;
• subsidizing the cost of new looms so that they could purchase their own equipment;
• upgrading their skills so they would be able to produce their traditional patterns but in a much finer quality;
• and later, teaching the best of the weavers to read graph patterns so they would be able to introduce more colors and new designs.

Through local home economics agencies, the women were gathered together and the project was discussed with them. It was discovered that the new vertical looms could not be introduced into their homes because the roofs were too low and there was not enough light. This problem was solved by suggesting that the subsidy to cover the cost of the loom also include the cost of materials to build a very simple shed attached to the home where two looms could be put back to back. The beams, the supports, and tin sheets for the roof would be given as a grant by the government, but the women, along with their families, would construct the shed, giving their labor as a contribution to the project.

A government subsidy covered half the cost of the looms and the women paid the rest: 10 percent as an initial deposit with the remainder to be paid over the next year from the women's earnings. This was feasible because earnings for a year were projected at three times the cost of the loom. The 10 percent initial deposit (approximately $15) was a small amount for the women to raise from family sources. The women did this with great enthusiasm because ownership of the loom made them creditworthy in the village economy.

The women were then given the raw materials from local coopera-

Weaving palm mats in the South Pacific *(International Women's Tribune)*

tives, along with instructions on design and quality. A master weaver assisted in the initial mounting of the warp on the new looms, started them off, and provided periodic supervision. The master weaver was located in the village and the women could go to him if they ran into difficulties. One master weaver supervised fifteen looms with great ease. While the carpet weaving was in progress, the cooperative extended credit to the women to cover their daily needs such as flour, salt, oil, tea, sugar, and lentils, items that women generally provide for their households.

After one carpet was finished, which took from three to seven months, the woman could sell it either to the cooperative or to the trader, whoever paid her a better price. The cooperative society would pay the woman a price based on the basic weaving costs of the carpet immediately upon production, after deducting any advance she had taken. The carpet was then evaluated by an expert who fixed the actual price at which it could be sold. As this price was often higher than the basic unit cost, 50 percent of the market price, in addition to the unit cost, also was paid to the woman. This acted as a good incentive to induce the women to produce very fine carpets, and slowly they became absorbed in the overall system of carpet production. Later, private dealers decided that women were more reliable than men, kept their promises better, and worked more regularly. Eventually the dealers began to induce women in nearby districts to take up fine quality weaving. This process was also helped by the fact that men were migrating to the towns in search of better job opportunities.

This project worked because it was based on careful assessment of prevailing socioeconomic conditions, locally available skills and raw materials, and because there was a strong demand for the product. The opportunity to own their own looms, along with initial supervision and support provided in a flexible manner, enabled the women to enter a commercial operation formerly accessible only to men. Eventually they were able to be independent of any continuing government assistance.

Diversifying Products

Other approaches to expanding craft incomes are to (a) introduce new products or alter a traditional product without substantially changing existing skills, and (b) introduce new skills and products. In both cases the feasibility study is even more important.

An example of developing new or improved products based on existing skills comes from a potters' village in India where the families for years had made water jars for the local market. The weekly earnings from these items never went above $6 per family. The introduction of a few new items requiring the same skills but directed to a modern market, such as candle holders, cut work lamps, garden lights and perforated small stands, brought not only a new clientele but also allowed them to charge higher prices for their hand labor and thus increase their incomes.

In another case, Turkoman women wove beautiful silk but in narrow widths, for which there was a limited local market. By changing the beam and the combs of the looms, they were able to produce silk of 90 cm., for which there was a growing market, and thereby triple their earnings. In this way, a very nominal expenditure and less than one week's training in the use of the new loom revived a dying craft and gave a regular source of income to a large village of women weavers.

In some cases a skill can be diverted to a totally new line of production for which there is a growing demand. Recently a project was developed in Ethiopia to divert the skills of traditional potters, who were making storage jars and cooking pots, to the manufacturing of indigenous construction materials such as bricks, tiles, pipes, and large water storage jars. This answered the local need for building materials and replaced imported tin and asbestos sheets. Without this diversion, these craftswomen would have very soon faced competition from the new plas-

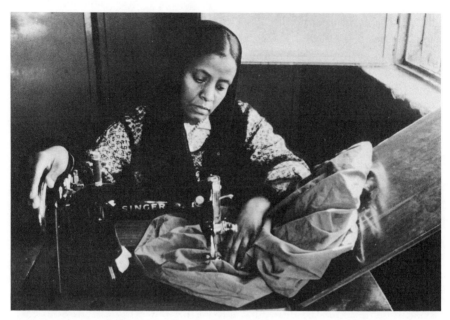
Sewing is an activity traditionally associated with women. *(United Nations: B.P. Wolff)*

tic and pressed aluminum industries which produce lighter, unbreakable storage and cooking utensils.

The second means of diversifying products is to introduce new skills and materials. Some good examples of training women in crafts that they have not practiced before are glass cutting in India, screen printing in Kenya, and wood-block printing combined with tie and dye embroidery in Ethiopia.

Introducing new products usually requires training women in skills they do not have, substantial investment in new equipment, much trial and error in production, careful supervision, and so on. It should not be done except when existing products show no prospect for upgrading. It is imperative that the feasibility study be very carefully done with particular attention to market analysis and availability of raw materials, technical expertise, and supervision.

Wherever possible inexpensive, locally available materials should be used. In Bangladesh the use of the simple jute fiber for making pothangers, bags, mats, and a variety of utility articles, started by a cooperative society organized for the rehabilitation of war widows, has had unprecedented success. On the other hand, the use of imported materials for crafts generally fails. An example of a poorly selected new skill and material was a scheme in the traditionally rich craft area of flower making in Ghana. This project failed because the synthetic material, imported at a high cost, was affected by the humid climate. The end result was artificial flowers that wilted faster than natural ones.

Marketing

Marketing is a critical element in any handicrafts project and marketing problems have plagued most handicraft projects started by welfare organizations in the developing world. These centers often decide to start a handicrafts project without looking into the question of consumer requirements, available skills, existing market prices or regular outlets for their products. It is imperative to make a thorough market study before any commercial handicrafts activity is started and the study should be carried out by an expert.

There are certain aspects of the marketing of handicrafts which must be borne in mind when starting a commercial enterprise:

- You must produce a high quality product. A badly finished article, not suitable for the purpose for which it is intended, will find few buyers and is poor publicity.
- Price your product competitively. An object which is available at a lower cost at other shopping centers will not attract customers.
- Always test a market with samples of your new products before taking up large-scale production.
- Rotate your designs and always have new designs to offer. Variety and change in products is crucial. Keep abreast of consumer preferences and do not be left with stock on your shelves.

A women's organization in Kenya, Maendeleo ya Wanawake (also discussed in Chapter 1), which has members all over the country, has a number of groups working on handicrafts. The organization started a shop in Nairobi to sell their products. Though the shop was located in a commercial area and in front of a large, busy tourist hotel, it was not very successful. It lacked working capital to pay cash for goods on delivery from the women's groups. The lack of funds also prevented the marketing unit from developing new products and designs, since they were unable to supply the needed raw materials or buy the finished products from women on a cash basis.

A regional agency for assisting women in developing income-generating activities assessed the situation and found that Maendeleo's initial setback should not be taken as a failure. They assisted the organization in the development of a new approach which includes provision

A Guatemalan weaver
(United Nations)

of working capital and also supports a designer to develop new lines of production and a field worker to upgrade the skills of the women in order for them to produce a new range of merchandise. A key element in this approach is a well-motivated and competent technical staff who do outreach work and train women to organize themselves into associations, cooperatives, or private production units.

While diversifying and upgrading skills and developing new markets is important, it is also very important not to break links with traditional markets, which are regular markets. This has happened with bad consequences in numerous cases. Two well-known instances have occured in India. One was the case of the "bleeding madras," a checked cotton lungi material with running colors which became a short-lived fashion in the United States. Local weavers' cooperatives switched to the production of this new material, using dyes not available locally, and ignored the traditional market for the sarong, used by the local men. Suddenly the demand for the bleeding madras in the U.S. ceased and the cooperatives found themselves with huge stocks and no market. This drove a number of cooperatives into bankruptcy and a large number of weavers to the point of starvation.

In another case, the producers of *cire perdu* metal deities in central India received large orders from the government for export, for two years running. In the meantime they failed to supply the local tribal population, that had been their regular market and with whom they maintained a close cultural link. The link was broken and when the government failed to place an order in the third year, the workers faced real hardship.

Experience has shown that attention should first be focused on finding markets within the country, first near the area of production, and then farther away in other towns or regions. These local markets are regular outlets and present minimal transport and marketing problems. In addition, the home market is a discerning market in which it is relatively easy to establish consumer preferences. It also provides quick feedback to assist in setting acceptable standards of production and maintaining quality control.

Production for export, on the other hand, poses many very difficult problems: generally large and steady levels of production are required; products must be designed and quality maintained to suit foreign and often unknown tastes; and there are often complicated government regulations to deal with, to say nothing of transport problems. Given these problems, much larger financial resources generally are needed to organize a successful export marketing operation.

In developing projects for the marketing of handicrafts, the needs of the women are a priority but the requirements of the commercial market also must be kept in view. A balance must be struck between development activity and commercial operation. This requires experienced management. The well-known Central Cottage Industries Emporium in New Delhi, India, is an excellent example of a successful operation of this nature. This organization was set up by a group of motivated social workers with government assistance. In a systematic way they began to apply sound commercial practices. New and old production centers were assisted in innovating new products, quality control procedures were set up, and sales promotion campaigns began. Through their efforts they succeeded both in providing employment for low-income women and creating the best in handicrafts. Their retail store is currently the finest shop for handicrafts in India.

Institutional Support: Financial Resources and Protection

There has been a tendency in women's organizations, be they private or governmental, to set up activities in different ways without linking them with existing institutions that could help them develop technical training, marketing, and credit. Utilization of existing institutions can lead to a very successful program.

For instance, the Tunisian Government has developed a range of protective and supportive policies for small-scale industries under a decentralization plan that provides special privileges to technically qualified entrepreneurs. Creative use of these policies is demonstrated by the Tunisian program of "Production Families." This program was organized by the Ministry of Social Welfare but has close links to the Tunisian Handicrafts Promotion Centre, another government organization. The two organizations jointly identified the crafts to be developed and a training program was financed and initiated by the Ministry of Social Welfare. The instructor for the training, the raw materials, and the designs came from the Handicrafts Centre so that the training was up to the standard needed for commercial production.

The trainees were given a stipend during the nine-month course so they could afford to participate. Also, the organization of the training program was arranged so that they would be able to work independently on completion of the training. The nine months of training were divided into two periods: during the first five months, the trainees worked under one roof with strict supervision; in the next four months, the tools and equipment were installed in their homes and they were taught to work on their own. Once independent, they still maintained their contacts with the commercial wing of the Handicrafts Centre and could either market their products through the Centre or to traders. The link with an existing specialized institution protected the program from the usual failure caused by low standards in skills, poor production, problems in marketing, exploitation by the traders—problems that, sadly, are common to most handicrafts centers initiated for women.

Organizational Strategy—Groups Dynamics

Another important element in designing a program in which women participate and benefit is to develop a good organizational structure. Whether it is a cooperative, association, registered society or traditional women's group, it is important that the women are assisted in forming viable economic units that prevent exploitation. The government and voluntary organizations can channel assistance to organized groups that they cannot provide to dispersed family units or individuals. Further, officially registered organizations can receive funds and disburse loans on a flexible basis to their members, whereas the conditions for loans to individuals are often far more strict and require collateral.

One effective way to build an organization is to build upon the foundation of traditional associations among women. These groups take many forms. One of the most common is the thrift society, such as the *tontin* of the market women in Togoland or the *arisan* in Indonesia. Here women meet regularly and at each meeting deposit a sum of money.

Young women attending a sewing class in Egypt *(United Nations)*

The total amount is then made available to each of the members in rotation. This allows each woman to have sufficient capital at one time to make a major investment, such as repairs on the house, buying bulk commodities for sale, purchasing tools, or any other outlay that would be beyond her individual capacity. When such a group works well it can even provide guarantees for individual members who take out loans from outside agencies; it can act as a pressure group to see that loans are repaid and, if a member is unable to make a payment due to unforeseen circumstances, members can pool their resources to pay back a loan at the specified time.

Unfortunately, most development projects ignore traditional social groups and try to introduce new institutional structures. Acceptance of innovations and long-run success may often be greater if they instead attempt to strengthen existing associations.

The type of institutional structure usually introduced in connection with handicrafts projects is the western model of a cooperative organization. This generally means that a system is introduced which requires detailed recordkeeping and therefore a relatively high level of literacy for the cooperative's leaders. Since women in many parts of the world are either nonliterate or only marginally literate, leadership roles in such groups very often fall into the hands of literate men. It is therefore not hard to understand why women members in such groups soon lose interest. If cooperatives are to be used successfully to help women, it is necessary either to simplify the procedures or give expert managerial assistance. For example, in Iran a cooperative organizer was made available to assist in the organization and maintenance of rural women's cooperatives. Members were helped with complicated bookkeeping, financial transactions, purchase of raw materials, and sale of finished goods. The organizer also served as a link between the individual cooperatives and the cooperative marketing organization. This model has been very successful in Iran and could possibly be an effective way to provide needed assistance to women's groups.

Another method, developed by the handicrafts cooperatives in India, involves provision of managerial assistance at the inception of the cooperative and for the first few years on a declining basis. At the end of this period it is expected that the cooperative members will either have acquired the necessary managerial skills or will have sufficient income to pay a professional manager. (See also chapter 6.) Perhaps the most effective method would be a blend of these two schemes along with a component to train members to assume managerial tasks. Selected members would receive short-term, intensive training to prepare them for leadership roles within the organization.

It should be stressed that cooperatives are not the only answer. In the early stages, women may prefer to opt for a less highly structured form of organization. There are a number of intermediate forms of association that may be used to advantage, such as the collective renting of space or buying of materials, or organizational structures that provide a fixed wage for women, plus an opportunity for profit sharing. The structure should be the one best suited to the needs and resources of the members.

In addition it should be remembered that an association of women is not just a way of organizing commercial enterprises. It also has a social function that makes the members feel a part of the community. In areas where social custom does not allow women to participate in activities outside the home or among men, a women's association can be a first step towards the outside world. It provides a place where members can meet other women with different life experiences and can participate in activities that bring them out of the enclosed environments in which they often live.

Handicrafts can be a means of increasing income for women in some settings, but only under the conditions outlined above, since crafts are specialized activities that have limited markets and offer limited potential as a means of employment. The following points summarize a few of the key issues that must be addressed when considering a handicrafts program for women:

1. **Feminine crafts are not the best choice for income-generating activity.** They are essentially time-consuming, give poor returns, and offer little possibility for upgrading skills.

2. **Therefore, before embarking on a handicrafts scheme, study the existing conditions in which women are working.** Include in the study the possibilities that are open to them based upon traditional skills or easily acquired new skills and the prospects for creating and managing the organizational structure needed to provide support for a handicrafts project. Remember that handicrafts are often a more complicated way of generating income for women than other choices, such as food processing for local markets.

3. **Think creatively about income-generating opportunities for women.** Women can do any of the jobs which are done by men, provided they have access to the training and to the employment market.

4. **It is imperative to make a thorough market study before any activity of a commercial nature is undertaken.**

5. **Links with the traditional market—which is a regular market—should not be broken while exploring new outlets for products.**

6. **Key elements of a successful project are a well-motivated and competent technical staff and proper management.** These can give necessary guidance and help the group to diversify, uphold quality in the product line, and maintain access to markets.

It is necessary to exercise caution when developing the field of handicrafts. It can be a means of providing a viable income, but it can also be a means of exploitation, serving only to increase the burdens women already shoulder and cutting them off from opportunities to improve their economic and social position.

Further Information

The following are sources of information about regional handicrafts programs, including technical assistance.

Africa
African Training and Research Centre for Women (ATRCW)
United Nations Economic Commission for Africa
P.O. Box 3001
Addis Ababa, Ethiopia

Asia
Women's Programme Centre, ESCAP
U.N. Building
Rajdamnarn Avenue
Bangkok, Thailand

All India Handicrafts Board
Government of India
Ramakrishna Puram
New Delhi, India

Latin America
Women's Programme Unit
CEPAL
Castilla 179/D
Santiago, Chile

Caribbean
Women in Development Unit
Extra-Mural Centre
University of the West Indies
Pinelands
St. Michael, Barbados

International
International Labour Organization
CH 1211
Geneva 22, Switzerland

International Trade Centre
CH 1211
Geneva 22, Switzerland

Seeds for a New Model of Development: A Political Commentary

Vina Mazumdar

The women and development debate that began during the United Nations Decade for Women has been haunted, even constricted, by certain concepts that emerged fairly early in the debate. The time has come to critically examine the value, or the universal validity, of these terms, to prevent the debate, and action precipitated by the debate from succumbing to stagnation, or self-defeating restrictions on organized efforts to unleash women's power—to ensure a sane and livable future, at least for the children we have brought into the world.

Three of the most frequently used concepts that emerged during the Decade—"sexual division of labor," "sex-role stereotypes," and "traditional roles"—are already under attack from investigations of poor women's lives. Each of the Seeds case studies shows that these divisions, or stereotypes, or traditions were fictions in the minds of urban, middle class people—the scholars, planners, men and women of the media, political and religious leaders, and the industrial bourgeoisie. As far as the preservation of tradition goes, this has always been a powerful weapon in the hands of political and religious authorities, however little basis it actually had in historical or empirical reality. Here again, women's studies has challenged the immutability of women's traditional roles, both across cultures and over time. Why then must we continue to argue that breaking traditional roles is the most important criterion for success? Any attempt to freeze tradition in order to refuse to question it *is* wrong in my opinion. Where tradition gives women facing adverse forces the courage to defy the powers that be, however, it can become an asset.

It is in this context that I find the SIRDO story from Mexico the most exciting in the series, because it has mobilized women to control their environment through an age-old tradition devised by women: the conservation and recycling of waste. The instinct is old, but in this case it addresses a problem that is a creation of our present-day civilization. Extension of the debate about women and development from a narrow definition of economics to encompass the wide range of challenges facing humanity today, such as environmental problems, will be, in my opinion, the "great leap forward" in women's search for our lost power. Maybe this reflects the traditions of my own culture, whose myths depict power for women only in times when the universe faces extinction—to protect. Most of us would any day choose to protect rather than to destroy humanity.

The women and development debate has also given rise to efforts to offer alternative, operative instruments with which to mobilize and organize women. The goals for such organization or mobilization may vary—from narrow economic or local level social ends, to far broader social and political objectives, as the Seeds case studies indicate. But the operative strategies of the Seeds projects show a marked commonality: a *collective approach* in preference to the earlier emphasis on the individual woman's right to self-fulfillment; an emphasis on *women's economic and decision-making roles,* instead of the earlier focus on the right to choose one's life style, or partner in marriage; and a plea for *professional services as critical inputs* in enabling women to organize, plan, and sustain their activities. As a political scientist, my focus is on the political implications of the implementation of these strategies.

Many of the Seeds projects are small, collective efforts by women working at the local level. Few indicate a need for political support and, in fact, there is an occasional hint of fear, suspicion, or rejection of things political in some cases. The Kingston Women's Construction Collective advocates a "neutral" political identity in order to avoid being identified with either of Jamaica's two major political factions; in the exploration of the myth and reality of women and handicrafts there is no mention of the role of the political process, domestically or internationally, that determines the structure of the handicrafts market and the scale of investment in its growth. Yet the underlying story that runs through most of the chapters is one of political struggle, to win for women not "a place in the sun," but visibility and acknowledgement of our capacity and determination, and a *new* way of achieving change by sharing benefits, by resolving conflicts through discussion, and gaining greater confidence in the process of such resolution of conflict.

Yes, the efforts are small, hence the title *Seeds*. But seeds have a tendency to sprout and grow into mighty forests, unless felled by acts of nature or people. To me, *any collective action for change is a political action,* especially if the action carries in its core a message of equality—the end of women's subordination, invisibility and powerlessness. The Working Women's Forum, for instance, explicity describes itself as "anti-politics," yet the forum goes on to describe itself as pro-women, anti-caste, and pro-secular. Founded by a political activist, from the beginning it has applied techniques of political organization. In the Indian context, these are explicitly *political positions.* As defined in the ideological foundation of the Indian political system, they form the core of the message of Indian nationalism and its greatest mobilizer, Mahatma Gandhi. He measured India's salvation not merely in terms of its freedom from colonial rule, but by the inclusion in its reconstruction following independence of the political mobilization of women as partners and leaders and not just passive observers of the political process.

What the Kingston Women's Construction Collective in Jamaica struggled for, and achieved, was a breach in political monopolies. It was common practice in Jamaica for construction jobs to be awarded on the basis of political patronage, thereby keeping people divided in the interest of maintaining the status quo. The collective saw no value to women from this system. Their "neutral" political stance is in fact one kind of politics. Movements that try to break up monopolies or challenge divisive systems such as caste and religion, as in the case of the Working Women's Forum, are political by their very nature.

On the other hand, I view BRAC's approach as apolitical, even though it is stated that "programs designed for the poor must challenge the rural power structure, which keeps not only power but also resources in the hands of the few." The women of BRAC have been helped to subsist, and to intervene in cases of injustice against women, but I wonder if this focus on the processes that keep them dependent and subordinate might be too limited. While I agree that most of the eleven lessons drawn from the BRAC case study are immediately useful strategies in the given context, constant vigilance is necessary to be certain that utilization of traditional skills and occupations, even though they may prove immediately viable, do not confine rural women to projects and markets that are "less complicated to manage." Programs can build upon, but should not be confined by, the present pattern of sexual division of labor.*

A related, and most important, point is made in the study of handicrafts in chapter 9. The message is that there is, in fact, no universal rationale in this division of labor. The division is neither common across geographical regions nor over time in a single region. Major historical upheavals and national disasters, as well as changes in technology, production systems, and control over the resources of production, have all destroyed, changed, or reorganized such divisions.

There are two common characteristics in the women portrayed in these case studies. The first is poverty. Whether in rural or urban areas, they are part of the great majority of the world's population who, by and large, have not thus far benefited from the process of development. All have been ignored and many have been victimized. The second characteristic is their common voice of protest, challenge, and the initiative for change.

The degree of challenge, or initiative, depends not only on the sociocultural context, but on the ideology of the catalysts, whom I call "intermediaries," involved in the projects. Some of these intermediaries humbly concede from the beginning that these women know what they want and should be free to make their own decisions, even if this involves making mistakes. It is the intermediary's role to provide information and access to resources and services and generally to give support. These features are apparent in the stories of the Markala Cooperative and the Mraru Bus Service in Africa, in the later phases of the construction collective in Jamaica, and in the extraordinary story of the SIRDO in Mexico. The professionals played an important role in each of these cases, but not as dominant partners.

Almost all of the studies described in this book illustrate the need for professional support in the form of market and feasibility surveys, training by experts, and even assistance in management for a period of time (though all advocate the need to break such dependence as early as possible). The studies also project "a commitment to grassroots leadership as a means of strengthening and nourishing the dormant power of poor women" (chapter 3, Working Women's Forum). Many contain very specific, significant lessons about the nature of this leadership, about its values and the methods it rejects, and about how the approaches taken differ from the established theories of the behavior of political elites. I am sure some credit for this must be given to the

---

*One of the four major thrusts of the BRAC women's program is to establish employment for women in "traditionally 'male' skills and occupations."—Ed.

selection of the studies, because there are many cases in which the leaders of women's groups do not behave differently from men in similar situations.

In terms of the use of professional services, the Working Women's Forum stands in a class by itself. While it has used the services of professionals for particular activities, such as operation of its credit program or provision of health and family planning services, still it has developed its own definitions of "productive" and "economic" activities and "creditworthiness," instead of accepting the commonly accepted definitions.

In my view, the value of these Seeds studies lies in the authenticity of the experiences and struggles that they document, the inspiration they can offer to women's groups seeking not only to earn income but to meet other basic human needs, and the immediate operative value of some of the lessons from these cases to a wide variety of women's organizational efforts. The world needs far more of these case studies of women's courage, capacity, and collective strength, given the multiple crises that face us. My only request is that we do not treat *politics* as a dirty word, but rather recognize the inherently political aspects involved in any process of change. I would also hope that we would bring to the fore lessons from the past that can break the unquestioning acceptance of the myth that "integrating" women into development was nothing more than an unnecessary creation of the Decade for Women.

Seeds: An African Perspective

Aminata Traore

As an African, I believe strongly that income-generating projects are of primary importance. Throughout all of the long hours and days of the African woman, the driving motivation for her hard work is always the crucial need for money. Women do not always receive remuneration for what they provide—food, water, fuel, care—but as these essential commodities grow increasingly scarce they more and more often must be paid for within the cash economy. Life, or the quality of life, depends upon purchasing power. As with the rest of the world, African women too have learned to consume that which they do not produce. They too seek initiatives that can augment their incomes, while avoiding those that appear to be an imposition upon their time; for time is a scarce commodity and must be managed well. Projects that lose sight of economic constraints and realities will, sooner or later, arrive at an impasse. While the African woman does not overestimate the importance of money, she manifests the will to acquire and control one of the means of economic survival.

The Seeds case studies present the women of the Third World in action: organizing themselves against the innumerable frustrations and material deprivations that are imposed on them by underdevelopment and that are often compounded by economic recession and debt. As the providers of basic needs (food, water, fuel), women are hardest hit by the economic and ecological deterioration of their environment. Often on the fringe of the cash economy, they have no access to appropriate means of action, particularly to technology, and the resources of production. Despite this, they continue to struggle to meet their needs armed only with their courage, ingenuity, and perseverance.

The governments of African nations have learned, over the past two decades, to understand women's economic roles and realize that women play a major role in the move towards national development. The United Nations Decade for Women has been a determining factor in this new awareness. During these ten years attitudes have changed, new alternatives have been explored, and perspectives have been widened; these gains must now be maintained and strengthened.

Much of the material presented in these chapters stems from projects initiated within the historic context of the Decade. If we hope to arrive at a more equitable society, we must learn from these experiences, examine them, augment them, benefit from them, and work for their wider implementation. Such action is imperative and urgent, given the grave economic situation in underdeveloped countries, the extreme vulnerability of the large majority of women, and the difficulties currently encountered in implementing most projects designed for women's development.

Income-generating projects, due to their immediate relevance to the quality of family life, often serve as an important means for involving women and their families in related activities in a variety of fields such as health, nutrition, population, environment, literacy, water supply, and sanitation. Programs that may not provide direct income, but assist in alleviating some of the drudgery and time involved in daily tasks, are also beneficial as the time gained allows women to engage themselves more productively in income-generating activity.

Access to credit is another important aspect of the economic promotion of women, and attempts at providing such access are touched upon in several of the chapters. The moneylenders of Nicaragua and Bangladesh, have counterparts in the market towns of Africa. African women too are often victims of traditional development financing policies that favor large enterprises that generally benefit only men. The Asian and Latin American experiences in this regard provide an interesting indicator of the methods that might be explored in Africa.

The Seeds case studies deal with a number of subjects that fall within the domain of development projects in Africa, from food, health, and employment, to transport and environmental issues. They also present information on experiences in fields not commonly associated with women's work, such as providing access for women to jobs traditionally reserved for men and recycling of waste materials. In effect, they provide a range of new possibilities to explore, possibilities that will certainly evolve and grow with time and that concern women at all levels.

In any attempt at organizing income-generating activities for women, I believe that several points must be kept in mind. First, in order to sustain the enthusiasm of any target group involved in a development activity, and to maintain a high level of beneficiary participation in the operation of the program, it is essential for the benefit, both in time and money, to be immediately evident. A loss of time and money is to be expected in any process entailing the transfer of technology, especially during the initial phase when start-up expenses and training time are involved. This loss must be compensated for by the sponsors of development projects or, in any event, the risks of initial short-falls should be shared. Underprivileged women can scarcely be expected to undergo further sacrifices.

Another important consideration is that any attempt to organize women for financial gain *must* be backed by assistance in the form of training, equipment, materials, and marketing; also, and this often is overlooked, the women must be receptive to the activity in question. In Africa, and many other parts of the developing world, women traditionally tend towards group rather than individual activity. However, to be successful, such group activity, albeit encouraged and sustained by a support network, must grow out of the goals and initiative of the group itself: cooperative movements that were imposed upon communities against their will have left bitter memories, and sometimes have served as a means of exploitation and oppression.

The experiences presented in the Seeds case studies also suggest that it is not always best for women to be channeled into being artisans simply because this work is considered to be traditional, for in some cases, especially when women work for others, they are open to exploitation. On the other hand, when an artisan is genuinely engaged in earning an income through her craft, it is essential to help her derive the maximum benefit from her occupation. In order to do so, she must be assisted in ensuring that her products are competitive and of high quality. Support personnel play a determinate role here: they must keep in mind the objectives the women seek to achieve. They need to be available when needed to provide advice and assistance, while not becoming overbearing.

Finally, the financial investment required of each participant in a group activity must be relative to the means of even the most underprivileged women in the group. Otherwise the project will exclude precisely those who would benefit most from participation.

Certainly, the experiences in these studies often are small-scale activities implemented in countries far removed from each other—but these are the small streams that flow together to make a river. I hope that initiatives such as these will multiply and will be integrated, in the not-so-distant future, in actual program strategies for women in development.

Seeds of Change in Latin America and the Caribbean

Marguerite Berger

Profound changes are occurring in the lives of women in Latin America and the Caribbean. Three key trends present challenges and opportunities for the integration of women in the development process and provide the backdrop against which the experiences of the women's groups documented by Seeds should be viewed in relation to this region: the increasing number of women in the recognized and counted labor force; increasing levels of female education in most countries in the region; and the significant presence of women-headed households, especially among the poor.

Official statistics show that women's participation in the paid labor force has grown rapidly over the last twenty-five years, and it is likely that the current debt crisis in Latin America and the associated austerity policies and recessionary economic conditions will accelerate this trend. However, higher rates of ''economic participation'' have not necessarily meant greater economic benefits for many women. ''Real'' wages have deteriorated, especially in the last ten years; the gap between male and female earnings has not declined; and, at the same time, the bulk of household work responsibilities still remains in the hands of women.

For the many women in the region who provide the primary economic support to their households, the situation is even more critical. According to a 1983 United Nations study of five major Latin American cities, between 18 and 38 percent of poor households in those cities were headed by women. Two years later, data revealed that this proportion had risen in all but one of the cities. In the Commonwealth Caribbean even higher percentages of female-headed households have been reported.

While levels of educational enrollment for boys and girls have reached near parity in the region as a whole, this achievement has not been even across countries, and has not eliminated the differences in education among the older population. Even in those countries where educational opportunities for girls have been greatest, increased education has not translated into greater equality of earnings between the sexes. For the most part, women remain concentrated in the lowest paying occupations, especially in the informal sector, and have a greater tendency to be unemployed and underemployed than men.

The Seeds case studies provide examples of how women from Latin America and the Caribbean, and other parts of the Third World, have come together to develop more advantageous ways of participating in the market economy. They document efforts to bring productive resources within the reach of poor women, thus enabling these women to improve their own livelihoods. In the years since the first cases were published, the number of efforts by and for women has grown, but these projects have not fully resolved a number of critical issues facing women's projects in the region and elsewhere. Of these, I would like to address four major points that stand out: the importance of economic benefits for poor women; the question of whether to build on traditional activities or to introduce new, nontraditional ones; the issue of project sustainability or economic viability; and the role of outside technical assistance to projects.

Focus on Economic Benefits. As Adrienne Germain points out in the introduction to this volume, most development projects ignored women until recently, transferring new productive technologies and assistance only to men. This often hastened the erosion of women's existing productive base without replacing it with new opportunities (Boserup 1970). Although development agencies finally "discovered" women in the 1970s and 1980s, the programs they supported generally placed women in nonmarket, "traditional" roles and were based on the stereotyped model of the nuclear family purportedly prevalent in industrialized countries (Rogers 1979). Traditional women's civic and philanthropic groups too frequently have failed to design interventions that actually bring economic benefits to women because of the welfare orientation of these groups (Buvinic 1986, 653–64).

As Aminata Traore also points out, poor Third World women face severe time constraints because of their household and market work responsibilities. Yet, given their lack of resources and property, time is the primary element that they have to invest in an activity. Therefore, the success of projects for poor women will lie in their ability to increase economic benefits to women and to give women control over these benefits.

There are, however, limits to what any individual project can accomplish. Even successful income-producing projects may not be able to go beyond stop-gap measures and marginal improvements in women's income. Ultimately, we must face the question that comes out most clearly in the Bangladesh Rural Advancement Committee case: is it possible for women to raise themselves out of poverty without political change that challenges the existing power structure? Even if the answer to this question is no, it does not necessarily mean that a project itself is the most appropriate or effective vehicle for bringing about such political change.

Traditional or Nontraditional. Another major question that confronts anyone trying to design productive projects for women is whether the project should follow the existing sexual division of labor, and perhaps recoup some status and recognition for ''women's work,'' or whether to try to break with tradition. In the short-run, it seems that many more women can be reached by targeting traditional occupations (meaning occupations that are very common for women). In Latin America and the Caribbean, two such traditional female activities are sewing and selling.

In the long-run, however, getting women involved in new activities may be one of the few means available to affect their economic situation significantly. Changes in the structure of production and the sexual division of labor are part of the development process, and should be exploited, if possible, for the benefit of women. After all, there is nothing natural or permanent about what are so often labeled as ''traditional'' (again, meaning common or typical) female occupations. For example, some activities, such as secretarial work or sewing, are not traditionally female occupations in the historical sense, but have become feminized in some countries. Others, such as heavy labor in construction and farming, which in the West are not generally considered to be traditionally female activities, are in reality commonly performed by women in many parts of Latin America and the Caribbean. New job areas such as export processing have opened up to women, but only because manufacturers can offer them lower wages than men would earn in comparable occupations.

The study of handicrafts production points out the dangers of favoring women's work which is low paying and dead end. On the other hand, the Seeds projects in India and Nicaragua have been successful in helping women because they focus on an occupation where women already predominate—petty trading. And some efforts, like those in Mexico and Africa, provide a new approach to women's household roles—reorienting them toward the production of income or other concrete benefits.

Finally, the Kingston Women's Construction Collective in Jamaica shows that barriers can be broken. Women whose vocational aspirations tended toward predominantly female occupations—secretaries or beauticians—were trained and employed successfully as skilled construction workers. In another part of the world, BRAC has been able to encourage women to undertake aspects of agricultural production that previously were taboo, including field work. In these cases, peer groups have provided a support network to help the women involved enter a nontraditional field and deal with the pressure and negative reactions they faced.

Equally important, however, has been the provision of financial resources necessary to break into these activities. Typical women's jobs tend to be those that require very low capital investments, while nontraditional jobs may require a substantial up-front financial commitment (such as the saws or other tools construction workers need in Jamaica). Because few women control much property independently of men and their earnings are generally low, it is very difficult for them to amass the resources necessary to launch themselves in a new trade or business. A group, therefore, can help women to pool resources and gain access to required funds.

Sustainability and Economic Viability. Very few projects for women, and for that matter very few projects designed to reach the poor, have been able to sustain themselves—to cover their operating and indirect costs, not to mention recouping their initial investments—without repeated donations, usually from international agencies. However, at some point these projects must face the issue of economic viability. That does not mean that any subsidization should be ruled out. However, it is necessary to examine subsidized efforts closely to ensure that they eventually will lead to self-sustainability. This is particularly important today, when donors' resources are more scarce than in the past.

Paradoxically, part of the problem of attaining self-sufficiency often is that the amounts of money invested in these projects do not allow them to reach a scale of operations that would make them look economically attractive. Another is that these projects often are implicitly compared with enterprises that receive a host of hidden subsidies through government policies designed to favor growth of certain sectors of the economy (generally, large-scale industry or agriculture). Still another problem is the lack of institutional development within many of the young organizations that are undertaking projects for women.

Nevertheless, despite the harsh economic reality in which they operate, some projects are relatively successful in economic terms. As the case studies show, those projects that seem to have been most successful in approaching self-sufficiency have generally started out simply and worked with a single focus. Diversification has come, if at all, only when the first activity has proven a success. The lesson here may be that, in order to do something well, groups should not attempt to do too much. As the Spanish saying goes, *lo mejor es enemigo de lo bueno.* (The best is the enemy of the good.)

The Role of Outside Experts. For the most part, the projects described here do not seem to have suffered from the "leveling" tendency, often found in grassroots efforts, whereby the participants must do everything themselves for the project to be considered successful. Neither have they become victims of paternalism by relying too heavily on outside experts and administrators, thus creating a shell with no meaningful local participation that would fall apart as soon as donor funds were withdrawn. Rather, they have had to confront over and over the questions: how much technical assistance, where, when, and from whom? Should members of the local groups gradually take over all skilled tasks, such as financial management, fundraising, and marketing? Or should experts continue to advise and work with them, providing technical services on a permanent basis? And if the latter option is chosen, how should it be financed? While it is clear that outside experts should not control the operations, it is not so clear if and when they should withdraw, possibly leaving the local women with no access to technical services.

Each of the projects profiled in this book has had to deal with a number of these thorny issues. They provide different answers to these problems in different situations. The point is not that new projects can look to Seeds for a model of what to do when faced with similar problems; instead, organizations can learn to anticipate these problems and think creatively about solutions appropriate within the local context and their institutional abilities.

Works Cited

Boserup, Esther. 1970. *Women's Role in Economic Development.* London: Allen and Unwin.

Buvinic, Mayra. 1986. "Projects for Women in the Third World: Explaining Their Misbehavior." *World Development* 14 (May).

Rogers, Barbara. 1979. *The Domestication of Women: Discrimination in Developing Societies.* New York: St. Martin's Press.

Planting *Seeds*
in the Classroom

Kathleen Staudt

One clear outcome of the United Nations Decade for Women from 1975–1985 is an internationalization of women's studies. At the Decade conferences, women from diverse cultures, classes, and political systems built and sustained ties with one another. They communicated about women's struggles in the household, community, and larger society. The grassroots struggles of women, however, remain less visible in these communication networks. Seeds cases make prominent the activities and priorities of grassroots women from around the world.

The field dubbed "Women in Development" is an important part of internationally oriented women's studies. This field, drawing on a variety of disciplines, has embraced two approaches. First, it examines how the state, laws, economic strategies, public policies, and programs affect women, men, and the relations between them. All too often, as studies have documented, women's circumstances have worsened in the course of the seemingly progressive or benign process of development. In a second approach, studies document women's experiences as they vary by class and culture. Such experiences often have been rendered invisible in typical mainstream approaches to understanding development. In reporting women's experiences, studies also reveal the ways in which women or gender issues affect this process called "development." We need to learn much more about women's experiences, in all their intricate variations, so that they can serve as models to women elsewhere.

For this reason *Seeds* is a welcome addition to the classroom. These real-life cases are an inspiring contrast to the grim record of many development projects. Frequently, development projects fall short of goals, aggravate income inequalities, and tie people tighter into national and international political economies in which they exert little control. Projects are usually oblivious to women or to the gender inequalities that the projects may have helped to foster. With a track record like this, instructors, students and activists might very well throw their hands up in despair. Fortunately, many women have not been defeated by this fatalistic thinking.

Women struggle in a variety of ways, achieving mixed successes, as the Seeds cases show. In women's efforts to achieve a better and fairer return for their labor, they challenge the sexual division of labor and rewards, or temporarily accommodate themselves to that division, as in Bangladesh. Organizationally, some women join hands with men, as in Mexico, or they share capital, resources, and risks, as in Kenya and even among usually competitive market women in Nicaragua and the street vendors in India. Whatever the country or cultural context, women in these development projects have joined forces in *organizations,* thus controlling the decision-making processes to some degree.

Several key issues rise to the surface in the consideration of the Seeds cases as a whole: *development, empowerment, and feminism.* I can think of virtually no course on women in development that doesn't (or shouldn't) touch at least one of these topics. Are Seeds projects examples of *development,* and how is this value-laden term defined and operationalized? To answer these questions, comparisons of several schools of thought can be useful. One might contrast capitalist and socialist strategies, nationalist self-sufficiency and international integration, and reformist variations within capitalist growth strategies such as ''growth with equity'' and ''basic human needs'' approaches. Are women *empowered* in these types of organizations? Importantly, participants will need to consider what they mean by power and how it might be measured, implicitly critiquing mainstream approaches to understanding power in a public sphere alone. And finally, are these efforts *feminist?* Participants many want to discuss whether there is either a single standard by which to judge feminism (in its various ideological hues as socialist-, liberal- or radical-feminism), or a co-existence of multiple feminisms. As Gita Sen and Caren Grown for DAWN (Development Alternatives with Women for a New Era) have stated: ''There is and must be a diversity of feminisms, responsive to the different needs and concerns of different women, and *defined by them for themselves.* This diversity builds on a common opposition to gender oppression and hierarchy . . .'' (Sen and Grown 1987, 18–19.)

In this brief essay, I outline some of the classroom uses to which *Seeds* might be put, drawing from the experience of three users of Seeds pamphlets and from curriculum materials published in my article "Women in Development: Courses and Curriculum Integration" (1986). Marianne Schmink of the University of Florida used nine of the Seeds cases in a graduate seminar on women in development; Gay Young of the University of Texas at El Paso used the Mexican case in an undergraduate class, Introduction to Women's Studies; and I used both the Kenyan and Mexican cases in an upper-division course on development administration, also at the University of Texas at El Paso. These are only a few of the many kinds of courses in various disciplines in which *Seeds* might be planted. Curriculum ideas follow for both contextual themes and specific course content.

Seeds Cases in Their Contexts

To grapple with the big questions—development? empowerment? feminism?—course participants will need to situate the Seeds case studies in their national and international contexts. For example, in Mexico, "La Crisis," the downturn in the country's economy which followed the drop in petroleum prices, along with the waxing and waning of interest in popular constituencies over politicians' terms of office, has great bearing on prospects for the success of SIRDO-like projects. A dramatic indication of the effect of the crisis is the rapid fall of the value of the peso from 167 to the dollar, when the SIRDO project was first profiled, to well over 2,000 per dollar in 1988. Money earmarked for the provision of basic services during a boom period quickly evaporates in times of economic belt-tightening, resulting in a need to re-think by both politicans and communities as to what technologies are acceptable and affordable. In addition, the battle over control of the Mexico City SIRDO illustrates well the challenges that a community-managed project poses to the status quo of clientelistic politics. Nicaragua, too, has undergone an internal transformation under the Sandanista government since the FUNDE project was first written about. Its policies affect the price and supply of market goods. The country has been besieged, from the outside and within, and national defense takes policy priority under such circumstances.

In these wide-ranging political and economic contexts, course participants will want to examine the degree to which women in Seeds cases were dependent on larger political-economic forces and if so, what this meant for their organizations. National governments, bilateral assistance agencies, and nongovernmental organizations were linked to various of the cases in different ways. What "strings" did these institutions pull, with what effects on the women's organizations?

Of particular interest in political science courses are the varying stances women take toward politics. In India and Mali, women consciously avoided the political process, while in Bangladesh they used it for their benefit. Those who avoided politics, however, did not seem to include government bureaucracy as part of the whole political process. What is it about elections and political parties which creates general unease? What links exist between politics and bureaucratic policies or staff? Do female leaders, women's organizations, or women's bureaus connect any links on this chain? Under what *political* conditions are Seeds nurtured?

Seeds projects have operated in capitalist or so-called free market economies, about which great debates have been generated in terms of their conduciveness to women's emancipation. To what extent are markets "free" for women, with both reproductive and productive responsibilities? Classroom participants may well want to carry on those debates, speculating about how women's conditions would or would not change under socialism. Ultimately, participants might want to assess the worth of different types of organizational strategies—developmental and/or political—under market economies. The Bangladesh Rural Advancement Committee's attention to class differences among women also merits discussion. Can feminist outcomes occur in class-based societies?

Seeds projects also operate in states where men virtually dominate political and bureaucratic decision-making processes. Multilateral and bilateral assistance organizations are similar in that regard. (For a critique of the U.S. Agency for International Development, see Staudt 1985 on international organizations.) In the Seeds cases, readers should take note of the extent to which development resources were channelled to men. India's subsidized interest rates for the "weaker section of society," bank officials admitted, had previously been applied *only* to poor men; even though the women of Nepal were the chief collectors and users of forest products, *all* the forest extension workers in Nepal were men, who were unaccustomed to working with women. In the past, administrators have conveniently fallen back on handicraft projects as a solution, though such projects tend to be time consuming and offer little return for labor, as Seeds author Jasleen Dhamija details. A student project might involve checking the *development plan* of a particular country for how and where women actually and potentially fit.

Clearly, the women in the Seeds projects struggle in an environment of considerable constraints. Whatever those constraints, women have confronted fundamental aspects of the organizational process. They have fused personal and political concerns and realities, which makes for fascinating possiblities in the transition from subordination in *any* kind of political-economic system. Once confronted, how were organizational and policy matters resolved? Virtually all Seeds projects faced the chronic issue of how to distribute incentives and rewards for labor; this is not an uncommon question, from debates in Chinese communes to those in the United States Congress over tax policy. Women are asking these basic, time-worn questions: To each according to her merit (merit being defined as labor time, productivity, capital contribution, talent, or some mix)? To each according to her need? Or to all in equitable parts?

Determining management structure is another recurring challenge, but all too often the development mainstream assumes that some universal standard exists for "good management." Defying Western management techniques, do women spread responsibility to all members, regardless of educational achievement, in order to avoid potential abuses of power by the literate? Among Kenyan women, officers received modest compensation for their skills and time, and group decision making followed majority rule/secret ballot principles. Those who have followed the history of the U.S. feminist movement will recognize some familiar *process* themes.

Seeds in Specific Course Content

Seeds will be ideal in the many kinds of courses offered in international studies and development, from anthropology and economics to women's studies and management. The projects illustrate the ways women can or do affect components of development studies such as health, water, and sanitation. The projects also are a testimony to the enormous difficulties posed in any and all development efforts, from a lack of transportation to insufficient capital; these difficulties often are more problematic for women due to their limited resource base, time-consuming household responsibilities, and the conventional (male?) wisdom that women's development efforts cannot succeed. Who can forget the taunts that Mexican women faced in the SIRDO waste recycling project—"crazy women playing with shit"?

One feature I particularly like about the Seeds series is its frank discussion of problems encountered and lessons learned. This represents a marked departure from the project histories/evaluations written in many development agencies, which tend to be superficial, glossing over mistakes to protect the image of the staff or their prospects for funding. Moreover, evaluations tend to be number-oriented, consulting only the staff and document files rather than, in agency language, the "beneficiaries.'' In the real world of projects in development, numerous problems are encountered that can be overcome with participation and flexible management.

Still, a top-down preplanned mentality prevails in many development agencies and among governments, requiring designers to determine precise goals, implementation strategies, and evaluation indicators before the project even begins (the ''blueprint approach''). Designers usually work either in capital cities, far removed from rural participants, or in the headquarters of bilateral/multilateral foreign assistance agencies. Implementation of projects designed in this way is virtually destined to fail owing to coordination problems, data inadequacies, delays, and human error, their rigidity making them inimical to participation from the very people who are supposed to benefit from the project. In contrast, a ''learning process approach'' embraces the idea of learning from trial and error; ideally, projects pass through stages of learning to be effective, to be efficient, and to expand. This approach, also called social or people-oriented development, has a literature almost a decade old, but its techniques defy the standard operating procedures of most large development agencies. Curiously, however, social development practitioners have been oblivious to women's development activities (Korten 1984, 176–88). The Seeds project permits a perfect hybrid. With a learning process approach in mind, students might role-play alternative scenarios for further project development. After researching the political-economic context, students could take on the roles of organizational members or government and other officials to address the question: Where do we go from here?

The Seeds cases raise specific issues for classroom dialogue, such as: How are projects initiated? What is the optimal balance between leaders' and members' participation? Can women join forces across class lines? What is the nature of outside intervention, by women or by foreign governments? What role can women's advocacy organizations play— should they initiate projects? broker resources from other agencies? advise or monitor other government agencies? nurture women's political constituencies? How do the projects enrich the ''conventional administrative wisdom'' that assumes that only large-scale projects can spend significant sums efficiently? In the Indian project, large numbers of small loans could be moved without high administrative overhead. The Nicaraguan project was able to accommodate daily repayments to suit women's circumstances just as the convenient, but much more highly priced moneylenders were able to do.

Personnel issues are also worthy of discussion, since little incentive may exist for government staff to serve women well. Management tends to work to please those to whom they report, who are *rarely* project participants. Although FUNDE in Nicaragua hired the cooperative manager, she reported to cooperative members. Why can't this become more common?

Sample Course Projects

The Seeds cases lend themselves to a variety of writing assignments, loosely organized around project design and evaluation. Marianne Schmink assigned Seeds and other cases for students to read and thus acquire advanced technical knowledge on project design. Students can also write compare-and-contrast essays, evaluating Seeds cases on different criteria. Ideas from Seeds can be applied to hypothetical problem situations, which is what I did in one midterm examination: Students were asked to put themselves in the position of the Mraru bus project or Mérida waste management project representatives and to consider ''What happens next?''

In my development administration course, students designed development projects over the semester through a staggered set of assignments, broken up into manageable parts. They first did background research on the country, culture(s), and policy area of their choice, culminating in an administrative strategy which charted the various people and institutions they needed to mobilize. Students then prepared a draft of the entire project design, complete with implementation schedule, evaluation plan, budget, and participation strategy. They then presented this plan to the class for feedback and to me for written comment. Completed projects were then placed on library reserve, and the final examination consisted of peer review of projects, using a project evaluation sheet with this bottom line question (after scores for each criterion were tallied): Would you fund this project? Student reviewers were also asked to evaluate the likely impact of the project on women. Armed with two Seeds cases, as well as a thoroughly women-integrated course, students considered complexities that went beyond how many women were involved or what resources came women's way, such as alteration/reinforcement of the sexual division of labor, increased/decreased labor time, increased self- and partner-respect, provision of support networks, and more.

Discussion about issues such as these throughout the course permitted a workshop-like session on project evaluation techniques. I outlined the evaluation guidelines used by the U.S. Agency for International Development—a formidable chart on which designers outline goals, outputs, inputs, objectively verifiable indicators, methods, and assumptions. Although this demanding exercise requires the designer to think through the many dimensions of the project, it can promote—even if unintentionally—a form of "blueprintism" that often develops in large-scale organizations. Seeds cases offer a way to critique and expand these kinds of evaluation techniques.

Bringing Development Home

Students can apply the women's experiences that have been collected for the publication of *Seeds* to development problems in their own communities, or to women in transition from subordination. Students might also consider the kinds of government policies that support and deter international, and specifically women's, development. For course wrap-ups, Seeds cases can generate the kind of dialogue necessary to bring development home, both in terms of addressing analagous issues in the students' own communities and in supporting the kind of development assistance which empowers women all over the world.

Works Cited

Korten, David. 1984. "Rural Development Programming: The Learning Process Approach." In *People-Centered Development*. D. Korten and R. Klauss, eds. West Hartford, CT: Kumarian Press.

Rogers, Barbara. 1979. *The Domestication of Woman*. New York: St. Martin's Press.

Sen, Gita and Caren Grown. 1987. *Development, Crisis and Alternative Visions of Third World Women's Perspectives*. New York: Monthly Review.

Staudt, Kathleen. 1985. *Women, Foreign Assistance and Advocacy Administration*. New York: Praeger.

Staudt, Kathleen. 1986. "Women in Development." *Women's Studies Quarterly,* vol. 14, no. 3/4 (Fall/Winter).

Notes on Contributors

Susan Caughman, after serving as a Peace Corps volunteer in Togo, held various positions with international development projects. She analyzed women's small business projects in Mali for the Ford Foundation and then trained East African managers in economic development practices for the Carnegie Corporation. She then joined the American Friends Service Committee and launched a development project to employ rural women in Senegal, Mali, Upper Volta, and Guinea-Bissau. After returning to the United States and completing a Masters Degree in Public and Private Management at Yale University in 1983, she joined Time, Inc., where she is currently the Circulation Manager for *Life* magazine.

Marguerite Berger is an economist who works with the International Center for Research on Women, where she has been involved in a wide variety of activities since 1983 dealing with women's economic participation. In 1985 and 1986 she was also a Visiting Scholar at the Instituto Latinoamericano de Investigaciónes Sociales in Quito, Ecuador. Marguerite Berger has a Ph.D. in economics from The American University and has published extensively in the area of women and economic development.

Judith Bruce is a Senior Associate of the Population Council and a founding member of the Seeds Steering Committee. She has coordinated a program of policy oriented research on, and documentation of women's roles in, social and economic development over the past twelve years. She has written extensively on women's perspectives on reproductive health technologies and services.

Marty Chen is currently a Research Associate at the Harvard Institute for International Development, where she is working on a research project on women and household livelihoods in rural India. From 1981 to 1987, she was the Oxfam America field representative for India and Bangladesh, based in New Delhi. During the 1970s she lived in Bangladesh and worked with the Bangladesh Rural Advancement Committee (BRAC) on the development of its women's project. Fluent in both Hindi and Bengali, she has traveled widely through the subcontinent and written numerous articles on women and development.

Jasleen Dhamija has been involved in craft development, rural non-farm employment, and cross-cultural studies throughout her professional life. She began her career in India thirty-two years ago in pioneering work to develop handicrafts and rural industries. She worked in Iran for more than six years in rural non-farm employment, handicrafts production, and curriculum development in applied arts and Asian culture at Farabi University. For four years she served as Chief of the joint International Labour Organization and U.N. Economic Commission for Africa project "Small Industries and Handicrafts Division for African Women," located in Addis Ababa, Ethiopia and serving twenty-one African countries. For the past five years, she has been back in India, living in the state of Gujarat and carrying out in-depth studies of living traditions, folk arts, and crafts. She has been publishing books on Indian folk arts and crafts since 1970 and also has written about Iran. She has lectured in India, the United States, and Europe on crafts, the history of textiles, symbolism, cross cultural traditions, and women's employment.

Adrienne Germain is Vice President and Program Director of the International Women's Health Coalition in New York. From 1972 through 1986 she was with the Ford Foundation, where her main concern was programs in support of women in the Third World. From 1981 through 1985 she was the foundation's Resident Representative in Bangladesh. Adrienne Germain holds an M.A. in sociology from the University of California at Berkeley and has published a number of articles on various aspects of Third World women's lives and policies that affect them.

Jill Kneerim is a writer and editor based in Boston, Massachusetts. She creates books, magazines, pamphlets, and articles for nonprofit organizations and has worked as an editor for various publishing houses. She is the author of *Revelations of New England Architecture,* published by Grossman/Viking in 1975. She has overseen many projects, including *All Our Children* for the Carnegie Council on Children; the final report to President Carter for the National Commission on the International Year of the Child; and *The Exchange Report,* a magazine on women in developing countries based on the mid-decade meeting of the U.N. Decade for Women.

Ann Leonard is a consultant in communications working primarily in the areas of health and family planning, women's issues, and education. She is particularly interested in the design of materials appropriate for specific audiences, from policy makers to those who cannot read. Prior to becoming an independent consultant in 1981, Ann Leonard was with the Ford Foundation's Population and Development Communication Project for six years. Previous affiliations were with the Southwest Regional Laboratory for Education Research and Development, CBS, and the Center for International Education of the University of Southern California. She has been the editor of the Seeds pamphlet series since its inception.

For sixteen years, **Vina Mazumdar** was Professor of Political Science and Department Head at the Universities of Patna and Berhampore in India. From 1972 to 1974, she served as Member Secretary of the Committee on the Status of Women in India, and from 1975 to 1980 as the Director for Women's Studies of the Indian Council of Social Science Research. Since 1980, Mazumdar has been Director of the Centre for Women's Development Studies in New Dehli. She earned both her M.A. and Ph.D. at Oxford University.

Vina Mazumdar is the author of *Education and Social Change: Three Studies in 19th Century Bengal, Towards Equality: Report of the Committee on the Status of Women in India,* and various papers on education, political development, and women and development. She has served as a member of the board of the Population Council in New York, as a consultant to the International Labour Organization and the U.N. Secretariat for the Mid-Decade Conference on Women, and on several expert groups of ILO, UNICEF, UNESCO, ESCAP, INSTRAW and the government of India on women and development issues.

Ruth McLeod, Executive Director of the Construction Resource and Development Center in Kingston, Jamaica, has worked in the Caribbean since 1975 as an educator, project coordinator, and documentor, with particular emphasis on urban development. In 1983, she was asked by the Masterbuilders Association of Jamaica to coordinate the establishment of the Construction Resource and Development Centre. Also in 1983 she founded the Kingston Women's Construction Collective, which has since become the first all-female construction company in Jamaica and which devotes its profits to the training of unemployed women from low-income communities in the city of Kingston. Ruth McLeod has published work on various aspects of the construction industry, the role of women in urban development and provision of shelter, income-generating strategies among the urban unemployed, informal sector shelter survival, and the actual and potential role of women within the horse racing industry.

Augusta Molnar is a development anthropologist who earned her Ph.D. in Nepal on the economic and social roles of Magar women in Western Nepal. During this time she was also involved in the Status of Women in Nepal Project, which collected anthropological data on women's roles and status that would provide solid information for planners. For the past eight years, Augusta Molnar has worked in the field of community forestry in India, Nepal, and Bangladesh. She has participated in a number of evaluations of the Nepal Community Forestry Development and Training project. She is currently working with the World Bank on development of a set of guidelines for women's involvement in all of the Bank's forest-related projects.

Mariam N'diaye Thiam is responsible for women's programs in the Ministry of Agriculture in Mali. Together with Susan Caughman, she founded the Mali Rural Women's Advisory Service, a program that now provides technical assistance to some five hundred women in producer cooperatives in rural Mali.

Marianne Schmink is Associate Professor of Latin American Studies and Anthropology at the University of Florida. Since 1980, she has served as Executive Director of the Amazon Research and Training Program at the Center for Latin American Studies, and from 1983–1987 she was co-director of the Women in Agricultural Development Program at the University of Florida. She has worked as a consultant in the field of women and development for more than a decade. From 1981–1987 she served as co-manager of the Population Council/U.S.A.I.D. project entitled "Women, Low Income Households, and Urban Services in Latin America and the Caribbean," which supported interdisciplinary working groups in Peru, Mexico, and Jamaica. Her publications include: *Gender Issues in Farming Systems Research and Extension* (with S. Poats and A. Spring); *Learning About Urban Services for Women in Latin America and the Caribbean* (with J. Bruce and M. Kohn); *Frontier Expansion in Amazonia* (with Charles H. Wood); and numerous articles on development in Latin America.

Kathleen Staudt is Professor of Political Science at the University of Texas at El Paso. She has published articles on agricultural policy and women's politics in various journals, including *Development and Change*,

Comparative Politics, Rural Sociology, and *Women and Politics.* She has co-edited *Women, the State, and Development* with Sue Ellen Charlton and Jana Everett (SUNY/Albany Press, 1989). Her *Women, International Development, and Politics: The Bureaucratic Mire* is forthcoming in 1990 from Temple University Press.

Aminata Traore is currently a researcher at the Institute of Ethno-Sociology of the National University of the Ivory Coast. She was formerly the director of Studies and Program Planning of the Ministry on the Status of Women. She received her doctorate in social psychology from the University of Paris VII, a *licence* in psychology from the University of Caen and a diploma in psycho-pathology from the University of Paris V. Dr. Traore has written extensively about women in development, the family, and children in Africa and has participated in numerous international conferences on these subjects.

The Feminist Press at The City University of New York offers alternatives in education and in literature. Founded in 1970, this nonprofit, tax-exempt educational and publishing organization works to eliminate sexual stereotypes in books and schools and to provide literature with a broad vision of human potential. The publishing program includes reprints of important works by women, feminist biographies of women, and nonsexist children's books. Curricular materials, bibliographies, directories, and a quarterly journal provide information and support for students and teachers of women's studies. Through publications and projects, The Feminist Press contributes to the rediscovery of the history of women and the emergence of a more humane society.

New and Forthcoming Books

Always a Sister: The Feminism of Lillian D. Wald, a biography by Doris Groshen Daniels. $24.95 cloth.

Bamboo Shoots after the Rain: Contemporary Stories by Women Writers of Taiwan, 1945–1985, edited by Ann C. Carver and Sung-Sheng Yvonne Chang. $29.95 cloth, $12.95 paper.

A Brighter Coming Day: A Frances Ellen Watkins Harper Reader, edited by Frances Smith Foster. $29.95 cloth, $13.95 paper.

The Daughters of Danaus, a novel by Mona Caird. Afterword by Margaret Morganroth Gullette. $29.95 cloth, $11.95 paper.

The End of This Day's Business, a novel by Katharine Burdekin. Afterword by Daphne Patai. $24.95 cloth, $8.95 paper.

Families in Flux (formerly *Household and Kin),* by Amy Swerdlow, Renate Bridenthal, Joan Kelly, and Phyllis Vine. $9.95 paper.

How I Wrote Jubilee *and Other Essays on Life and Literature,* by Margaret Walker. Edited by Maryemma Graham. $29.95 cloth, $9.95 paper.

Lillian D. Wald: Progressive Activist, a sourcebook edited by Clare Coss. $7.95 paper.

Lone Voyagers: Academic Women in Coeducational Universities, 1870–1937, edited by Geraldine J. Clifford. $29.95 cloth, $12.95 paper.

Not So Quiet: Stepdaughters of War, a novel by Helen Zenna Smith. Afterword by Jane Marcus. $26.95 cloth, $9.95 paper.

Seeds: Supporting Women's Work in the Third World, edited by Ann Leonard. Introduction by Adrienne Germain. Afterwords by Marguerite Berger, Vina Mazumdar, Kathleen Staudt, and Aminata Traore. $29.95 cloth, $12.95 paper.

Sister Gin, a novel by June Arnold. Afterword by Jane Marcus. $8.95 paper.

These Modern Women: Autobiographical Essays from the Twenties, edited and with a revised introduction by Elaine Showalter. $8.95 paper.

Truth Tales: Contemporary Stories by Women Writers of India, selected by Kali for Women. Introduction by Meena Alexander. $22.95 cloth, $8.95 paper.

We That Were Young, a novel by Irene Rathbone. Introduction by Lynn Knight. Afterword by Jane Marcus. $29.95 cloth, $10.95 paper.

What Did Miss Darrington See? An Anthology of Feminist Supernatural; Fiction, edited by Jessica Amanda Salmonson. Introduction by Rosemary Jackson. $29.95 cloth, $12.95 paper.

Women Composers: The Lost Tradition Found, by Diane Peacock Jezic. $29.95 cloth, $12.95 paper.

For a free, complete backlist catalog, write to The Feminist Press at The City University of New York, 311 East 94 Street, New York, NY 10128. Send book orders to The Talman Company, Inc., 150 Fifth Avenue, New York, NY 10011. Please include $1.75 postage and handling for one book, $.75 for each additional.